SEASPEAK
TRAINING MANUAL

Essential English for
International Maritime Use

Other related publications

SEASPEAK REFERENCE MANUAL

SEASPEAK TRAINING MANUAL CASSETTE

Information on the above listed, and other Pergamon publications,
is available from Pergamon Press.

SEASPEAK TRAINING MANUAL

Essential English for International Maritime Use

Supplemented by an optional audio cassette

Capt. **Fred Weeks,** MA (Exon.), FNI, Extra Master
Faculty of Maritime Studies, Plymouth Polytechnic
Lt. Cdr. **Alan Glover,** Royal Navy, MNI, Master Mariner, Airline Pilot
Faculty of Maritime Studies, Plymouth Polytechnic
Edward Johnson, B.Ed. (Cantab.), MA
Wolfson College, Cambridge
Peter Strevens, MA, FIL
Wolfson College, Cambridge

PERGAMON PRESS

OXFORD · NEW YORK · BEIJING · FRANKFURT
SÃO PAULO · SYDNEY · TOKYO · TORONTO

U.K.	Pergamon Press, Headington Hill Hall, Oxford OX3 0BW, England
U.S.A.	Pergamon Press, Maxwell House, Fairview Park, Elmsford, New York 10523, U.S.A.
PEOPLE'S REPUBLIC OF CHINA	Pergamon Press, Room 4037, Qianmen Hotel, Beijing, People's Republic of China
FEDERAL REPUBLIC OF GERMANY	Pergamon Press, Hammerweg 6, D-6242 Kronberg, Federal Republic of Germany
BRAZIL	Pergamon Editora, Rua Eça de Queiros, 346, CEP 04011, Paraiso, São Paulo, Brazil
AUSTRALIA	Pergamon Press Australia, P.O. Box 544, Potts Point, N.S.W. 2011, Australia
JAPAN	Pergamon Press, 8th Floor, Matsuoka Central Building, 1-7-1 Nishishinjuku, Shinjuku-ku, Tokyo 160, Japan
CANADA	Pergamon Press Canada, Suite No. 271, 253 College Street, Toronto, Ontario, Canada M5T 1R5

Copyright © 1988 Pergamon Books Ltd.

First edition 1988

Library of Congress Cataloging in Publication Data
Seaspeak training manual.
(Essential English for international maritime use)
Includes index.
1. Radio in navigation — Terminology —
Handbooks, manuals etc.   2. English language —
Conversation and phrase books (for seamen)
I. Weeks, F.   II. Glover, A.   III. Johnson, E.
IV. Strevens, P.   V. Series
VK39.7S43   1986   428.3'4'0246238   86–2555

British Library Cataloguing in Publication Data
Seaspeak training manual: essential English
for international maritime use
1. English language — Conversation and phrase
books (for seamen)   2. Seamanship — Terminology
I. Weeks, F.   II. Glover, A.   III. Johnson, E.
IV. Strevens, P.
428.3'4'0246238   PE1131
ISBN 0–08–031555–0

Printed in Great Britain by A. Wheaton & Co. Ltd., Exeter

Contents

Contents

GENERAL

This book is an expansion of the **SEASPEAK Reference Manual**, that is to say, it contains the full text of the **Reference Manual** together with additional explanations and examples. The purpose of the additional material is to help those who are learning to use SEASPEAK, and their instructors.

THE RELATION BETWEEN THE REFERENCE MANUAL AND THE TRAINING MANUAL

The **Reference Manual** is a precise statement of recommended usage for maritime communications using VHF radio. It assumes that the reader is a trained seafarer, and that he has a good command of the English language. The **Reference Manual** is not intended to supply help either to those who are still engaged in being trained as seafarers or to those who require further assistance in learning English for the purpose of maritime communications.

The **Training Manual**, by contrast (i.e. this volume), is designed to help seafarers in training and those requiring further help with the English language; the additional material contained in this book is intended to assist in such training.

Since the training which this book provides is training in using SEASPEAK, two principles have been followed: (i) the full text of the **Reference Manual** is included in the **Training Manual**: no sections are omitted, and the student who works through the **Training Manual** will therefore meet the whole of the system of Essential English for Maritime use known as SEASPEAK; (ii) the numbering of the Sections and paragraphs used in the **Reference Manual** is maintained in the Training Manual: the officer who has worked with the **Training Manual** will find, when he comes to use the SEASPEAK **Reference Manual** on the ship's bridge or as a shore station officer or VTS controller, that its layout and numbering are familiar.

ADDITIONAL FEATURES INCLUDED IN THE TRAINING MANUAL BUT NOT IN THE REFERENCE MANUAL

Basic principles for VHF radio operation

Many officers in training will not be familiar with the basic operating principles of VHF radio communication. For that reason a new Introductory Section has been provided in this volume only.

Additional explanations included in the Training Manual

Throughout Sections 1 to 6 a good deal of additional explanation is included. Some of this takes the form of training introductions and notes; there are also suggestions for further learning strategies.

EXERCISES

At the end of Sections 1 to 4 and 6 exercises are provided. They are intended not only as a direct means of assisting the learning and teaching of the content of each Section, but also as a guide to ways of creating additional exercises.

RECORDINGS

Since SEASPEAK is, by definition, spoken language, many of the examples in the text are supported by recordings, these are to be known as the SEASPEAK Training Manual Tapes. These are available as additional training material to this volume. Each example so recorded is clearly marked by a symbol 📼 in the text. The Manual can be used with or without these 'model' recordings but the use of a tape recorder for personal recording is highly recommended throughout as an aid to learning.

DIFFERENT LEVELS OF ATTAINMENT

Many students will be able to get a firm grasp of SEASPEAK by working solely from this **Training Manual** and the recordings, either alone or with the help of a teacher or instructor. However, the **Training Manual** assumes a certain grasp of English; it is not designed for use by complete beginners with no previous knowledge of English.

SEASPEAK IS A SYSTEM

Students and their instructors should realise from the beginning that although SEASPEAK is made up entirely from English and contains nothing that is not English, it is more than just a restricted part of English. SEASPEAK is a system for speech communication, and it is intended for use in situations where it is essential that communication should be as clear, brief and accurate as possible. It contains several elements, all of which may be present in any conversation.

The principal elements in SEASPEAK are:

(i) **VHF conventions (Section 1):** the use of VHF radio at sea (and also on the ground and in the air) is regulated by the International Telecommunications Union (ITU). In order to use SEASPEAK it is necessary to follow ITU conventions, which include: the proper selection of suitable radio frequency bands or channels; standard ways of identifying oneself and addressing other ships or stations; conventional ways of pronouncing the letters of the alphabet, numbers and other quantities; also internationally-agreed conventions for speaking the time and for defining positions and bearings.

(ii) **VHF procedures (Section 2):** every conversation by VHF radio must conform to accepted procedures for initiating a call, continuing a conversation, interrupting, terminating, etc. SEASPEAK follows these procedures, and in order to use SEASPEAK it is essential to learn the English employed in such procedures.

(iii) **Distress, urgency and safety procedures (Section 3):** by international agreement, all communications dealing with distress, danger, rescue etc. must follow certain rigid rules, which are incorporated in SEASPEAK.

(iv) **VHF messages (Section 4):** once a conversation is initiated, the message content has to follow an agreed pattern. In the construction of messages, SEASPEAK employs a number of **Standard Phrases, Message Markers** and **Reply Markers**, and **Message Checks**. The purpose of all these is to increase to the maximum extent the listener's chances of hearing the message accurately and without ambiguity.

(v) **Major communications subjects and Full conversations (Sections 5 and 6):** maritime communications on VHF radio deal with a range of subjects or topics. Thirty-two SEASPEAK subjects are listed on p. 118, and examples are given of conversations within them.

In addition to the elements outlined above, a 'core' maritime vocabulary is included.

LEARNING SEASPEAK

The Sections used in the **Reference Manual** are placed in the same order in the **Training Manual**. However, the sequence which is most logical and appropriate for a reference manual is not necessarily the most appropriate order for learning and training purposes. Students and their instructors should realise that they are free to decide for themselves the order in which the content would best be taught and learned.

In many cases, we suggest, the most appropriate learning sequence might be as follows:

(i) **Section 2. VHF procedures,** which make the student familiar with the basic construction of VHF conversations, including the essential sequence of transmissions within a conversation.

(ii) **Section 4. VHF messages,** which then enables the student to produce simple, accurate and unambiguous messages in the required form, and within the procedures already learned from Section 2.

(iii) **Section 3. Distress, urgency and safety procedures,** which can be mastered with greater confidence once the student already has a mastery of the techniques for producing normal messages according to the general rules.

(iv) **Section 1. VHF conventions,** which provide a quantity of detail that can gradually be absorbed, once the principal techniques have been learned.

Students and instructors will certainly wish to be flexible in their programme of learning and teaching. They will find valuable assistance by using as examples the many conversations and messages to be found throughout the **Training Manual**.

FFW   AG   EJ   PS
Spring 1987

Preface to the Reference Manual

NB: This Preface is reprinted here because it contains considerable historical and general information.

I. The need for international maritime English

Many features of modern sea transport have combined to produce radical changes in maritime communications. These features include: technological changes in the design of ships leading to faster vessels and greater navigational hazards; changed patterns of shipping routes with new areas of traffic density; the increase in numbers of professional bridge officers from many language backgrounds, no longer predominantly from among native speakers of English; the availability of VHF radio on the bridge, permitting direct communication, albeit within a limited range, intership, ship to shore, and ship to aircraft; and the growth of satellite and other long-range communications and navigation systems.

In these changed conditions, mariners need to be sure that their speech communications are as precise, simple and unambiguous as possible, and that predictable areas of language confusion and error are avoided. International agreement on English as the required language provides a starting point. Existing IMO and ITU regulations concerning navigational safety and radio procedures take the process further. The next requirement is for the English language as used by mariners to be freed from ambiguity, to be organised in message form according to accepted rules, to embody agreed conventions — in short, to reduce possibilities of confusion, to maximise 'guessability' and listener's expectancies, to concentrate on effective communication.

In the light of these requirements, a project was set up in 1980 to produce Essential English for International Maritime Use (referred to as SEASPEAK, for brevity) financially sponsored by the Department of Industry of the Government of the United Kingdom, and Pergamon Press. The work was undertaken on contract by Specialists in Language Management Ltd. and its end-product is the present Reference Manual, containing recommendations for the language to be used by mariners, for intership, ship to shore, and ship to aircraft communication, principally by VHF radio. (N.B. SEASPEAK does not in any way contradict or diminish such established signalling codes and procedures as the morse code, the International Code of Signals, etc.)

The SEASPEAK recommendations relate chiefly to communication by VHF radio; they embody recommended procedures for initiating, maintaining, and terminating conversations, as well as recommended language (i.e. relevant portions of English grammar and vocabulary) and recommendations for the structure of messages, the whole within the range of the great majority of maritime subjects for communication. (See Elements of SEASPEAK, below.)

These recommendations are based on intensive research carried out by specialists in maritime communications and applied language studies working at the Faculty of Maritime Studies, Plymouth Polytechnic, and at Wolfson College,

Cambridge University. The researchers have had the benefit of criticisms and advice from many quarters across the globe, including a number of serving ships' officers, communications specialists, and professionals in maritime education. The research and development work has also been greatly assisted by the presence, on the project's steering committee, of senior officials from the International Maritime Organisation and the Departments of Trade and Industry of the Government of the United Kingdom. Their advice and comments have been most welcome and helpful: any defects remain the responsibility of the SEASPEAK team.

In devising the SEASPEAK recommendations, the team had the advantage of building on the pioneering work of the IMCO Standard Marine Navigational Vocabulary (SMNV) (1977). SEASPEAK extends the coverage of the SMNV. It makes possible not simply the use of the phrases included therein but the construction of very large numbers of messages, not directly arising from SMNV.

II. Elements of SEASPEAK

The recommendations for essential maritime English have the intention of bringing together the conventions and procedures already established for VHF radio communications at sea, together with rules for using the English language to construct messages appropriate in maritime conditions, procedures for checking the accuracy with which messages transmitted by one speaker are heard by his respondent, a glossary of terms specifically defined in SEASPEAK, and an outline of essential maritime communication subjects.

The central principle of SEASPEAK is that the receiver should be alerted to the type of message that follows, at the very beginning of the message. This aim is achieved by the use of 'message markers', Question, Instruction, Advice, Request, Information, Warning, Intention.

The principle is entirely in agreement with the IMO Assembly Resolution A14/Res. 578, Guidelines for Vessel Traffic Services, which states 'Any message to a vessel should make it clear whether it is information, advice, or instruction'.

In addition to copious examples of particular usages in SEASPEAK which are provided throughout the body of the Manual. Section 6 contains the texts of several long conversations, typical of maritime communications, which illustrate the utilisation of SEASPEAK. An appendix contains a comprehensive Vocabulary of Maritime English.

III. Future revisions

It is in the practical use of SEASPEAK by mariners of all nations that its value and its shortcomings will be seen. There is little doubt that as seafarers become familiar with SEASPEAK they will suggest ways of improving it. Therefore it will be desirable to set up machinery for reporting difficulties, suggesting improvements, making systematic revisions, and promulgating subsequent versions. For the moment, the progenitors of SEASPEAK offer this first version in the hope that it will be seen as a contribution to better communications and therefore to enhanced safety at sea.

Capt. Fred Weeks, MA (Exon.), FNI, Extra Master
Faculty of Maritime Studies, Plymouth Polytechnic
Lt. Cdr. Alan Glover, Royal Navy, MNI, Master Mariner, Airline Pilot
Faculty of Maritime Studies, Plymouth Polytechnic
Edward Johnson, B.Ed. (Cantab.), MA
Wolfson College, Cambridge
Peter Strevens, MA, FIL
Wolfson College, Cambridge

Acknowledgements

The sponsors, publishers and authors of this Manual wish to express their thanks for the great assistance they received from over a thousand people in twenty-six maritime nations, in conducting the research which led to the production of the SEASPEAK Reference Manual and developing the recommendations contained therein. Help was given by professional seafarers, ships' pilots, search and rescue personnel, shipping company officers and executives, air traffic controllers, vessel traffic services operators, nautical college lecturers, nautical students and university professors, from around the world. It is their collaboration and suggestions that have made this publication possible.

Special thanks are also due to C. P. Srivastava, Secretary General, IMO, for his encouragement and support.

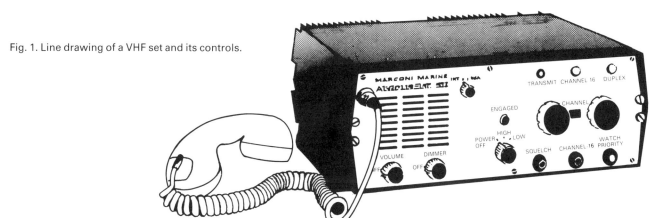

Fig. 1. Line drawing of a VHF set and its controls.

Introductory Section

Basic principles of VHF radio communications

This Introductory Section (which does not appear in the **Reference Manual**) is intended to provide an explanation of the working of a typical Very High Frequency (VHF) radio set. The Section includes:

(i) VHF sets and the operation of their controls;

(ii) the propagation of VHF radio waves;

(iii) special restrictions on maritime VHF, including the difference between **simplex** and **duplex** working.

0.1 VHF SETS

Marine VHF sets are of many different makes and types. However, some basic controls are common to all (See Fig. 1).

0.1.1 Controls

(i) **On/Off Switch**: When a set is switched **on** it at once acts as a VHF **receiver**; it is available to act instead as a **transmitter** if the operator should so decide. VHF sets require only a few seconds at most to warm up.

(ii) **Power Switch**: This is normally marked **High** and **Low**. In order to reach its maximum range the set will need to use all the power available, and this is provided on **High**. But the power switch should only be set on **High** when maximum range is required, since high power may interfere with other ships' transmissions (see **Capture Effect,** 0.2.5). Unless maximum range is a primary consideration the power switch should always be in the **Low** position.

(iii) **VHF Channel Selector**: VHF frequencies in the maritime band (156.025–162.025 MHz) are divided for operational convenience into VHF **channels** by the International Telecommunications Union (ITU). This International body governs all radio communications. The VHF channels are each given a number ranging from 0 to 28 and from 60 to 88. There are also some 'private' channels e.g. VHF channel 'M' is for Marina use in Great Britain. The use of these channels is not at present internationally agreed; however, they are within the band of VHF maritime frequencies, consequently their use outside the precise circumstances for which they are designed may cause unacceptable interference on the agreed VHF channels. For example, since VHF channel 'M' utilises half of a two-frequency international VHF channel it should not be used outside the UK.

It is not necessary to memorise the frequency or frequencies of each VHF channel; the VHF set is tuned by selecting the appropriate VHF channel number. The selection is made either from a keyboard on the front of the set or by dialling the required VHF channel on suitably marked knobs. The VHF channel selected will be displayed in a window on the front of the set in two-digit form: 09, 12, 63 etc.

(iv) **VHF Channel 16**: VHF channel 16 is important because it is used for many purposes: distress and urgency communications are conducted on it; shore stations usually make 'all ships' calls on it; it is the channel most frequently used for making initial contact ship to ship. To enable users to tune to this channel quickly, some sets are provided with a VHF Channel 16 selector (usually in the form of a push button) which immediately selects this channel.

In many parts of the world there is either a legal requirement or a practical need to listen to (i.e. keep watch on) more than one VHF channel. In order to do this, some sets are fitted with a facility called Dual Watch, which enables two VHF channels to be selected. The set will then receive on both of them alternately but will lock into one of them when a transmission is received. When the transmission ceases, the set will then resume dual watch. In order to transmit it is first necessary to re-select a single channel.

The controls necessary to achieve dual watch vary from one VHF set to another, depending on the design choice of the manufacturer. The dual watch controls are usually to be found near the VHF channel selector, particularly where the channel selector is a keyboard.

(v) **Loudspeaker on/off, Volume and Dimmer**: These are the remaining controls to be found on the VHF set. When the loudspeaker is switched off, the received transmissions are heard in the earpiece of the handset. This provides a certain amount of privacy for the user of the VHF set. The volume knob controls the volume in the loudspeaker and the handset, in the same manner as on a radio set. The dimmer reduces the brilliance of the panel front lights for night time use on ships' bridges.

(vi) **Handset**: The handset resembles a normal telephone handset or radio microphone. Mounted on the handset is the pressel switch which operates the transmitter. (NB: Although the VHF handset looks like an ordinary telephone, it is essential to realise that there are many fundamental differences between the two.)

(vii) **Pressel Switch**: The pressel switch may be either a small button or a long bar, mounted on the part of the handset which is held in the hand. It is marked 'Press to talk', or is conspicuously coloured.

0.1.2 | Using the VHF handset

0.1.2.1 The handset contains a microphone and an ear-piece loudspeaker, and it looks very like a telephone. However, unlike a telephone, in normal operation **either** the microphone **or** the ear-piece will operate, but **not** both together. Until the pressel switch is operated, the VHF set acts as a receiver only; the user hears in the ear-piece any transmission in progress on the channel to which the set is tuned. (If no transmission is in progress, the user will usually hear background noise or static.) When the pressel switch is operated, the set changes from being a receiver to being a transmitter. The user can no longer hear any conversation that may be in progress, nor background noise. Instead the user now speaks, and the VHF set transmits his speech. This either/or, receive/transmit type of operation is known as **simplex working** and is a feature of typical VHF operations.

0.1.2.2 During the change from receive to transmit, it is necessary to pause briefly before speaking. This is because the transmitter requires a short period to become energised. If the user speaks immediately he presses the pressel switch his first few words may be lost because the transmitter is not yet fully energised. When the user stops speaking he should also pause briefly before releasing the pressel switch, to avoid the common error of releasing it too quickly and therefore losing the last few words because the transmitter has already de-energised.

0.1.2.3 Operating the pressel switch will cause a break in the background noise, and on some sets a warning light indicates that the transmitter is energised.

0.1.2.4 The pressel switch is spring-loaded. Releasing the switch automatically cuts out the transmitter. It is most important that the pressel switch should not be accidentally operated, for example by contact with other objects caused by the ship's motion, because the handset has not been returned to its proper place. Accidental operation must be avoided, because while the pressel switch is down:

(a) you cannot hear any other ship or station that is transmitting, and

(b) without your knowledge, your own transmitter may be blocking all use of the channel selected, anywhere within the range of your transmitter, i.e. within a circle of 30–40 miles radius.

0.1.2.5   **Operator's Manual**: Different VHF sets have different features. When joining a ship, check whether you are familiar with the type of VHF set on board. If not, always read the operator's manual (**before** you have to use the set), or ask a colleague to explain the working of the set to you.

0.2   PRINCIPLES AND PROPAGATION OF VHF RADIO

0.2.1   Frequency

The initials VHF stand for Very High Frequency. It is usual to distinguish radio stations by the frequency in cycles per second (referred to as **Herz**, abbreviated *Hz*) of their radio signal. All the maritime VHF channels are situated in the range from 156.025 megaHerz (MHz) to 162.025 MHz. In comparison, television is transmitted in the 90–100 MHz band, and commercial marine radar at about 9000–10000 MHz.

0.2.2   Modulation

The basic radio signal has additional information (in the case of maritime VHF this is speech) imposed upon it. The signal is said to be **modulated** by the additional information. Modulation can be of two kinds. One is **amplitude modulation**, in which the additional information is coded into the radio signal by varying the strength (amplitude) of the signal. Amplitude modulation (AM) is easily degraded by atmospheric conditions such as rain or electrical storms.

The method used in maritime VHF is **frequency modulation** (FM). In this case the information is coded into the radio signal by slightly varying the frequency of the signal. It has the advantage that it is little affected by atmospherics. FM is used for commercial broadcasting of music in stereo for the same reason.

0.2.3   Range of VHF

There is an important restriction upon the use of VHF for maritime purposes: VHF radio signals travel in straight lines. Any solid object between the transmitter and the receiving station (such as a headland, or the transmitting ship's funnel, or the horizon) may block the transmission. (See Fig. 2.)

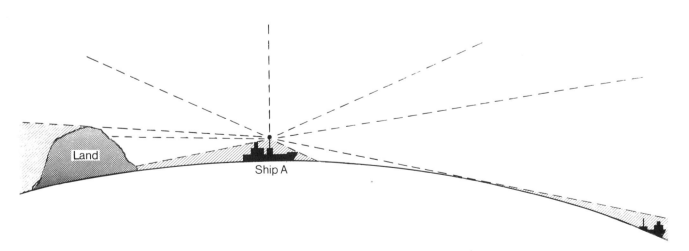

Fig. 2. The shaded areas are those in which the VHF transmissions of ship A will not be received.

The operational range of VHF is limited chiefly by the horizon, and the distance from the transmitting aerial to the horizon is a function of height above sea level. (The **radio horizon** is at a slightly greater distance than the **visual horizon** because the radio waves bend slightly as they approach the horizon.) The surface range of a VHF set is therefore the same as the distance to the radio horizon. And since the VHF set is almost always at some height above sea level, it is clear that in calculating the VHF range it is necessary to take into account the height of the transmitting aerial, and also the receiving aerial, above sea level. (See Fig. 3.)

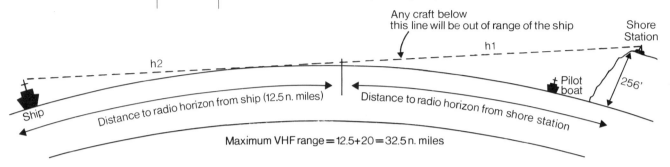

Fig. 3. VHF radio range depends on the horizon and the height of the transmitting and receiving aerials above sea level.

Introductory Section

In the example shown in Fig. 3 the maximum range at which the shore VHF station (on the right) can be received by the ship (on the left) is calculated as follows:

(i) The distance to the radio horizon in nautical miles is:
$1.25 \sqrt{h}$ (where h is the height of the aerial above sea level, in feet)
or $2.21 \sqrt{h}$ (where h is the height of the aerial above sea level, in metres).

(ii) In this example, the maximum range is the sum of the two distances, shore station to its radio horizon (h1) plus ship to its radio horizon (h2):

ie: $1.25 \sqrt{h1} + 1.25 \sqrt{h2}$ nautical miles (height in feet)
or $2.21 \sqrt{h1} + 2.21 \sqrt{h2}$ nautical miles (height in metres)

(iii) using the height in feet shown in Fig. 3.
$$1.25 \sqrt{100} + 1.25 \sqrt{256}$$
$$= (1.25 \times 10) + (1.25 \times 16)$$
$$= 12.5 + 20$$
$$= 32.5 \text{ n miles}$$

0.2.4 Limitations on VHF range

(i) **Power setting**: It was pointed out in para 0.1.1 (ii) that sets can typically be operated with either high power or low power. On high power the signals will travel beyond the radio horizon as shown in Fig. 3. Consequently the ship will still receive the VHF transmission from the shore station even though it is a further 10 miles beyond the radio horizon of the shore station.

On *low power* the signals will not travel beyond the radio horizon. In normal conditions all VHF communication with vessels closer than the radio horizon should be conducted on *low power*.

(ii) **Abnormal propagation**: The term *propagation* refers to the whole process by which radio waves are produced and spread through the earth's atmosphere. Some meteorological conditions can have the effect of reducing or distorting the normal process of radio transmission. Such conditions produce *abnormal propagation*, and one effect is to increase or decrease the maximum range of VHF signals, up to over 100 miles, or down to 9 or 10 miles. Increased range is more common than reduced range; increased range is most likely to occur in the northern Indian Ocean, and in temperate latitudes where high barometric pressure prevails. Decreased range is likely only in polar latitudes. In either case such effects are temporary and unpredictable: they should not be relied on in calculating maximum VHF ranges.

0.2.5 | Capture effect

0.2.5.1 VHF signals radiate in straight lines in all directions from a transmitter. At a given moment, many ships or shore stations may be within range of a ship which is transmitting. All of them will hear the transmission, not only the one for whom the transmission is intended. This is another way in which VHF differs from a land-based public telephone service: VHF conversations cannot be private.

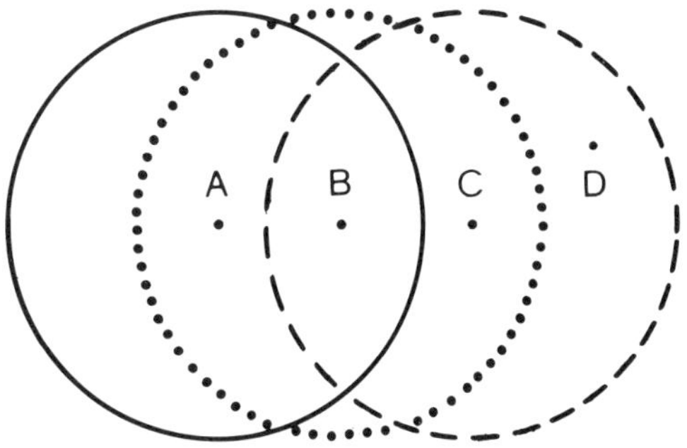

Fig. 4. Overlapping ranges and the capture effect.

0.2.5.2 A major limitation upon VHF radio transmissions may follow from the overlapping ranges of transmitting ships and shore stations. Fig. 4 represents four ships: A, B, C and D. The VHF ranges of ships A, B and C are shown as circles. Suppose that ships A and B are speaking to each other by VHF radio.

Then:

(i) Ship A can hear ship B;

(ii) Ship B can hear ship A;

(iii) Ship C can hear ship B but not ship A;

(iv) Ship D can hear neither ship A nor ship B.

0.2.5.3 Ship C is not actively involved in the VHF exchange between ships A and B. However, ship C is 'captured' by that exchange, because C could not transmit on that channel: the channel is already occupied by the A-B conversation. The capture can cause difficulties, especially since it can take place over quite long distances. A ship's efforts at initiating a transmission on a given channel (for instance, ship D in Fig. 4) may be blocked because the channel is captured by two ships, A and B of whose existence ship D may not even be aware. Ship A may be 90 miles from ship D, and 60 miles from ship B, yet they may be directly preventing D from transmitting on a particular channel. When the channel concerned is the **calling channel**, e.g. channel 16 in European waters, the capture effect can cause great difficulties.

0.2.5.4 Three points about the capture effect need to be kept in mind:

(i) The operator should at all times remember that his transmissions may affect more ships than those actually visible, or in radar range, or within direct VHF contact, and that his transmissions may be producing a capture effect on some unknown ship.

(ii) All transmissions should be kept as brief as possible, especially on the calling channel, so that any capture effect is of short duration.

(iii) The use of low power whenever possible can reduce the extent of capture effect. See Fig. 5. If all four ships are using low power their radio ranges are reduced and communications are possible, on the same channel and simultaneously, between A and B, and between C and D.

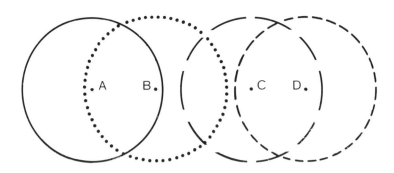

Fig. 5. Low power transmissions may avoid capture effect.

Introductory Section

0.2.6 Simplex and duplex channels: i.e. single-frequency and dual-frequency working

0.2.6.1 A radio frequency can accept only one signal at a time. Therefore, if one station is transmitting another station cannot also transmit on that frequency at the same moment. As stated in para 0.1.2, this is known as **simplex** working. In terms of the rules for conducting a conversation between two stations on a particular channel, simplex working means that a listener must wait until the speaker has finished transmitting before he can reply. The speaker indicates the end of his transmission by using the standard phrase **Over** (or **Out** if the whole conversation is completed) and then releasing the pressel switch on his handset. The listener can now become the speaker, pressing the pressel switch and thus transmitting on the same channel. An example of a simplex channel is VHF channel 16, using a frequency of 156.800 MHz for both transmission and reception — for both speaking and listening.

0.2.6.2 There are also some **duplex channels**, in which two different frequencies are used simultaneously, one for transmission and one for reception. An example is VHF duplex channel 82, using a transmission frequency of 157.125 MHz and a receiving frequency of 161.725 MHz. This makes it possible to transmit and receive at the same time, as on a telephone ashore.

0.2.6.3 All duplex channels are used for working with shore stations, particularly **public correspondence stations**. (See Section 1.2.2 for list of VHF channels indicating simplex and duplex working.) Suppose a ship makes a call to a telephone subscriber ashore, by a **link call** through a Coast Radio Station: when the telephone subscriber answers the speaker on the ship can talk as if on a direct telephone line. However, it is recommended that appropriate SEASPEAK principles should be observed even when working through VHF duplex channels, in order to maintain accuracy of communications.

0.2.6.4 Note also that if each ship transmits on 157.125 MHz and listens on 161.725 MHz when using VHF channel 82, then all the ships will be transmitting on one frequency and nothing will be coming in on the listening frequency. This applies to all duplex VHF channels and means that they are not usable for intership purposes. However, a shore station using duplex working will transmit on the ship's listening frequency and receive on the ship's transmitting frequency. A VHF set installed ashore for duplex working will thus have the opposite arrangement of frequencies on each duplex channel to one installed in a ship, although the VHF channel designator numbers will be the same.

SECTION | 1.0

VHF conventions

1.1

1.1.1

.1 This section outlines the basic principles for using VHF radio and provides guidance on the communication in speech of **numbers, letters, standard units of measurement, time and position.**

.2 The operation of a ship station is under the supreme authority of the master or the person responsible for the ship or other vehicle carrying the station. The person holding this authority will require each operator to comply with the ITU radio regulations and ensure that the radio station is always used in accordance with those regulations. The person holding this authority shall also ensure that all persons who have knowledge of the existence of, or text of, a radio message, observe the obligation to maintain secrecy of correspondence. The foregoing requirements are to be observed at all times when using VHF radio.

USING VHF RADIO

General principles

.1 Do not make unnecessary transmissions. (Training Note 1.)

.2 Always follow the recommended VHF procedures. (Training Note 2.)

.3 *Speak slower than in normal conversation.*

.4 Speak more slowly if the addressee is writing down your message.

.5 *Maintain a constant voice level.*

.6 *Pronounce each word clearly.*

.7 Always follow VHF message recommendations, particularly the use of Message Markers (see Section 4.2).

.8 Always be concise and unambiguous.

.9 Use fixed formats, e.g. MAREP, BAREP, etc. where applicable. (See Section 5.12.)

TRAINING INTRODUCTION TO SECTION 1:
VHF CONVENTIONS

This section contains a number of basic VHF conventions. No attempt should be made to learn the whole section at this stage. Instead, certain critical points, listed below as Points for Special Attention, should be learned now. The rest of the section should be read through for later use.

Ultimately, a thorough knowledge of the whole section is required for efficient VHF maritime radio use, but many learners would be best advised to learn Sections 2, 4 and 3 first, and to learn the contents of this section as required.

Points for special attention

1. Certain items which are italicised in *Using VHF Radio* (1.1)
2. Use of VHF channels (1.2)
3. Identification of stations (1.3)
4. The transmission of letters — phonetic alphabet (1.4.1)
5. Certain abbreviations which are **bold** in 1.4.2
6. The transmission of numbers (1.5)
7. The transmission of standard units of measurement (1.6)
8. The transmission of time (1.7)
9. The transmission of position (1.8)

TRAINING NOTES to 1.1.1: Using VHF radio (general principles)

The nine points given above are explained in detail here. Those which should be carefully considered at this stage are marked with an asterisk (*). The numbering is the same as above.

General principles: points to be noted

1.   **Do not make unnecessary transmissions**. There are only 56 internationally-agreed VHF Channels for the use of the tens of thousands of VHF stations in the world. Do not speak unless you really have to. It is an offence, for which you can be prosecuted, to make annoying or misleading transmissions. (ITU Rules)

2.   **Always follow the recommended VHF procedures**. The VHF procedures have been carefully designed to ensure rapid and efficient communication. As with any standard system, success depends on everyone working to the same set of rules: use of non-standard procedures will lead to chaos.

3.* **Speak slower than in normal conversation**. VHF communicators cannot see each other, their voices may be distorted, they may be trying to hear above a lot of background noise, and they may not be familiar with the accent of the speaker. Speaking slowly saves time, due to the above reasons.

4.   **Speak more slowly if the addressee is writing down your message**. If you speak too quickly you will get requests for repetition of your message. The end result will be that the exchange will take longer to complete. If you are not sure how fast to speak in these circumstances, try writing down the message as you transmit it.

5.* **Maintain a constant voice level**. It does not help to shout or to try to give meaning by the tone of voice. Where there is severe stress, for example in emergency conditions such as collision or fire, the act of forcing yourself to speak slowly and steadily will make you more careful about what you say. This will save time and, perhaps, life.

6.* **Pronounce each word clearly**. If you are faced with an unfamiliar word (a geographical name, for example) and are unsure of the pronunciation, then spell the word out using the phonetic alphabet (1.4.1).

7. **Always follow the VHF message recommendations, particularly the use of Message Markers** (see Section 4.2). These recommendations have been made to ensure that all users of VHF radiotelephony use language in the same way. The use of message markers is particularly important since the marker alerts the listener to the *type* of message he is about to hear. Markers are an important aid to comprehension.

8. **Always be concise and unambiguous**. Messages like: 'You can, at least, umm, I think you can, er, go through the other, er, the channel. You know, the one they used before the jetty was finished' should be avoided. Choose words carefully, keep the language simple, keep the messages short, keep to the subject, and remember that your listener's actions may be determined by what you say.

9. **Use fixed formats, e.g. MAREP, where applicable.** (see Section 5.12). Fixed formats (defined in the Glossary) are designed to enable a large number of items of information to be contained in one transmission. When the circumstances are relevant (see Section 5.12) fixed formats should always be used. The VHF operator ashore will be expecting them and they will greatly ease your communication workload.

1.1.2   Before transmitting (See Training Notes to 1.1.2)

.1   Make sure that your call is really necessary.

.2   Plan what you want to say before starting. Write it down if necessary.

.3   *Check that the VHF set is switched to the correct VHF channel.*

.4   *Listen to find out if the VHF channel you intend to make the call on is already in use.*

.5   Before making the Initial Call listen to find out if the VHF channel you intend to select as the working VHF channel is already in use.

.6   Do not interrupt another station's transmissions.

TRAINING NOTES to 1.1.2: Before transmitting
    *Denotes points which should be considered at this stage.

1. **Make sure that your call is really necessary**. Do not jam VHF channels with trivial communications.

2. **Plan what you want to say before starting. Write it down if necessary**. By doing this, you will be able to ensure that you actually say what you want to, and that you eliminate unnecessary repetition. It is much easier to do this kind of thinking *before* you start talking.

3.* **Check that the VHF set is switched to the correct VHF channel**. It is very easy to transmit on the wrong channel, to forget to switch over to the working channel, or to forget to cancel the dual watch before transmitting.
   When calling shore radio stations on their working VHF channel, check carefully in the most up-to-date copy of the ITU list of Coast Radio Stations, the Admiralty List of Radio Signals, or the equivalent publication carried on board your ship, to ensure that you are using the correct VHF channel

4.* **Listen to find out if the VHF channel you intend to make the call on is already in use**. There is no excuse for accidentally interrupting other people's VHF exchanges. It only takes a minute of listening to ensure that you will not be interrupting anyone. Should you unnecessarily interrupt a Mayday exchange, you might find legal action being taken against you.

5.* **Before making the Initial Call, listen to find out if the VHF channel you intend to select as the working VHF channel is already in use**. If you are going to call another ship, you will be expected to tell that ship which working VHF channel should be used for the exchange. It will save problems later if, **before** you choose a working VHF channel, you make certain that it is not already in use.

6. **Do not interrupt another station's transmissions**. It is illegal to interrupt distress and urgency communications and it can be dangerous to interrupt other exchanges. Always behave in this respect as you would like others to behave towards you.

1.1.3 When transmitting (See Training Notes to 1.1.3)

.1 *Check that the transmit switch is on before starting to speak.*

.2 *Keep the microphone about 3 cm from your mouth when speaking.*

.3 *Do not release the transmit switch until you have finished speaking.*

.4 *Use simplex working, i.e. do not hold the transmit switch down when listening.*

.5 Only use duplex for making link calls through Coast Radio Stations.

.6 *Always use the low power setting unless it is necessary to use the high power setting due to distance, interference etc.*

TRAINING NOTES to 1.1.3: When transmitting

1.* **Check that the transmit switch is on before starting to speak**. Do not speak and press the switch simultaneously; it does not work. Always press first, then speak, then release the switch, in that order.

2.* **Keep the microphone about 3cm from your mouth when speaking**. If it is at the wrong distance, your speech may be distorted.

3.* **Do not release the transmit switch until you have finished speaking**. (see 1 above).

4.* **Use simplex working, i.e. do not hold the transmit switch down when listening.** See Introductory Section, para. 0.2.6: *Simplex and Duplex Channels: i.e. single-frequency and dual-frequency working*, p. 6. The procedural rules, i.e. the method of working, for simplex, can be applied to duplex but not vice versa. It is therefore better to learn the simplex rules first.

5. **Only use duplex for making link calls through Coast Radio Stations**. (see 4 above).

6.* **Always use the low power setting unless it is necessary to use the high power setting due to distance, interference, etc**. Unnecessary use of the high power setting can cause problems for other people. Unnecessary use of the high power setting by other people can cause problems for you. See introductory section *Basic principles of VHF Radio.*

1.2 USE OF VHF CHANNELS

1.2.1 Use of VHF channel 16

TRAINING INTRODUCTION to 1.2: USE OF VHF CHANNELS

1. The use of VHF channels is controlled by regulations drawn up by the ITU (see 1.2.2 below).
    It is not necessary to learn the whole of the table shown at 1.2.2 below. However, you should learn the Intership channels, the order of selection of Intership channels and the channels which are preferable in coastal waters.
    This section on the use of VHF Channel 16 is important and should be studied carefully (1.2.1.1). VHF channel 16 is the distress, safety and urgency channel, and therefore should be treated with respect.

2. Misuse of VHF channel 16 is dangerous and may cost lives.

.1 If a station's working VHF channel is known it should be used for calling in preference to VHF channel 16.

.2 VHF channel 16 is only to be used for calling in cases of:
    (a) **distress, safety** and **urgency;**
    (b) where the other station's working VHF channel is not known;
    (c) where the other station's working VHF channel is known but is engaged.

.3 Calls on VHF channel 16 may be made up to three times at intervals of two minutes. If no reply is received after the third call the interval between calls is to be extended to three minutes. Calling is not to be continued after it becomes obvious that no reply is going to be received.

.4 VHF channel 16 is not to be used for communications other than those connected with distress, safety and urgency situations, except that an exchange less than one minute in length concerning the safety of navigation may be made on VHF channel 16, if it is important that all ships within range hear it. All other communications must be conducted on a VHF working channel.

.5 A listening watch must be kept on VHF channel 16 at all times while the bridge is manned, except when the local regulations require a watch to be kept on another VHF channel and dual watch facilities are not available.

TRAINING INTRODUCTION to 1.2 continued
   Anyone who may be required to keep watch on, or to use, a VHF set must know the contents of this sub-section and of Section 3. (Distress, Urgency and Safety Procedures).

1.2.2 Table showing ITU approved usage of VHF channels

.1   This table is drawn from the International Telecommunication Union (ITU) **Manual for use by the Maritime Mobile and Maritime Mobile Satellite Services,** 1982 edition. (Rev. 1985)

VHF channel designator	Notes	Intership	Port operations: simplex	Port operations: duplex	Ship movements: simplex	Ship movements: duplex	Public correspondence
01				10		15	8
02				8		17	10
03				9		16	9
04				11		14	7
05				6		19	12
06	g	1					
07				7		18	11
08		2					
09	m	5	5		12		
10	l	3	9		10		
11	n		3		1		
12	n		1		3		
13	n	4	4		5		
14	n		2		7		
15	j	11	14				
16		DISTRESS, SAFETY AND CALLING					
17	j	12	13				
18	f			3		22	
19	f			4		21	
20	f			1		23	
21	f			5		20	
22	f			2		24	
23							5
24							4
25							3
26							1
27							2
28							6
60	h			17		9	25
61				23		3	19
62				20		6	22
63				18		8	24
64				22		4	20
65				21		5	21
66				19		7	23
67	l	9	10		9		
68	n		6		2		
69	n	8	11		4		
70	p	DIGITAL SELECTIVE CALLING FOR DISTRESS AND SAFETY					
71	n		7		6		
72	m	6					
73	l	7	12		11		
74	n		8		8		
75	k	NOT AVAILABLE, GUARD BAND BELOW VHF CHANNEL 16					
76	k	DIRECT PRINTING FOR DISTRESS AND SAFETY PURPOSES					
77		10					
78				12		13	27
79	f/n			14		1	
80	f/n			16		2	

SECTION

1

VHF conventions

VHF channel designator	Intership	Port operations: simplex	duplex	Ship movements: simplex	duplex	Public correspondence
Notes						
81			15		10	28
82			13		11	26
83						16
84			24		12	13
85						17
86	o					15
87						14
88	h					18

NOTES REFERRING TO THE TABLE

a The figures in the column headed 'Intership' indicate the normal sequence in which channels should be taken into use by mobile stations.

b The figures in the columns headed 'Port operations', 'Ship movement' and 'Public correspondence' indicate the normal sequence in which channels should be taken into use by each coast station. However, in some cases, it may be necessary to omit channels in order to avoid harmful interference between the services of neighbouring coast stations.

c Administrations may designate frequencies in the intership, port operations and ship movement services for use by light aircraft and helicopters to communicate with ships or participating coast stations in predominantly maritime support operations under the conditions specified by ITU. However, the use of the channels which are shared with public correspondence shall be subject to prior agreement between interested and affected administrations.

d Channels, with the exception of channels 06, 15, 16, 17, 75 and 76, may also be used for highspeed data and facsimile transmissions, subject to special arrangement between interested and affected administrations (see also notes **k** and **p**).

e Except in the United States of America, channels, preferably two adjacent channels from the series 87, 28, 88 with the exception of channels 06, 15, 16, 17, 75 and 76, may be used for direct-printing telegraphy and data transmission, subject to special arrangement between interested and affected administrations (see also notes **k** and **p**).

f The two-frequency channels for port operations (18, 19, 20, 21, 22, 79 and 80) may be used for public correspondence, subject to special arrangement between interested and affected administrations.

g The frequency 156.300 MHz (channel 06) may also be used for communication between ship stations and aircraft stations engaged in coordinated search and rescue operations. Ship stations shall avoid harmful interference to such communications on channel 06 as well as to communications between aircraft stations, ice-breakers and assisted ships during ice seasons.

h Channels 60 and 88 can be used subject to special arrangement between interested and affected administrations.

i The frequencies in this Table may also be used for radiocommunications on inland waterways in accordance with the conditions specified by ITU.

j Channels 15 and 17 may also be used for on-board communications provided the effective radiated power does not exceed 1 W, and subject to the national regulations of the administration concerned when these channels are used in its territorial waters.

k   The frequency 156.825 MHz (channel 76) is used exclusively for direct-printing telegraphy for distress and safety purposes subject to not causing harmful interference to channel 16.

l   Within the European Maritime Area and in Canada these frequencies (channels 10, 67, 73) may also be used, if so required, by the individual administrations concerned, for communication between ship stations, aircraft stations and participating land stations engaged in coordinated search and rescue and anti-pollution operations in local areas, under the conditions specified by ITU.

m   The preferred first three frequencies for the purpose indicated in note c are 156.450 MHz (channel 09), 156.625 MHz (channel 72) and 156.675 MHz (channel 73).

n   These channels (68, 69, 11, 71, 12, 13, 14, 74, 79 and 80) are the preferred channels for the ship movement service. They may, however, be assigned to the port operations service until required for the ship movement service if this should prove to be necessary in any specific area. Channel 13 is also used on a worldwide basis for intership navigation safety communications.

o   This channel (86) may be used as a calling channel if such a channel is required in an automatic radiotelephone system when such a system is recommended by the CCIR.

p   This channel (70) is to be used exclusively for digital selective calling for distress and safety purposes as from 1 January 1986 (see Resolution 317 Mob-83).

1.3   IDENTIFICATION OF STATIONS

1.3.1

.1   ITU regulations state that a station must always identify itself each time it makes a transmission. (See Training Notes to 1.3.)

.2   Shore and coast stations will be identified by the use of their geographical name followed by the type of service that they provide. (See Training Note 2 below.)

e.g. | Niton Radio | Coast radio station

| Colombo Radio | Coast radio station

| Gris Nez Traffic | VTS Station

| Sabine Pilot | Pilot service station

The correct identification of coast and shore radio stations will be found in the ITU **List of Coast Radio Stations.**

.3   *Ship stations* will be identified by their name and/or their international call-sign. International call-signs will be spoken using the phonetic alphabet (Section 1.7).

e.g. G X B C (See Training Notes to 1.3).

| Golf Xray Bravo Charlie |

.4   If the name or call-sign of a ship is not known it should be addressed by the phrase '*All ships (in . . . area)*', followed by one or more of the following:
(a)   ship-type and special features;
(b)   position;
(c)   course and speed.
These elements should be spoken in that order.

SECTION

VHF conventions

If *position* is used it must be given by one of the methods described in Section 1.8. e.g.

> *All ships in West Cape area, calling unknown ship,* position: bearing: two-seven-zero degrees true, from West Cape, distance: six mls.

N.B. Never use relative directions from your own ship.

.5 A portable station (e.g. a hand-held set) must identify itself by the name of its parent station, followed either by the location in which it is operating or by a number. (See Training Notes to 1.3.) e.g.

Name of parent station (in this case a ship); | Whitegate

Bow of ship Whitegate identifies itself as: | Whitegate bow

TRAINING NOTES to 1.3: Identification of stations

1. Remember that a VHF set does not provide a direct and private link like a telephone. VHF transmissions radiate from the aerial in all directions. It is therefore critical that you identify yourself at the beginning of a transmission. Failure to do this has caused collisions. For the same reasons, it is also necessary to say who you are speaking to, i.e. to properly address that station, using its correct identification.

2. There are 4 types of station:
   1. Coast Radio Stations (stations in the public correspondence service)
   2. Shore Radio Stations (stations in the maritime operational service)
   3. Ship Stations (fixed stations on board ships)
   4. Portable Stations (hand-held sets)

3. The international call sign for your ship will be found on the ship's radio licence or in the radio room. It should be prominently displayed near the VHF set for easy reference.

4. A failure to identify has led to collision. A call 'Bow: this is bridge, let go the port anchor' was obeyed on another ship nearby; her sudden stop caused a third ship to collide with her.

1.4 TRANSMISSION OF LETTERS

1.4.1

The phonetic alphabet must be used when giving call-signs, when spelling a word or when speaking individual letters.

TRAINING NOTE to 1.4:
TRANSMISSION OF LETTERS

There is considerable variation in the pronunciation of letters throughout the world, e.g. Z is 'ZED' in British English, 'ZEE' in American English. Use of the phonetic alphabet is essential for mutual understanding.

Letter	Word	Pronunciation guide
A	Alpha	AL FAH
B	Bravo	BRAH VOH
C	Charlie	CHAR LEE
D	Delta	DELL TAH
E	Echo	ECK OH
F	Foxtrot	FOKS TROT
G	Golf	GOLF
H	Hotel	HOH TELL
I	India	IN DEE AH
J	Juliett	JEW LEE ETT
K	Kilo	KEY LOH
L	Lima	LEE MAH
M	Mike	MIKE
N	November	NO VEM BER
O	Oscar	OSS CAH
P	Papa	PAH PAH

Letter	Word	Pronunciation guide
Q	Quebec	KEH <u>BECK</u>
R	Romeo	<u>ROW</u> ME OH
S	Sierra	SEE <u>AIR</u> RAH
T	Tango	<u>TANG</u> GO
U	Uniform	<u>YOU</u> NEE FORM
V	Victor	<u>VIK</u> TAH
W	Whiskey	<u>WISS</u> KEY
X	Xray	<u>ECKS</u> RAY
Y	Yankee	<u>YANG</u> KEY
Z	Zulu	<u>ZOO</u> LOO

The underlined syllables are to be emphasised when pronouncing the words.

1.4.2 Abbreviations

TRAINING NOTE to 1.4.2:
Abbreviations

It is not necessary to memorise all these abbreviations at an early stage of learning Seaspeak. However, the ones which are printed in bold type are constantly in use and must be memorised early.

Some common names and terms are known by their initial letters. There are two types of such abbreviations: (i) where the initial letters are pronounced separately e.g. ETA; (ii) where the initial letters are pronounced as if they formed a word e.g. RoRo (See Training Note to 1.4.2)

(i) List of common abbreviations spoken as initial letters, showing the full spelling from which the initials are taken:

Initials	From the spelling of:
AC	alternating current
AM	amplitude modulation
BHP	brake horsepower
CG	centre of gravity; or coastguard (UK), or Coast Guard (US)
CPA	closest point of approach
CO_2	carbon dioxide
CRT	cathode ray tube
DC	direct current
DF	direction finding
EP	Estimated position
ETA	**Estimated Time of Arrival**
ETD	**Estimated Time of Departure**
FM	frequency modulation
GM	metacentric height
GMT	**Greenwich Mean Time**
HF	high frequency
IHP	indicated horsepower
IMO	International Maritime Organisation
LF	low frequency
LNG	liquefied natural gas
LOP	Line of position
LPG	liquefied petroleum gas
MCT	moment to change trim
MF	medium frequency
PPI	plan position indicator (radar screen)
RT	radio telephony
SAR	**search and rescue**
SHP	shaft horsepower
SI	Système Internationale d'Unités
SSB	single side band
TPC	tonnes per centimetre

Initials	From the spelling of:
TPI	tonnes per inch
TRS	tropical revolving storm
UHF	ultra high frequency
ULCC	ultra-large crude (oil) carrier
UN	United Nations
UTC	**co-ordinated universal time**
VHF	**very high frequency**
VLCC	very large crude (oil) carrier
VLF	very low frequency
WT	wireless telegraphy

(ii)   List of words pronounced as if the initial letters formed a single word:

Abbreviation	From the spelling of:
AMVER	Automated Mutual Vessel Rescue system
IALA	International Association of Lighthouse Authorities
LASH	Lighter Aboard SHip system
OBO	Oil/Bulk Ore ship
RAS	Replenishment At Sea
RoRo	Roll On-Roll Off
SATCOM	SATellite COMmunications
SATNAV	SATellite NAVigation

1.5   TRANSMISSION OF NUMBERS

.1   Numbers are pronounced as in normal English except for a few numbers which have modified pronunciation to ensure that they are more clearly received (see table below).

.2   The decimal point is expressed by the word *decimal* (pronounced day-see-mal).

.3   Each digit must be given separately.

.4   If the number is a whole thousand, e.g. 25,000, the number of thousands is given by separate digits followed by the word *thousand*. If it is not a whole thousand, e.g. 25,256, it is given by separate digits without using the word *thousand*.

Figure	Spelling of number	Pronunciation guide
0	zero	ZERO
1	one	WUN
2	two	TOO
3	three	TREE
4	four	FOWER
5	five	FIFE
6	six	SIX
7	seven	SEVEN
8	eight	AIT
9	nine	NINER
1000	thousand	TOUSAND

The underlined syllables are to be emphasised when pronouncing the words.

SECTION

VHF conventions

.5 **Examples**

Figure	Spelling of number as spoken	Pronunciation guide
2	two	TOO
15	one-five	WUN-FIFE
34	three-four	TREE-FOWER
217	two-one-seven	TOO-WUN-SEVEN
25,000	two-five-thousand	TOO-FIFE-TOUSAND
25,256	two-five-two-five-six	TOO FIFE-TOO-FIFE-SIX
250,000	two-five-zero-thousand	TOO-FIFE-ZERO-TOUSAND
36.04	three-six decimal zero-four	TREE-SIX DAYSEEMAL ZERO-FOWER

1.6 STANDARD UNITS OF MEASUREMENT

TRAINING INTRODUCTION to 1.6:
STANDARD UNITS
OF MEASUREMENT

It is important that the units used for expressing measurements are standard. This avoids confusion and prevents potentially dangerous misunderstandings. Consider for example the considerable difference between a draught of 30 metres and 30 feet. Also the use of standard units means fewer mathematical conversions. Such conversions are time-consuming and a potential source of mistakes.

The list below of Standard Units of Measurement to be used in SEASPEAK is divided into three columns. The left hand column headed. **To Measure** lists the item being described. The centre column headed **Unit** lists the appropriate Standard Units to be used and the right hand column headed **SEASPEAK term** gives the words to be used when speaking that unit on VHF.

To measure	Unit	SEASPEAK term	Notes
Barometric pressure	millibars	*millibars*	
Bearings and courses	360-degrees three-figure notation	*degrees*	Always 009°, 090°, etc.: never 9°, 90°.
Depth	metre	*metres*	
Directions	cardinal	Name of cardinal point e.g. *North, West*	Do not use half or quarter points.
Distance	nautical miles	*miles*	
Draught	metres	*metres*	
Height	metres	*metres*	
Linear dimensions	metres	*metre(s)*	For all dimensions less than 1 mile (1852 metres)
Radio frequencies	Hz	*hertz*	
	kHz	*kilohertz*	
	MHz	*megahertz*	
Speed	knots	*knots*	
Temperature	degrees Celsius	*degrees Celsius*	
Tonnage	DWT	*deadweight tonnes*	
	NRT	*net tonnes*	
	GRT	*gross tonnes*	
VHF frequency	ITU VHF Channel number	*VHF channel*	
Visibility to one mile	metres	*metres*	
Visibility over one mile	nautical miles	*miles*	
Volume	cubic metres	*cubic metre(s)*	
Weight	kilograms	*kilograms*	
	tonnes	*metric tonnes*	
Wind speed	Beaufort Scale	*force*	(See Training Note to 1.6)
	knots	*knots*	

SECTION

VHF conventions

TRAINING NOTE to 1.6:
Wind Speed

Some authorities ashore use the unit Metres per Second (m/s) for reporting and forecasting wind speed. This unit is not used internationally but is common in some areas, particularly Northern Europe. A useful approximation is to multiply the wind speed in m/s by 2, the answer being roughly equivalent to knots.

However, when transmitting wind speed it is advisable to use the standard units of knots or Beaufort Scale; let the shore station do the conversion themselves if they wish to.

1.6.1 Transmission of measurements and quantities

TRAINING INTRODUCTION to 1.6.1:
Transmission of measurements and quantities

It is necessary not only to use the standard units of measurement but to state them clearly before stating the numbers that apply. The reason for this procedure is that the same (or nearly similar) numbers may apply to quite different measures. For example, the information that a ship expects to reach buoy 15 at 1500 GMT and that her draught is 15 metres, could easily lead to confusion. Speak the message as below:

e.g.

> 'My ETA at **position** buoy number one-five is **time** one-five-zero-zero GMT and my **draught** is one-five metres'.

The basic rule is first to say what you are referring to, e.g. *draught*, DRAUGHT, then to say the numbers, e.g. 15, then to say the units or conventional term, e.g. metres.

e.g.

> My draught is one-five metres

.1 Measurements must always be given in the following order:
  (i) what is being measured (length, draught, speed, etc.); (See Training Introduction to 1.6.1 above)
  (ii) the numbers (e.g. two-five-zero, etc.);
  (iii) the units of measurements (metres, knots, tonnes, etc.)

e.g.

> length: two-five-zero metres

.2 Quantities of items (e.g. cylinders, brushes) must be expressed by the word *quantity* followed by the number and the name of the item.
e.g. **24 cylinders** would be spoken as:

> quantity: two-four cylinders

.3 Changes in measurements and quantities are to be expressed by giving the final measurements or quantities required to be indicated by the use of the word *new* before the final value required.
e.g.

> reduce speed, new speed: one-zero knots

.4 Different ways of expressing the thing measured: If the measurement or quantity e.g. for draught: *salt water* draught, *fresh water* draught, draught *forward*, draught *aft*, *maximum* draught, *loaded* draught; then the category used must be stated.
e.g.

> My salt water draught is: two-five metres

> My draught forward is: two-five metres

page 17

SECTION

VHF conventions

1.7 TIME

1.7.1 General rules

.1 Time is given in the same way as other measurements. The word *time* or a phrase containing the word *time* (e.g. *ETA, ETD*) will precede the numbers used.

.2 The unit to be used is either *GMT* or *UTC*, or *local*.

.3 At sea, prior to entry to a port, harbour or other terminal facility, time will be given in *GMT* or *UTC*.

.4 Inside a port, harbour or other terminal facility time will be given in local time.
  e.g. A time 1500 GMT or UTC is to be spoken as:

> time: one-five-zero-zero GMT

or

> time: one-five-zero-zero UTC

An arrival estimate of 1030 is to be spoken as:

> ETA: one-zero-three-zero GMT

or

> ETA: one-zero-three-zero UTC

1.7.2 Periods of time

.1 Periods of time are to be given in the same way as other measurements. The word *period* will precede the numbers used.

.2 The units to be used are hours and minutes.
  e.g. A delay of thirty minutes is to be spoken as:

> delay is period: three-zero minutes.

1.7.3 Time Zones

.1 Time zones are to be indicated using the following convention. The sign to be applied to a time zone is that which would be required to convert it to *GMT* or *UTC* i.e. easterly zones are — (minus) *GMT* or *UTC*, and westerly zones are + (plus) *GMT* or *UTC*.

.2 Time zones are to be given in the same order as other measurements. The words *zone minus* or *zone plus*, as appropriate, are to precede the numbers.

.3 When a time zone is not an exact number of hours different to *GMT* or *UTC*, the number of minutes over are to be expressed as minutes and not as fractions of an hour.

e.g. A time zone of 2½ hours East of Greenwich is to be given as follows:

> zone minus: two hours three-zero minutes

A time zone of one hour West of Greenwich is to be given as follows:

> zone plus: one hour

1.7.4 | Dates

TRAINING INTRODUCTION to 1.7.4: Dates

In principle, it is best to avoid the use of words such as **tomorrow, yesterday** etc. and convey all dates by the use of the day of the month.

It is not normally necessary to use names of days of the week (Monday, etc.) and months of the year.

The standard calendar for international communications purposes is the Gregorian calendar.

.1 The prefixes for giving dates are year, month, day, in that order.

.2 The day of the week (*Monday* etc.) is not to be used.
e.g. Sunday 13 May 1982)

> year: one-nine-eight-two, month: zero-five, day: one-three

1.8 | POSITION

TRAINING INTRODUCTION to 1.8: POSITION

Always be accurate when giving a position. Observe the rules in this section at all times.

With the widespread use of modern rescue equipment, fewer problems now occur in the safe evacuation of people from distressed vessels. The greatest problems are usually experienced in finding the distressed vessel in the first place. Often this is an unfortunate result of partial, inaccurate or poorly-communicated positional information coming from the distressed vessel itself. If you get into the habit of giving positions in the correct manner, you are less likely to make mistakes in an emergency.

1.8.1 | Methods of giving a position

.1 Position can be given in five ways:
   (a) latitude and longitude;
   (b) bearing and distance;
   (c) reference to a navigation mark;
   (d) by reporting points;
   (e) electronic position-fixing references.

1.8.2 Which method to use

.1 **Latitude and Longitude**
This method should be used when clear of land, when near a featureless coast, when confusion with geographic names might arise and when giving positions obtained by electronic position fixing equipment such as Decca Navigator (see .5 below).

.2 **Bearing and Distance**
This method should be used when near land or a conspicuous sea mark. It is recommended that this method be used when there is any possibility of charts with differing datums being used.

.3 **Reference to a Navigation Mark**
This method should be used in the approaches to ports and harbours. The marks should, if possible, be those delineating the fairway being navigated or approached at the time.

.4 **By Reporting Points**
This method is to be used in those areas where designated Reporting Points have been marked on the charts.

.5 **Electronic Position-Fixing References**
This method is only to be used when you are sure that the other station has the necessary charts or equipment to interpret the information that you are giving him. In other cases it is to be converted to latitude and longitude before transmission.

.6 In a distress, safety or urgency situation the position is always to be transmitted in the form in which it was observed.

.7 Always use the most rapid and unambiguous method.

1.8.3 How to use the methods

.1 When giving a position by VHF the positional information must be preceded by the word *position*.

.2 Time of position is to be transmitted after the word *position* and before the first element of the positional information.

.3 If required, the method of obtaining the position and its accuracy may be given after the last element of the positional information in the order:
(a) method (e.g. *Sat-Nav, Radar, Loran* etc.)
(b) accuracy (e.g. *good, poor* or *bad*)

e.g.

> My position, time: one-four-three-zero UTC, latitude:
> ... North, longitude: ... East, loran, good.

1.8.4 Latitude and Longitude method

.1 Latitude is always to be given before longitude.

.2 Latitude is to be spoken before the numbers.

.3 The units to use are *degrees* and *minutes*.

.4 Parts of a minute are to be given as decimals.

.5 Preliminary zero(s) is to be transmitted, (e.g. Longitude zero-one-eight degrees)

.6   The names *North* and *South* are to be spoken after the units.

.7   Longitudes are to be given in the same manner except that the names *East* or *West* are to be used.
   e.g. 30° 50′N 018° 25′.02E

> position: latitude: three-zero degrees five-zero minutes North; longitude: zero-one-eight degrees two-five decimal zero-two minutes East.

1.8.5   Bearing and Distance

.1   The bearing is to be given first before the point of reference.

.2   The bearing to be given is that *from* the point of reference being used.

.3   The word *bearing* is to be given before the numbers.

.4   The units to be used are *degrees true* in the 360° notation form.

.5   The word *distance* is to be given before the numbers.

.6   The units to be used are nautical *miles*.

.7   The word *from* is to be spoken before the name of the reference point.
   e.g.   194° (T) from Cape Otway: distance: 12.4 miles

> position: bearing: one-nine-four degrees true; from Cape Otway distance one-two decimal four miles.

1.8.6   Reference to a Navigation Mark

.1   The order of transmission is to be direction-distance-progress-name(s) of navigation mark(s).

.2   Direction is to be given from the navigation mark using points of the compass (e.g. *North, Southwest*, etc.).

.3   Distance may be given in miles and decimals of a mile, or in metres.

.4   Progress may be expressed by the words *passing, approaching, between, near, leaving.*

.5   In a buoyed fairway, position should be given relative to the buoys lying on the starboard side of the ship.
   e.g.

> position: Northeast from Rangitoto Beacon.
> position: approaching Goeree Light Tower.
> position: between buoy number: one-three and buoy number: one-five

1.8.7   By Reporting Points

.1   Observe the rules for the particular system as given in the official publications covering the navigation of the area.

.2   Generally the name of the ship, the Reporting Point and the time will be required.
   e.g.

> Gammon, position: point Alfa; time: one-zero-zero-one local

1.8.8 Electronic Position Fixing

.1 The order of transmission is to be name of system — name of stations or chain being used — receiver readout (e.g. LOP, Deccometer readings, etc.).

e.g.

> position: Decca, two bravo, red two-one decimal four, green three-two decimal five.

TRAINING NOTE to 1.8.8: Electronic Position Fixing

If the actual read out obtained from the instruments is given then the name of the system comes from the readout. e.g.

> position: Decca, two bravo, red two-one decimal four, green three-two decimal five.

If the readout of the system has been translated into Latitude and Longitude then the name of the system comes last. e.g.

> Position: Time: zero-zero-three-zero zone plus three hours. Latitude six-one degrees four-four decimal five minutes North; Longitude zero-three-one degrees five-six minutes West. Omega.

SECTION

1

VHF conventions

SECTION 1. EXERCISES

Ex. 1.A. Using VHF radio

Read aloud the example transmissions given below, taking care to:
(i)   speak slower than in normal conversations,
(ii) maintain a constant voice level,
(iii) pronounce each word clearly.

If possible, use a tape recorder to simulate a VHF radio. Play back and repeat until you achieve a satisfactory standard. Listen to these example transmissions on the Seaspeak Training Manual Tapes if you have them.

Several of the exercises on the remaining principles in Section 1.1 require access to live or simulated VHF equipment. These should be practised as soon as possible in order to become familiar with this medium of communication.

Example transmissions: ⬚⊙⊙⬚

(i)
> Offshore Star. This is Aberdeen harbour.
> Warning. The leading lights are not lit.
> Over.

(ii)
> All ships in River Weser. This is Weser Rivière Radio.
> Navigational Information: heights of tide.
> Information, one: position: Robbenplatz; height of tide one-decimal-five metres, time: now.
> Information, two: position: Fischereihafen, height of tide one-decimal-four metres, time; now.
> Over.

(iii)
> Gulf Trader, this is Nippon Maru.
> Switch to VHF channel zero-six.
> Over.

(iv)
> Nippon Maru, this is Gulf Trader.
> Agree VHF channel zero-six.
> Over.

Ex. 1.B. Transmission of letters; abbreviations

Phonetic Alphabet

(a)   Turn to Section 1.4.1, p. 13. Read the phonetic alphabet *silently* while listening to the recording. Repeat.

(b)   Now record your own voice, speaking the phonetic alphabet. Replay the original and your own version. Note any letters not spoken at a good standard in your own version. Replay the original, and record your own voice speaking the particular letters you noted down. Continue to listen, record and compare until you are satisfied with your performance on every letter of the phonetic alphabet.

(c)   Say the following groups aloud, using the phonetic alphabet:
1. SQV   2. NAM   3. TIR   4. JPZ
5. BWO   6. DEC   7. KFY   8. GLU
9. XH

(d)   Replay the recording which consists of 15 ships' call-signs. Write down the letters you hear and check the answers

CALL SIGNS: LLOYDS REGISTER 1984–85

1 AROSA SEXTO	EGHM
2 BRAVERY	VRGN
3 CHARLES R HUNTLEY	VDCX
4 DUBNO	UBFM
5 EURO CARRIER	DGDU
6 GORYN	UUVS
7 ILKE	PKMR
8 JIJIA	YQMW
9 LAGOVEN PARIA	YYBG
10 MARYUT	SYPY

SECTION 1. EXERCISES

11 NOJIMA	JAZP
12 OSHIMA MARU	JIIA
13 SEALAND PACER	KSLB
14 VILLE DU PONANT	DNPX
15 ENGADINE	GRBU

Ex. 1.C

Abbreviations

1. Turn to Section 1.4.2, p. 14. The recording lists 6 abbreviations: They are printed in bold type on P. 14 but on the recording they are spoken in 3 different sequences. Listen to the recording and write down the abbreviation in each case.

2. The recording gives a list of full names for which ETA, VHF etc. are the abbreviations. This set includes other terms from the lists on p. 14 in addition to the 6 in the recording.

3. Say the abbreviations for the following terms; record your voice, then compare with the recording:
   - (a) search and rescue
   - (b) International Maritime Organisation
   - (c) co-ordinated universal time
   - (d) satellite communications
   - (e) estimated time of departure
   - (f) roll on — roll off
   - (g) Greenwich Mean Time
   - (h) Very High Frequency
   - (i) Estimated Time of Arrival

Ex. 1.D. Numbers

1. Turn to Section 1.5, p. 15. The recording gives the required pronunciation of numbers. Listen to the recording.

2. Listen to the recording, Write down the number you hear, and check with the answer. Repeat this exercise until you can identify all the numbers spoken on the recording.

3. Say the following numbers and record your voice. Then check with the recording.

13,	30,	300,	103
99,	19,	191,	909
70,	170,	117,	777
21,	120,	111,	435

4. Work with a partner, read the following grid to each other. Repeat until there are no errors:

23	75	108	39	24	A reads to B
87	155	6	234	12	B reads to A
372	59	18	4	9	A reads to B
35	528	197	2	65	B reads to A
222	41	82	10	256	A reads to B
95	43	68	5	188	B reads to A

Ex. 1.E. Standard units; transmission of quantities

The following pieces of information are not expressed in a form suitable for transmission. Convert each one to SEASPEAK using the principles set out in Section 1.6 of this Manual. Practise transmitting the items. (If you have difficulty at first, write out the SEASPEAK in full before speaking it.)

Examples:

9°	=	zero-zero-nine degrees
twenty-five metres deep	=	depth: two-five metres
fifteen metres draught	=	draught: one-five metres

Now you try the following:

1. 90°
2. one-hundred-and-twenty nautical miles
3. 250 metres (length)
4. twenty-four coils of rope
5. 10 knots (wind speed)
6. increase speed to 10 knots
7. 10 metres (salt water draught)
8. 18 metres (draught)
9. My tonnage is 30,000 GROSS
10. My ETA at buoy 25 is 17.00 GMT

Ex. 1.F. Identification of Station

When you know the phonetic alphabet well, begin the following exercises on *Identification of Station*. The most important points to remember are:

(a) the four types of identification.

(b) the fact that it is essential to state the name of the station you are calling and your own station name *at the beginning of every transmission*.

Practise the following identifications and calls, using a tape recorder to check your performance. (Look up some more in lists of Radio Stations).

Example: Rattler GXBC to Niton Radio.

> 'Niton Radio: this is Rattler Golf Xray Bravo Charlie'. OVER.

Contacts between:

(**1**) Shore/Coast Station and ships

- (a) Elin Queen to Colombo Radio.
- (b) Almoussa 9KJS is calling Dubai Radio.
- (c) Boguslav UFLR to Ostend Radio.
- (d) Lands End Radio to Centaur DLCZ.
- (e) Gothenburg Traffic to Dae Jin 6MBA.
- (f) Dalia I, HZJK is calling Maas Pilot.
- (g) Dalibon YTRI is calling Yokohama Port Radio.

(**2**) Ship and ship
- (a) Dimitriy Zhloba UQOB to Drill Fish FUOY.
- (b) Gold Bond Trail Blazer D5BW to Atlantica HPRK.
- (c) Ambia Finjo ELBF5 is calling Genclik TCCF.
- (d) Batabano COGX is calling Cluj YQSQ.
- (e) Anco Chaser GTEX to Cattleya D7AW.

SECTION 1. EXERCISES

    (f)   Dorg Bang 6MGI is calling to Fenn Victory KHVU.

    (g)   Ferg Xiang BOWK to Global Mariner SXTW

(3) Ship and unknown ship
- (a) Annika N (SYDM) is trying to call an unknown ship of LASH type with red funnels near the North Goodwin buoy.
- (b) Bellyatriks ESSW is trying to call a car ferry in the sea area Maas approach, bearing 200 distance 2 miles from Maas Centre buoy.
- (c) Clytoneus GUWG is trying to contact an OBO ship in sea area Practicos Recalades course 126 degrees speed 13 knots.

(4) Portable Station and Portable Station (no call signs used)
- (a) Ferraz bow is calling Ferraz bridge.
- (b) Miranda stern to Miranda Bow.
- (c) Grand Youth gangway to Grand Youth bridge.
- (d) Glomfjord bridge to second officer ashore.
- (e) Coral Sea bridge calling Coral Sea lifeboat.
- (f) Canadia Number 3 calling Canadia Number 1.

Ex. 1.G. Time

Convert the following items of information into SEA-SPEAK and practise transmitting them.

1. local time 02:30.
2. local time 15:45.
3. one o'clock in the morning local time.
4. ETA (in UTC) 13:30.
5. ETA (local time) 11:00.
6. a delay of 45 minutes.
7. a delay of 1½ hours.
8. Estimated Time of Departure, two thirty in the afternoon.
9. Wednesday, 3rd October, 1984.
10. Thursday, April 19th, 1984.

Ex. 1.H. Position

Clear and accurate transmission of positional information in an internationally-agreed standard form is essential. Convert the following into a form suitable for transmission over VHF:

Example: 30° 50'N. latitude.
               18 25.02' E. longitude.
               23:30 UTC

Answer. position: at time: two-three-three zero UTC: latitude three-zero, degrees, five-zero minutes North, longitude: zero-one-eight. degrees, two-five decimal zero-two minutes East.

1. *Latitude and Longitude*
- (a) 03° 46' N, 08° 48'E.
- (b) 53° 14.2'N, 08° 28'E.
- (c) 12° 06'N, 68° 56.2'W. 15:00 GMT.
- (d) 12° 09 N, 69°.01 W. 01:00 GMT.
- (e) 63°.54 N, 38°.06 E. 10:00 GMT.

2. *Bearing and Distance*
- (a) 200°, 3.1 miles from Cap Couronne.
- (b) 340°, 4.6 miles from Uinga Island West Point.
- (c) 220°, 1.3 miles from Hoek van Baarland.
- (d) 180°, 2.1 miles from Fjard Hallan.
- (e) 090°, 0.1 miles from Red Fish Island South Point. 00.10 GMT.

3. *Navigational Marks*
- (a) Approaching Maas centre buoy.
- (b) NE from Goeree light beacon.
- (c) Between Eurogeul buoys E 11 and E 13.
- (d) Passing South from Deutsche Bucht light vessel.
- (e) Leaving Barrow Deep

4. *Reporting Points*
- (a) Approaching waypoint T.5, Texas City. 11:11 local.
- (b) Waypoint 10 Gryten. 12:00 local.
- (c) Waypoint 30 Klubbensborg 06:30 local
- (d) Waypoint, buoy number 135: Finkenwerder. 11:30 local.
- (e) Crayfordness Point. 20:00 local.

5. *Electronic Position Fixing References*
- (a) Decca: two Charlie oblique Mike Papa: Red A∅: Green C3∅ 17:50 UTC
- (b) Decca 6B/MP Red B 18 Green C36. 06:15 UTC
- (c) Satnav lat. 50° 15.5'N, long. 22° 36'W. 16:00 UTC
- (d) Omega lat. 61° 44.5'N, long 31°56'W. 00:30 zone Papa
- (e) Loran C. lat. 31° 03'N long. 76° 25'W. 10:00 UTC

Practise *receiving* positional information in the above form, and then write it down in navigational shorthand.

Take a suitable chart and mark positions at random. Transmit these positions to a partner using the correct SEASPEAK form. Your partner should then find the position on the chart. Reverse roles and repeat.

SECTION 1 ANSWERS

Ex. 1A

Oral. No answers.

Ex. 1.B

1. (a) Oral. No answers.
   (b) Oral. No answers.
   (c) 1. SEE AIR RAH, KEH BECK, VIK TAH
       2. NO VEM BER, AL FAH, MIKE
       3. TANG GO, IN DEE AH, ROW ME OH
       4. JEW LEE ETT, PAH PAH, ZOO LOO
       5. BRAH VO, WISS KEY, OSS CAH
       6. DELL TAH, ECK OH, CHAR LEE
       7. KEY LOH, FOKS TROT, YANG KEY
       8. GOLF, LEE MAH, YOU NEE FORM
       9. ECKS RAY, HOH TELL
   (d) Oral. No answers.

Ex. 1.C

1. Oral. No answers.
2. Oral. No answers.
3. (a) SAR
   (b) IMO
   (c) UTC
   (d) SATCOM
   (e) ETD
   (f) RoRo
   (g) GMT
   (h) VHF
   (i) ETA

Ex. 1.D

1. Oral. No answers.
2. Oral. No answers.
3. Oral. No answers.
4. Oral. No answers.

Ex. 1.E

1. zero-nine-zero degrees
2. one-two-zero miles
3. Length: two-five-zero metres
4. Quantity: two-four coils of rope

5. Wind speed: one-zero knots
6. Increase speed: New speed: one-zero knots
7. Draught: Salt water: one-zero metres
8. Draught: one-eight metres
9. Tonnage: three-zero thousand gross
10. ETA at Position: buoy number one-five is time: one-seven-zero-zero GMT

Ex. 1.F

1. (a) Colombo Radio, Colombo Radio. This is Elin Queen, Elin Queen. Over.
   (b) Dubai Radio, Dubai Radio. This is Almoussa, Nine Kilo Juliett Sierra, Almoussa, Nine Kilo Juliett Sierra. Over.
   (c) Ostend Radio, Ostend Radio. This is Boguslav, Uniform Foxtrot Lima Romeo, Boguslav, Uniform Foxtrot Lima Romeo. Over.
   (d) Centaur, Delta Lima Charlie Zulu, Centaur, Delta Lima Charlie Zulu. This is Land's End Radio, Land's End Radio. Over.
   (e) Dae Jin, Six Mike Bravo Alpha, Dae Jin, Six Mike Bravo Alpha. This is Gothenburg Traffic, Gothenburg Traffic. Over.
   (f) Maas Pilot, Maas Pilot. This is Dalia I, Hotel Zulu Juliett Kilo, Dalia I, Hotel Zulu Juliett Kilo. Over.
   (g) Yokohama Port Radio, Yokohama Port Radio. This is Dalibon, Yankee Tango Romeo India, Dalibon, Yankee Tango Romeo India. Over.

2. (a) Drill Fish, Foxtrot Uniform Oscar Yankee, Drill Fish, Foxtrot Uniform Oscar Yankee. This is Dimitriy Zhola, Uniform Quebec Oscar Bravo, Dimitriy Zhola, Uniform Quebec Oscar Bravo. Over.
   (b) Atlantica, Hotel Papa Romeo Kilo, Atlantica, Hotel Papa Romeo Kilo. This is Gold Bond Trail Blazer, Delta Five Bravo Whiskey, Gold Bond Trail Blazer, Delta Five Bravo Whiskey. Over.
   (c) Genclik, Tango Charlie Charlie Foxtrot, Genclik, Tango Charlie Charlie Foxtrot. This is Ambia Finjo, Echo Lima Bravo Foxtrot Five, Ambia Finjo, Echo Lima Bravo Foxtrot Five. Over.
   (d) Cluj, Yankee Quebec Sierra Quebec, Cluj, Yankee Quebec Sierra Quebec. This is Batabano, Charlie Oscar Gulf Xray, Batabano, Charlie Oscar Gulf Xray. Over.
   (e) Cattleya, Delta Seven Alpha Whiskey, Cattleya, Delta Seven Alpha Whiskey. This is Anco Chaser, Gulf Tango Echo Xray, Anco Chaser, Gulf Tango Echo Xray. Over.
   (f) Fenn Victory, Kilo Hotel Victor Uniform, Fenn Victory, Kilo Hotel Victor Uniform. This is Dorg Bang, Six Mike Gulf India, Dorg Bang, Six Mike Gulf India. Over.
   (g) Global Mariner, Sierra Xray Tango Whiskey, Global Mariner, Sierra Xray Tango Whiskey. This is Ferg Xiang, Bravo Oscar Whiskey Kilo, Ferg Xiang, Bravo Oscar Whiskey Kilo. Over.

3. (a) All ships, All ships. Calling unknown ship. Type: LASH. Funnels: red. Position: Near North Goodwin Buoy. This is Annika N, Sierra Yankee Delta Mike. Annika N, Sierra Yankee Delta Mike. Over.
   (b) All ships in sea area Maas approach. All ships in sea area Maas approach. Calling unknown ship. Type: Car ferry. Position: bearing two-zero-zero degrees true from Maas Centre buoy, distance two miles. This is Bellyatriks, Echo Sierra Whiskey, Bellyatriks, Echo Sierra Sierra Whiskey. Over.
   (c) All ships in sea area Practicos Recalades. All ships in sea area Practicos Recalades. Calling unknown ship. Type: OBO. Course: one-two-six degrees. Speed: one-three knots. This is Clytoneus, Gulf Uniform Whiskey Gulf, Clytoneus, Gulf Uniform Whiskey Gulf. Over.

4. (a) Ferraz bridge. This is Ferraz bow.
   (b) Miranda bow. This is Miranda stern.
   (c) Grand Youth bridge. This is Grand Youth gangway.
   (d) Glomfjord Portable. This is Glomfjord bridge.
   (e) Coral Sea lifeboat. This is Coral Sea bridge.
   (f) Canadia Number one. This is Canadia Number three.

Ex. 1.G

1. Time: zero-two-three-zero local.
2. Time: one-five-four-five local.
3. Time: zero-one-zero-zero local.
4. ETA: one-three-three-zero UTC.
5. ETA: one-one-zero-zero local.
6. Delay is period: four-five minutes.
7. Delay is period: one hour three-zero minutes.
8. ETD: one-four-three-zero local.
9. Year: one-nine-eight-four, month: one-zero, day: zero-three.
10. Year: one-nine-eight-four, month: zero-four, day: one-nine.

SECTION 1
ANSWERS

Ex. 1.H

1. (a) Position: Latitude zero-three degrees four-six minutes North; Longitude zero-zero-eight degrees four-eight minutes East.

   (b) Position: Latitude five-three degrees one-four decimal two minutes North; Longitude zero-zero-eight degrees two-eight minutes East.

   (c) Position at time: one-five-zero-zero GMT: Latitude one-two degrees zero-six minutes North; Longitude zero-six-eight degrees five-six decimal two minutes West.

   (d) Position at time: zero-zero-zero GMT: Latitude one-two degrees zero-nine minutes North; Longitude zero-six-nine degrees zero-one minutes West.

   (e) Position at time: one-zero-zero-zero GMT: Latitude six-three degrees five-four minutes North; Longitude zero-three-eight degrees zero-six minutes East.

2. (a) Position: bearing: two-zero-zero degrees true from Cap Couronne; distance: three decimal one miles.

   (b) Position: bearing: three-four-zero degrees true from Uinga Island West Point; distance: four decimal six miles.

   (c) Position: bearing: two-two-zero degrees true from Hoek van Baarland; distance: one decimal three miles.

   (d) Position: bearing: one-eight-zero degrees true from Fjard Hallan; distance: two decimal one miles.

   (e) Position at time: zero-zero-one-zero GMT, bearing: zero-nine-zero degrees true from Red Fish Island South Point; distance: zero decimal one miles.

3. (a) Position: approaching Maas centre buoy.

   (b) Position: Northeast from Goeree light beacon.

   (c) Position: between Eurogeul buoy number Echo one-one and Eurogeul buoy number Echo one-three.

   (d) Position: Passing South from Deutsche Bucht light vessel. *Note*: "Passing" at beginning of sentence to maintain English sentence construction.

   (e) Position: Leaving Barrow Deep.

4. (a) Texas City, position: approaching Waypoint Tango Five; time: one-one-one-one local.

   (b) Gryten, position: Waypoint one-zero; time: one-two-zero-zero local.

   (c) Klubbensborg, position: Waypoint three-zero; time; zero-six-three-zero local.

   (d) Finkenwerder, position: Waypoint buoy number one-three-five; time: one-one-three-zero local.

   (e) Position: Crayfordness Point; time: two-zero-zero-zero local.

5. (a) Position: Time: one-seven-five-zero UTC, Decca: Two Charlie Oblique Mike Papa Red Alpha Zero, Green Charlie Three Zero.

   (b) Position: Time: zero-six-one-five UTC, Decca: Six Bravo Oblique Mike Papa Red Bravo One Eight Green Charlie Three Six.

   (c) Position: Time: one-six-zero-zero UTC. Latitude five-zero degrees one-five decimal five minutes North; Longitude zero-two-two degrees three-six minutes West. SATNAV.

   (d) Position: Time: zero-zero-three-zero zone plus three hours. Latitude six-one degrees four-four decimal five minutes North; Longitude zero-three degrees five-six minutes West. Omega.

   (e) Position: Time: one-zero-zero-zero UTC. Latitude three-one degrees zero-three minutes North; Longitude zero-seven-six degrees two-five minutes West. Loran Charlie.

SECTION

VHF procedures

2.0 GENERAL INTRODUCTION

This section sets out the recommended procedures for communicating on VHF radio.

2.1 THE DIFFERENT TYPES OF PROCEDURE

Three types of procedure are to be distinguished:

(i) **exchange procedure;**
(ii) **broadcast procedure;**
(iii) **distress and safety communications.**

2.1.1 Exchange procedure (see 2.3 and 2.4)

This applies when two or more stations achieve communication with each other. An **exchange** is then said to be taking place.

2.1.2 Broadcast procedure (see 2.5 and 2.6)

This applies when:

.1 A station transmits without expecting a response from any other station.

.2 A station transmits without knowing if a response from another station will be received or not.

If another station responds to the **broadcast** then the communication becomes an **exchange** and the exchange procedure rules apply.

2.1.3 Distress and safety communications

Distress and safety communications and how to conduct them will be found in Section 3.1.

2.2 GENERAL PROCEDURE RULES

2.2.1 Order of priority of communications

(a) Distress calls, distress messages and distress communications. These will all be preceded by the word *Mayday*.

SECTION

VHF procedures

(b) Communications preceded by the urgency signal, *Pan-Pan*.

(c) Communications preceded by the safety signal, *Sécurité*.

(d) Communications related to radio direction finding.

(e) Communications relating to search and rescue.

(f) Communications relating to the navigation, movements and needs of ships and aircraft, including official meteorological messages.

(g) ETAT PRIORITY NATIONS communications (United Nations priority messages).

(h) ETAT PRIORITY communications (national government priority messages).

(i) Service communications (messages concerning the conduct of radio communications).

(j) Communications which do not fall into any of the above categories.

N.B. Stations must stop using any VHF channel which is needed for communications of a higher priority.

2.2.2 The Controlling Station (CS)

.1 The CS is responsible for making and maintaining contact.

.2 The CS is either:

    (a) The station that makes the initial call, or

    (b) A Coast or Shore Radio Station as soon as it becomes involved in an exchange or broadcast.

.3 What the CS does. The function of the CS is to:

    (a) nominate the working VHF channel;

    (b) conduct the change-over to the working VHF channel;

    (c) re-establish contact on the working VHF channel;

    (d) re-establish contact if it should be lost at any time;

    (e) terminate the exchange or broadcast.

.4 How the CS carries out its responsibilities is explained in Sections 2.3 and 2.4, with detailed explanations on how to conduct exchanges and broadcasts.

2.2.3 Interruptions: How to avoid interrupting and to deal with interruptions

.1 Sections 1.1.2.4 and .5 require that you listen to find out if a VHF channel is already in use before you transmit on it.

.2 If the VHF channel you select is already being used for a communication of higher priority you must:

    (a) wait until the other communication is finished, or

    (b) use another VHF channel. (See Training Note to 2.2.3).

SECTION

VHF procedures

TRAINING INTRODUCTION
to 2.2.3: Interruptions

In order to avoid interrupting others and to deal with interruptions from others, an accurate knowledge of the order of priority of communications and of exchange procedure structure is necessary.

The main problem experienced in VHF communications is of over-crowded VHF channels; hence the need for interruption rules. (see 1.1.1.1 and 1.1.2.1). In practice, however, many problems will resolve themselves.

.3 If it is necessary to interrupt a communication you must wait until a break between transmissions, then make the following transmission:

> *Interruption.*
> Address of at least one of the stations you are interrupting.
> *This is.*
> Identification of own station.
> Word or phrase indicating purpose of own communication, e.g. *Pan-Pan* or *Weather forecast.*
> *Stop transmitting.*
> *(x) minutes* (see .4 below).
> *Over.*

.4 If possible you should inform the interrupted station of how long the interruption will be.

.5 If any station's communications are unnecessarily interrupted by transmissions from another station, the following transmission may be made:

> *Interruption.*
> Address of the station(s) making the interruption.
> *This is.*
> Identification of own station.
> *Stop transmitting.*
> *(x) minutes* (see .4 above).
> *Out.*

.6 Because of the capture effect, any station may deal with interruptions to the communications in which they are involved.

2.2.4 Radio reception

TRAINING NOTE to 2.2.3:
Interruptions

VHF CHANNEL ALREADY
OCCUPIED

In most circumstances it will be better to wait, or to use another VHF Channel, even if your communication is of a higher priority than that of the communication in progress. The decision to interrupt or not will obviously depend on the urgency of your communication.

TRAINING INTRODUCTION to 2.2.4: Radio Reception: The Readability Code and the SINPFEMO Code

1. It is frequently necessary to know how well the other station is receiving you, especially when the message is of great importance. There is little point in continuing to transmit if the other station can hardly hear you, or make out your message. Equally, you may need to inform the other station that you can hear him only with difficulty.

2. Ability to make out the message is called **readability**, from the verb **to read**, meaning (in the special context of radio communications) 'to receive sufficiently well to make out the message'. *NB*: Readability has nothing to do with whether a message is **understood**, only with whether it is **heard**.

3. Information about the readability of a signal is reported by a simple code of numbers from 0 (**unusable**) to 5 (**excellent**). The form of the report is also simple:

Ex. **I read five**, or **I read two**, etc.

The code is designed for operational use and should be memorised by the student.

4. A more complex form of radio report, the SINPFEMO Code, provides radio engineers with eight categories of technical information. The student should be aware of the existence of the SINPFEMO Code but he does not need to memorise it, since it is unlikely he will encounter it in operational use.

5. Additional guidance in the use of the Readability Code is given in Section 4.1 (Standard Phrases).

.1 There are two codes for reporting radio reception. The overall readability of the received transmissions is reported by use of the Readability Code; detailed reports are made by use of the SINPFEMO Code.

.2 **The Readability Code**
   one = unusable
   two = poor
   three = fair
   four = good
   five = excellent

.3 The readability code is to be used by speaking the appropriate number.

e.g. | I read one | or | I read five. |

.4 A request for a readability report may be made at any stage of the exchange. The phrase to be used is:

| How do you read? |

.5 Only ask for a report if you think that the other station is not hearing you well.

.6 You may respond to a request for a report by including the appropriate response from the readability code in your next transmission.

.7 A report can be given without a request, e.g. to inform the other station that you are receiving him poorly.

.8 The SINPFEMO Code is to be used for specific radio checks and when reports are required on specific aspects of a station's transmissions.

.9 The SINPFEMO Code is only to be used when the station making a request for a report on its transmissions asks for it to be used.

.10 If no request is made, then proceed as follows:
   (a) use column heading word in SINPFEMO table e.g. signal strength;
   (b) use appropriate word in SINPFEMO table column e.g. excellent.

.11 The letter 'x' (spoken as *Xray*) shall be used instead of a numeral for SINPFEMO characteristics not being reported.

.12 **The SINPFEMO Code**

	S	I	N	P	F	E	M	O
rating scale		degrading effect of				modulation		
	signal strength	inter-ference	noise	propaga-tion dis-turbance	frequency of fading	quality	depth	overall rating
5	excellent	nil	nil	nil	nil	excellent	maximum	excellent
4	good	slight	slight	slight	slow	good	good	good
3	fair	moderate	moderate	moderate	moderate	fair	fair	fair
2	poor	severe	severe	severe	fast	poor	poor or nil	poor
1	barely audible	extreme	extreme	extreme	very fast	very fast	continu-ously over modulated	unusable

e.g. If the transmission being reported on was of:
excellent strength
moderate interference
slight noise
nil propagation disturbance
slow fading
fair modulation
no comment on depth of modulation
and overall was of fair quality,
then the report made using the SINPFEMO code would be:

> Darringer. This is Southport harbour.
> Signal check.
> INFORMATION: SINPFEMO: five, three, four, five, four,
> three, Xray, three.
> I say again, SINPFEMO: five, three, four, five, four, three,
> Xray, three.
> Over.

2.2.5 Lost Contact Rule

.1 If, without prior arrangement, nothing is heard for 20 seconds or more then both stations are to switch back to the calling VHF channel in use. (See Training Notes to 2.2.5).

.2 The Controlling Station must re-establish contact. (See Training Notes to 2.2.5).

.3 If the Controlling Station has difficulty in re-establishing contact on the calling VHF channel then VHF channel 16 is to be used. (See Training Notes to 2.2.5).

TRAINING NOTES to 2.2.5: Lost Contact Rule

1. In the context of open sea and intership communications, the effect of this rule is that after about 20 seconds of lost contact both stations switch back to the calling channel. Normally that channel is VHF channel 16. There may be many possible reasons for loss of contact, e.g.: interference by stations not directly involved; the capture effect; choice of working channel that turns out to be already in use; equipment failure; etc. Whatever the reason, when contact is broken for 20 seconds or more, this rule applies and both stations switch back to the calling channel. (*NB*: Twenty seconds is an approximate indication, not a precise measurement of time.)

2. The responsibility for re-establishing contact lies with the Controlling Station, as mentioned in Section 2.2.2. Obviously if both stations try simultaneously to call each other again, difficulties will arise. This rules states that the station which should first make the attempt is the CS. However, remember that when a shore station or coast radio station is involved, that will be the CS, even if the Initial Call was made by the other station. If the CS does not re-establish contact the other station may attempt to do so.

3. .3 of this rule applies in cases where the original calling channel was not VHF channel 16; for example, off the coast of the United States of America intership communications use VHF channel 13 for this purpose.

SECTION

| | 2.3 | EXCHANGE PROCEDURE |

VHF procedures

TRAINING INTRODUCTION to 2.3:
EXCHANGE PROCEDURE

(i) The following two subsections (2.3 and 2.4) contain essential information for the conduct of *exchanges* (conversations) on VHF radio. They are central to SEASPEAK. They are primarily concerned not with the content of messages but with the organisation of the exchange, so that at any point the communicators know what is happening, who should make the next move, and what that move should be. If VHF radio users keep to the standard routines set out here, much time and unnecessary talk can be saved, while establishing and maintaining contact with each other.

In some of the examples, actual maritime messages have been included, in order to make the examples realistic. No attempt should be made to learn message patterns (see Section 4) until a thorough knowledge of exchange procedure has been achieved.

(ii) There are, generally, four stages in a VHF exchange.

Stage 1
MAKE CONTACT (normally VHF Channel 16)

Stage 2
AGREE AND SWITCH TO A SUITABLE WORKING CHANNEL

Stage 3
EXCHANGE MESSAGES

Stage 4
TERMINATE

(iii) In some cases, however, the initial contact can be made on a working VHF Channel (as when calling a Port Radio Station).

The above procedure reduces the number of stages to three:

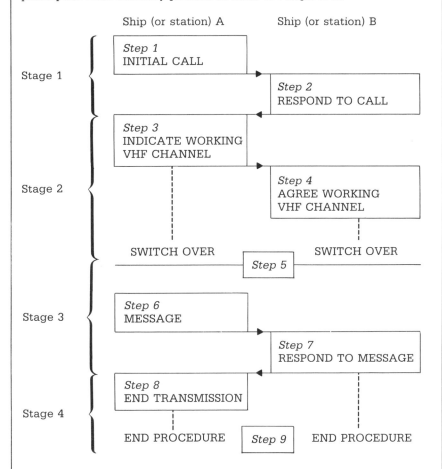

The following diagram shows the pattern of a simple VHF exchange in terms of the most usual four stage sequence, and the steps which each participant must normally perform in order to complete it.

The above diagram shows that the minimum number of steps in an exchange started on a calling channel is nine; ship A makes four transmissions and ship B makes three. Also both ships switch channels and both complete the end procedure.

This type of diagram, which provides a mental picture of a simple form of exchange is used extensively in the following subsection.

The best strategy for learning exchange procedure is to study and practise (with a partner if possible) each *stage* in turn; and then, finally, to practise running through the routine of a complete exchange. To make this easier, each stage is clearly marked in the text and exercises are provided stage-by-stage. Thus, stage 1 involves learning the procedure for making an initial call and responding to an initial call; stage 2 involves learning how to indicate a working channel, how to agree (or disagree) with that channel and how to switch channels; and so on.

VHF procedure makes frequent use of a few of the forty-two Standard Phrases used in SEASPEAK. The full list of Phrases (with definitions) is given at the beginning of Section 4.

SECTION

2

VHF
procedures

2.3.1	.1 This section explains how to make contact and maintain contact with another station. The construction and handling of the actual messages is dealt with in Section 4, VHF Messages.
2.3.2	.1 The diagram in Section 2.3.3 below outlines the transmissions and rules required to conduct an exchange. Detailed explanations of each transmission and the associated rules are given in Section 2.4. How to conduct an exchange.
	.2 Index numbers used in the explanations to be found in Section 2.4 relate to the segments of this diagram. e.g. .1 in the diagram INITIAL CALL is explained in detail at Section 2.4.1 entitled Initial Call. .2 in the diagram RESPOND TO CALL is explained in detail at Section 2.4.2 entitled Respond to Call etc.

2.3.3 Outline diagram of a two-ship exchange

Station making the call
(Controlling Station, CS)
(See training note to 2.3.3.)

Station responding to the call

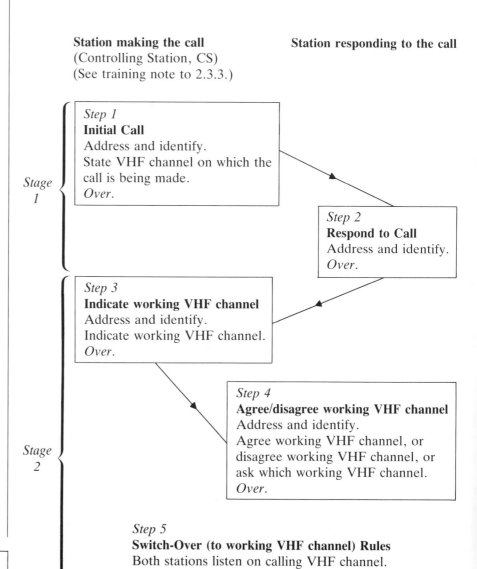

Stage 1

Step 1
Initial Call
Address and identify.
State VHF channel on which the call is being made.
Over.

Step 2
Respond to Call
Address and identify.
Over.

Step 3
Indicate working VHF channel
Address and identify.
Indicate working VHF channel.
Over.

Step 4
Agree/disagree working VHF channel
Address and identify.
Agree working VHF channel, or
disagree working VHF channel, or
ask which working VHF channel.
Over.

Stage 2

Step 5
Switch-Over (to working VHF channel) Rules
Both stations listen on calling VHF channel.
Both stations switch to working VHF channel.
Both stations listen to working VHF channel.
Ensure that the chosen working VHF channel
is free before proceeding with the exchange.

TRAINING NOTE to 2.3.3:
The concept of 'controlling station' (2.2.2) may be revised at this stage.

Stage 3

> **Step 6**
> **Message**
> Address and identify.
> Message.
> *Over*.

> **Step 7**
> **Respond to Message**
> Address and identify.
> Respond to message.
> *Over*.

> **Step 8**
> **End Transmission**
> Address and identify.
> Respond to previous transmission.
> Thank you. (optional)
> *Out*.

Stage 4

> **Step 9**
> Both stations listen for a short period before switching back to the appropriate watchkeeping VHF channel.

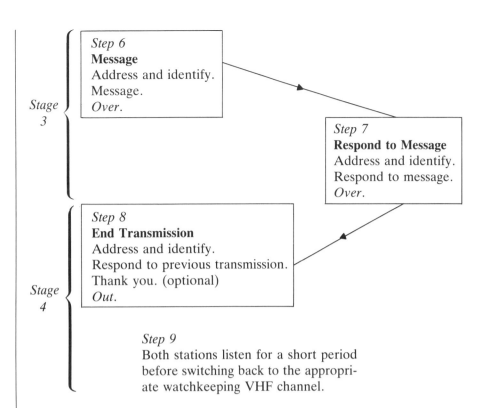

2.4 HOW TO CONDUCT AN EXCHANGE

(See Training Note to 2.4).

(Reference should be made to diagram at 2.3.3)

TRAINING NOTE to 2.4: HOW TO CONDUCT AN EXCHANGE

The following rules are set out for a four-step exchange where the first (initial) call is made on a *calling* channel. Of course, if the first call is made on a suitable *working* channel the steps which are necessary to reach agreement and switch to a working channel (steps 3, 4 and 5) are omitted.

2.4.1 Initial Call

MAKING CONTACT
(steps 1 and 2)

An Initial Call is the transmission by which a station starts or re-establishes an exchange.

.1 **Address**
This is the identification of the station being called and will normally consist of one or more of the following:

(a) name;   ⎫
(b) callsign. ⎬ Not more than three times.
            ⎭

If the name or callsign are not known the address will consist of one or more of the following, given in order of effectiveness, and preceded by the phrase *All ships... calling unknown ship...*

SECTION

VHF procedures

TRAINING INTRODUCTION to 2.4.1:
Initial Call (STEP 1)

An initial call is the transmission by which a station starts or re-establishes an exchange. *Only* those four items listed below should be transmitted. No other phrases such as 'can you hear me?' 'hello, hello. . .' should be included. Four items of information are required:

1. the proper form of ADDRESS
2. the proper form of IDENTI-FICATION
3. the VHF CHANNEL on which the call is being made
4. the RETURN word OVER

(c) ship description;
(d) position;
(e) course and speed. (see Training Note: 2.4.1).

Further details on identification of stations are in Section 1.3. The address is to be repeated once when making the Initial Call. It is not necessary to repeat it when addressing at other stages of the exchange.

.2 **Identify**

This is the identification of the station making the call, preceded by the phrase. *This is. . .*
It will normally consist of:

(a) name;
(b) callsign.

One or more of the following may be added if it will aid the addressee to recognise who is calling him, given in order of effectiveness.

(c) ship description;
(d) position;
(e) course and speed

Further details on identification of stations are in Section 1.3. The identification is to be repeated once when making the Initial Call.

.3 **State VHF channel on which call is being made**

This must be included in the Initial Call as most ship and shore stations listen on more than one VHF channel at the same time. The phrase to be used is: *on VHF channel...*

> On VHF channel one-six

.4 **Over**

The word *over* is to be used whenever a transmission is finished and a reply expected. It indicates to the other station that you have finished talking and are about to release the transmit switch, thus making it possible for him to reply, if he so wishes.

Example of an Initial Call:

> Rose Maru, Juliett Alfa Alfa Alfa.
> Rose Maru, Juliett Alfa Alfa Alfa.
> This is
> Rattler, Golf Xray Xray Xray;
> Rattler, Golf Xray Xray Xray;
> On VHF channel one-six.
> Over.

> TRAINING NOTE to 2.4.1:
> Course and Speed
> Caution: the course and speed information available about another ship may not be good enough for accurate identification purposes, unless it is being measured and communicated by a shore station.

2.4.2 Respond to Call

.1 This is the transmission which is used to reply to an Initial Call.

.2 **Address**

This is the identification of the station that made the Initial Call. It will consist of its name and callsign unless these have not been understood, in which case the phrase *station calling* will be used.

.3 **Identify**

This is the identification of the station making the Respond to Call transmission. It will consist of name and callsign plus a repeat of any extra elements which were used as part of the address of the Initial Call, (Section 2.4.1.1, c,d,e). This ensures that the calling station will recognise that the response is coming from the correct station.

SECTION

2

VHF procedures

.4 **Over**
Example of a Respond to Call transmission:

> Rattler, Golf Xray Xray Xray.
> This is
> Rose Maru, Juliett Alfa Alfa Alfa.
> Over.

.5 If the Initial Call was made on the working VHF channel the controlling station should now proceed to the message transmission as in 2.4.6 below.

END OF   Stage 1 ⬜—⬜—⬜   MAKING CONTACT

2.4.3 | Indicate Working VHF Channel

⬜—Stage 2—⬜—⬜

ESTABLISHING A WORKING CHANNEL AND SWITCHING TO IT (steps 3, 4 and 5)

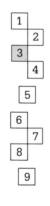

.1 This is the transmission by which the CS informs the other station of the working VHF channel to be used. If the station making the Respond to Call transmission, (Section 2.4.2) was a shore or coast station then it will give the working VHF channel to be used in its Respond to Call transmission.

.2 **Address and identify**
For the rest of the exchange the address and identify are to consist of name and/or call sign, (without repetition), whichever is the most convenient. The address and identify must never be omitted.

.3 **Indicate Working VHF Channel**
This is a statement of the VHF channel that the CS proposes should be used as the working VHF channel for this exchange. The phrase to be used is:

> Switch to VHF channel....

.4 **Over**
Example of an Indicate Working VHF Channel transmission:

> Rose Maru.
> This is Rattler.
> Switch to VHF channel zero-six.
> Over.

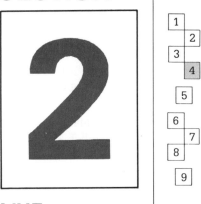
2.4.4

1	
	2
3	
	4
5	
6	
	7
8	
	9

Agree or Disagree or Ask Working VHF Channel

TRAINING INTRODUCTION to 2.4.4: Agree or Disagree or Ask Working VHF Channel (Step 4)

The Controlling Station is responsible for organising the selection of the working VHF channel. Before the exchange started the Controlling Station will have ensured by listening-in that the intended working channel is free.

When VHF Channels are busy it can take some time to find an acceptable working channel. There are, however, no shorts cuts, and no attempt should be made to switch channels until both stations are agreed. If switching over takes place prematurely then several things can go wrong: contact may be lost for a time; other stations may be unnecessarily interrupted; and there could be over-use of the calling channel.

.1 If possible the other station must agree with the CS's choice of working VHF channel. If it is not possible to agree, the other station must then make a Disagree VHF Channel transmission. If the CS neglects to state the working VHF channel, the other station must then make an Ask VHF Channel transmission.

.2 **Address and identify**

.3 **Agree VHF Channel.** The phrase to be used is:

> Agree VHF channel ...

e.g. An Agree VHF Channel transmission:

> Rattler. This is Rose Maru.
> Agree VHF channel zero-six.
> Over.

.4 **Disagree VHF Channel.** The phrase to be used is:

> VHF channel ... unable.

This is to be followed by an indication of which VHF channels it has available. The phrase to be used is either:

> VHF channels available ...,...,

or

> VHF channels available ... through ...

e.g. A Disagree VHF Channel transmission:

> Rattler. This is Rose Maru.
> VHF channel zero-six unable.
> VHF channels available zero-eight
> through one-zero, and seven-zero.
> Over.

.5 **Ask VHF Channel**
If the CS has not clearly specified which VHF channel to switch to, it then becomes the responsibility of the other station to request clarification. The phrase to be used is:

> Question: Which VHF channel?

e.g. An Ask VHF Channel transmission:

> | | Rattler. This is Rose Maru. |
> |---|---|
> | Question: | Which VHF channel? |
> | | Over. |

.6 The CS must respond to a Disagree VHF Channel or an Ask VHF Channel transmission with a new Indicate VHF Channel transmission. It is not possible to proceed to the next stage of the exchange until the other station has made a satisfactory Agree VHF Channel transmission.

SECTION

2

VHF procedures

1
2
3
4
5
6
7
8
9

TRAINING NOTES to 2.4.5:
Switch-Over rules

Note 1 Confusion could arise, for example, from misunderstanding of the indicated working VHF channel; from the Controlling Station starting to talk on the working VHF channel before the other station completes switching-over; and from the working VHF channel being found to be already in use.

Note 2 The other station must make a correct Agree VHF Channel transmission before the switch-over can take place. The switch-over rules allow a period for the Controlling Station to correct the other station should it make a mistake in the Agree VHF Channel transmission.

Note 3 The length of a listening period is a question of common sense. Remember that the Lost Contact rule (2.2.5) only allows approximately 20 seconds of silence before contact needs to be re-established on the calling VHF Channel.

2.4.5 | Switch-Over Rules

.1   These rules are designed to reduce the chances of confusion arising whilst the switch-over to the working VHF channel is being conducted. (See Training Notes to 2.4.5.)

.2   These rules are to be applied when the other station has made an Agree VHF Channel transmission. (See Training Notes to 2.4.5.)

.3   They apply to both stations.

.4   The Switch-Over Rules are that:
   (a)   Both stations listen on the calling VHF channel until they are sure that the number of the working VHF channel has been correctly transmitted and understood.
   (b)   Both stations switch their VHF sets to the agreed working VHF channel.
   (c)   Both stations listen on the working VHF channel to discover if it is already in use, and allow time for each other to complete the action of switching their VHF sets to the working VHF channel.
   (d)   The listening periods should be long enough to allow the specified actions to be completed, without being allowed to become excessive. (See Training Notes to 2.4.5.)

.5   If the working VHF channel is found to be in use, for a communication of higher priority (see Section 2.2.1):
   (a)   both stations switch back to the calling VHF channel;
   (b)   CS re-establishes contact by returning to step 2.4.1 (Initial Call);
   (c)   CS decides either to continue the exchange or postpone or cancel it;
   (d)   if the CS decides to continue he must nominate a new working VHF channel; (2.4.3)
   (e)   if the CS decides to cancel or postpone the exchange he must substitute and End Transmission (2.4.8) for the Indicate Working VHF Channel transmission.

.6   If the working VHF channel is found to be in use, but it is considered necessary to use that VHF channel for your communication, then the CS may employ the rules concerning interruption: (2.2.3.3).

e.g.
> Interruption.
> Rattler. This is Land's End radio.
> Weather forecast.
> Stop transmitting,
> two-zero minutes.
> Over.

.7   If the Initial Call is made on the working VHF channel there is no need to:
   (a)   indicate working VHF channel; (2.4.3)
   (b)   agree or disagree or ask working VHF channel; (2.4.4)
   (c)   apply the Switch-Over Rules.
   The CS will reply to the Respond to Call transmission (2.4.2) with the first message transmission, (2.4.6).

END OF 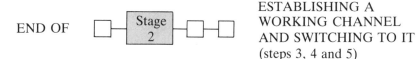 **Stage 2**   ESTABLISHING A WORKING CHANNEL AND SWITCHING TO IT (steps 3, 4 and 5)

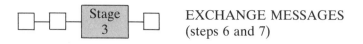

EXCHANGE MESSAGES
(steps 6 and 7)

TRAINING NOTE: Stage 3 Exchange messages
(steps 6 and 7)

Detailed guidance on messages themselves; their construction and content, is given in Section 4 of this manual. Since the purpose of the present section is to provide guidance on the structure of the total exchange from beginning to end, it is not necessary to give detailed attention to the form of the actual messages at this point. It is sufficient to know that a stage exists within the exchange (stage 3) for the inclusion of messages. This stage can involve a number of steps depending on the amount and complexity of the information to be transmitted. In the case quoted below, the message is a simple question requiring a straightforward answer and a subsequent acknowledgement; consequently only two transmissions (steps 6 and 7) are needed. The final acknowledgement is combined with the termination procedure in step 8.

2.4.6 | Message transmission

TRAINING INTRODUCTION to 2.4.6: Message Transmission (Step 6)

The content of a message transmission is the subject of a complete section (Section 4) of this manual. Briefly, the items within such a transmission should be:

1. the proper form of ADDRESS;
2. the proper form of IDENTIFICATION;
3. the MESSAGE or MESSAGES (not more than 2) which should be short, to the point, and expressed according to the guidelines provided in Section 4;
4. the RETURN word 'OVER'.

It is important to remember to address and identify in *every* transmission.

.1 **Address and identify** (See Training Notes to 2.4.6.)

.2 **Message.** The construction and handling of a message according to the SEASPEAK rules is to be found in Section 4, Constructing a Message.

.3 **Over.**

TRAINING NOTES to 2.4.6: Message transmission

Note 1. **Readability**

If circumstances permit, it is advisable to check that both participants can hear each other satisfactorily prior to the transmission of messages. The readability code (2.2.4) should be used for this purpose e.g. *How do you read?* — *I read...* Logically, a separate pair of transmissions is required for checking reception in this way but in urgent operational circumstances this may not be possible. It does not form an essential part of the simplified layout of an exchange, as represented in this section. However, remember that at any point in the exchange either station may request readability from the other, if there is some uncertainty about the quality of reception.

Note 2. **Coastguards and Shore Stations**

The Controlling Station is responsible for making the first transmission after the channel-switch has been accomplished. However, if a shore or coast station responds to the Initial Call and assigns the working channel, it effectively becomes the Controlling Station. Therefore even though it did not initiate the exchange, the coast or shore station will make the first transmission after the channel switch. This 'extra' transmission need contain no more than ADDRESS, IDENTIFY and the return word 'OVER'. This transmission is not included in the simplified layout of an exchange given here.

SECTION

2

**VHF
procedures**

2.4.7 | Respond to Message Transmission

> TRAINING INTRODUCTION to 2.4.7:
> Respond to Message Transmission
> (Step 7)
>
> Most messages require a response. The correct form of response is detailed in Section 4. For the purpose of this example it is assumed that step 7 includes simply the answer to a single question posed in the previous transmission (step 6). The term MESSAGE is used to cover all questions, statements, requests, warnings and the responses to them, which convey the purpose in making VHF radio contact.

.1 **Address and identify.**

.2 **Response to message.** The response to a message is covered by similar rules to constructing a message, (Section 4).

.3 **Over.**

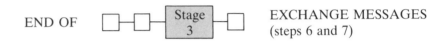

END OF · · Stage 3 · EXCHANGE MESSAGES (steps 6 and 7)

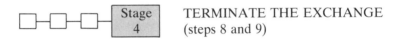

· · · Stage 4 · TERMINATE THE EXCHANGE (steps 8 and 9)

> TRAINING NOTE: Stage 4 Terminate the exchange
>
> These rules provide an orderly ending to the conversation. They cover the END TRANSMISSION itself (step 8) and the procedure to be adopted after this final transmission has been made. (step 9).

2.4.8 | End transmission

> TRAINING INTRODUCTION to 2.4.8: End transmission (Step 8)
>
> The END TRANSMISSION terminates the exchange. It is normally made by the Controlling Station. Use of the End Transmission must be followed by the END PROCEDURE (step 9) in the same way that an Agree VHF Channel Transmission (step 4) must be followed by the Switch-Over (step 5). The End Procedure cannnot commence until an END TRANSMISSION has been made.
>
> The END TRANSMISSION allows for readbacks (i.e. repetitions) of MESSAGES transmitted in the previous transmission, (see 4.4.5 Message checking steps). Thus, if step 6 contained a question and step 7 the answer to it, then step 8 would include a readback of the answer. However, if the conversation had ended with a readback in the previous transmission then the END TRANSMISSION need contain only:
>
> 1.   the proper form of ADDRESS
> 2.   the proper form of IDENTIFICATION
> 3.   the termination word 'OUT'

This is the transmission by which the exchange is terminated. It will normally be made by the CS.

.1 **Address and identify**

.2 **Respond to previous transmission.** This is optional. It will consist of one of the forms of message acknowledgement, (Section 4).

.3 **Thank you**
This phrase is optional.

.4 **Out**
This indicates that both this transmission and this communication are ended, that the station making the transmission does not expect a reply and that he will shortly be switching his VHF set back to the appropriate watchkeeping VHF channel.

Example of an **End Transmission:**

> Rose Maru. This is Rattler.
> Understood, ETA: one-five-four-zero GMT.
> Thank you.
> Out.

2.4.9 End Procedure

> TRAINING INTRODUCTION to 2.4.9: End Procedure (Step 9)
>
> This step applies automatically after an END TRANSMISSION has been made. The provisions of the END PROCEDURE apply equally to both participants in any exchange. They are made so that both stations are sure that the conversation is really finished.

This procedure is designed to avoid accidental premature termination of the exchange.

.1 Both stations listen on the working VHF channel for sufficient time to be certain that each has said all that he wants to say. (See Training Notes to 2.4.9.)

.2 Both stations switch back to the appropriate watchkeeping VHF channel. (See Training Notes to 2.4.9.)

> TRAINING NOTES to 2.4.9: End procedure
>
> *Note 1* As with all the other waiting times specified in the Seaspeak procedure rules, the *actual* period of time that the participants should wait will vary, at the discretion of individual operators and subject to prevailing circumstances. It is unlikely to exceed 20 seconds. The point of this waiting period is to allow the exchange to continue if it had been terminated prematurely.
>
> *Note 2* Watchkeeping will normally be on VHF Channel 16, in the open sea. Should either station wish to resume the exchange after switching back has occurred then a fresh exchange must be started with an INITIAL CALL (step 1).

END OF ☐—☐—☐—Stage 4   TERMINATE THE EXCHANGE (steps 8 and 9)

2.4.10 Example of Exchange Procedure

> TRAINING INTRODUCTION to 2.4.10:
> Example of Exchange Procedure (a) When the Initial Call is Made on a Calling Channel (e.g. VHF 16)
>
> The following is a complete example of an exchange which follows the same pattern as that used to explain exchange procedure above. The difference is that *all* the actual words spoken have been added.
>   With the exception of the actual messages transmitted in steps 6 and 7 and the message acknowledgement in step 8 the whole exchange is conducted by way of Standard Phrases. The small set of Standard Phrases can be seen therefore to do all that is necessary to make, maintain and terminate contact WHATEVER THE CIRCUMSTANCES. No language other than Standard Phrases is necessary for stages 1, 2 and 4 of any exchange.

SECTION

2

VHF procedures

Call made on a calling VHF channel (VHF 16 in this case)

Station making the call
(Controlling Station, CS)

Station responding to the call

Stage 1

.1 All ships, All ships, calling
Black tanker, position:
fairway buoy;
Calling
black tanker, position:
fairway buoy.
This is Rattler, Golf Xray
Xray Xray; Rattler, Golf
Xray Xray Xray. On
VHF channel one-six.
Over.

.2 Rattler, Golf Xray Xray Xray.
This is Rose Maru, Juliett Alfa
Alfa Alfa, black tanker, position.
fairway buoy.
Over.

Stage 2

.3 Rose Maru. This is Rattler.
Switch to VHF channel zero-six.
Over.

.4 Rattler. This is Rose Maru.
Agree VHF channel zero-six.
Over.

.5 Both stations listen on VHF channel 16.
Both stations switch their VHF sets to VHF channel 06.
Both stations listen on VHF channel 06.
For the purpose of this example VHF channel 06 is
assumed to be free.

Stage 3

.6 Rose Maru. This is Rattler.
QUESTION: What is your ETA?
Nothing more.
Over.

.7 Rattler. This is Rose Maru.
ANSWER: My ETA is one-five-
four-zero GMT
Nothing more.
Over.

Stage 4

.8 Rose Maru. This is Rattler.
Understood, ETA:
one-five-four-zero GMT.
Thank you.
Out.

.9 Both stations listen for a short period on VHF channel 06
Both stations resume watchkeeping on VHF channel 16

TRAINING NOTE to 2.4.10:
Use of the standard phrases
'Nothing more' and 'Stay on'

Note 1 The phrase 'Nothing More' is an optional **Standard Phrase** at the end of a Message Transmission or in a Respond to Message Transmission. It indicates that the station currently transmitting has no further messages to transmit; the other station may therefore, after responding, transmit messages and/or change the subject matter of the exchange. It is defined more fully in Section 4.1.2 (Standard Phrases).

The **Standard Phrase** 'Stay On' is the opposite of 'Nothing More'. Its use by one station means that the other participant *must not* change the subject or transmit a message, as the station which said 'Stay On' has further messages to transmit. It is more fully defined in Section 4.1.2 (**Standard Phrases**).

The use of these two **Standard Phrases** is designed to prevent premature termination of the exchange and to help maintain discipline in the exchange of messages.

Note 2 List of **Standard Phrases** used in the examples:

This is
On VHF Channel ....
over,
Switch to VHF Channel ....
Agree VHF Chanel ....
Nothing more
Understood,
Thank you
Out

With the exception of the messages themselves, all the language used is composed of these nine **Standard Phrases** plus names (such as 'Rose Maru') and numbers (such as 'one-six').

page 43

SECTION

2

VHF procedures

2.4.11 | Example of Exchange Procedure

TRAINING INTRODUCTION to 2.4.11: Example of Exchange Procedure (b) When the Initial Call is Made on a Suitable Working Channel

This example is included to demonstrate the simplicity of an exchange when stage 2 (ESTABLISHING A WORKING CHANNEL AND SWITCHING TO IT) is not necessary. It will be clear that a considerable saving of time can be achieved by the use of designated or pre-arranged working channels.

Call made on a working VHF channel (VHF channel 06 in this case)

Station making the call
(Controlling Station)

Station responding to the call

TRAINING NOTE to 2.4.11. Recommended learning sequence

Once the student has grasped the VHF Conventions (Section 1) and the basic rules for conducting an Exchange (Section 2, up to 2.4.11) the authors recommend that he should next move directly to Section 4 (Messages). The reasons for this recommendation are that the subjects of Section 3 (Distress, Urgency and Safety messages) require not only familiarity with VHF *procedures*, but also knowlege of how to construct *messages*. The remainder of this Section (Section 2.5, 2.6, Broadcast Procedure) can be left until after dealing with Sections 4 and 3, in that order.

.1 All ships, All ships, Calling
 Black tanker, position:
 fairway buoy;
 Calling
 black tanker, position;
 fairway buoy.
 This is
 Rattler, Golf Xray Xray Xray;
 Rattler, Golf Xray Xray Xray.
 On VHF channel zero-six.
 Over.

.2 Rattler, Golf Xray Xray Xray.
 This is
 Rose Maru, Juliett Alfa Alfa
 Alfa,
 black tanker, position:
 fairway buoy.
 Over.

.6 Rose Maru.
 This is Rattler.
 QUESTION: What is your
 ETA?
 Nothing more.
 Over.

.7 Rattler.
 This is Rose Maru.
 ANSWER: My ETA is:
 one-five-four-zero GMT.
 Nothing more.
 Over.

.8 Rose Maru.
 This is Rattler.
 Understood, ETA:
 one-five-four-zero GMT.
 Thank you.
 Out.

Both stations listen for a short period on VHF channel 06.
Both stations resume watchkeeping on VHF channel 16.

page 44

2.5

BROADCAST PROCEDURE

TRAINING INTRODUCTION to 2.5: BROADCAST PROCEDURE

Broadcasts are distinct from Exchanges in that there is only one station transmitting. The following procedure applies when:

(a)   a station transmits without expecting or requiring a response from any other station.

(b)   a station transmits messages without knowing if a response from another station will be received.

If another station responds to a broadcast then an Exchange is begun and the exchange procedure applies from that point on.

Typical subjects for broadcasts are:
Weather Forecasts
Weather Reports
Navigational Information
Decca Warnings
Sècurité Messages

2.5.1

.1   This section and Section 2.6 explain how a broadcast is to be conducted.

.2   The diagram in Section 2.5.2 below outlines the transmissions and rules required to conduct a broadcast. Detailed explanation of each transmission is given in Section 2.6, How to conduct a broadcast.

.3   Index numbers used in Section 2.6 relate to the segments of this diagram. e.g. (.1) in the diagram Initial Call is explained in detail at 2.6.1 entitled **Initial Call** etc.

2.5.2

Outline diagram of a broadcast
(See Training Notes to 2.5.2.)

TRAINING NOTE to 2.5.2:
Outline diagram of a broadcast
For training purposes, there are 4 steps in BROADCAST procedure:

Step 1: Initial Call
Step 2: Switch-over to Working Channel
Step 3: Message
Step 4: End Procedure

In Step 1 the transmission serves not only to make the initial call but also to announce the chosen working VHF channel. In Step 2 the CS and the stations listening switch to the designated VHF working channel. Step 3 contains the message which is the purpose of the broadcast. Step 4 returns all stations to keeping watch on the VHF calling channel.

Ships' officers and trainees should concentrate first on competence in receiving broadcasts and comprehending them, rather than on making them.

Station making the broadcast (Controlling Station, CS)	Stations listening
.1 Initial Call Address and identify. Indicate content of the broadcast. Advise VHF channel on which broadcast will be made. *Over.*	Is the broadcast for you? Is it of interest to you? If you did not receive the VHF channel on which the broadcast is to be made, request the CS to repeat it now by making an Ask VHF Channel transmission (Section 2.4.4.5).

Switch-Over Rules

.2 Station making the broadcast listens on the VHF calling channel.
All stations switch their sets over to the VHF working channel.
Station making the broadcast listens on the VHF working channel.
The CS ensures that the VHF working channel is free before proceeding with the broadcast.

| **.3 Message**
Address and identify.
Indicate content of the broadcast.
Broadcast message.
Out. | If you have not received the message satisfactorily, request a repeat of it at this stage. (See Section 4.1 Standard Phrases). |

End Procedure

.4 Station making broadcast listens on the working VHF channel.
All stations resume watch on appropriate watchkeeping VHF channel.

2.6 | HOW TO CONDUCT A BROADCAST

> **TRAINING INTRODUCTION to 2.6.1: Initial Call (Step 1)**
>
> It is necessary to warn prospective listeners to a broadcast (i) so that they can decide if it is intended for them, and (ii) to give them time to prepare for its reception and recording (usually in written form).
>
> There need be only five items in this transmission:
> 1. the proper form of ADDRESS
> 2. the proper form of IDENTIFICATION
> 3. an indication of the CONTENT of the broadcast
> 4. a statement of the WORKING CHANNEL to be used
> 5. the RETURN word 'OVER'

2.6.1 | Initial Call (Step 1) (See Training Note to 2.6.1.)

> **TRAINING NOTE to 2.6.1:**
> Initial Call (Step 1)
>
> While the broadcasting station is going through the above procedure, the receiving station will:
>
> (a) have identified this as a Broadcast (not as the beginning of an Exchange)
>
> (b) decide whether the broadcast is of operational relevance to them, from the ADDRESS used and the stated CONTENT of the broadcast.
>
> (c) prepare to switch channels if the decision at (b) is positive.

.1 This is the transmission a station uses to start a broadcast.

.2 **Address and identify**

This is done in the same way as in an exchange (2.4.1) except that if the broadcast is being addressed to more than one station it will be given as shown below:

(a)   All ships.

(b)   All ships (all *stations* if addressed to ships and shore).

(c)   All (type/nationality/company, etc.) ships.

(d)   Name(s) of station(s) for which broadcast is intended.

e.g.

> All ships in Malacca Straits;
> all ships in Malacca Straits.
> This is
> China Star, November Alfa Alfa Alfa;
> China Star, November Alfa Alfa Alfa.

.3 **Indicate content of the broadcast**

This is done so that other stations can decide if it is necessary to listen to the broadcast itself. The phrase to be used is to be selected from the list of major communication subjects. (Section 5.)

e.g

> Weather Report

> Navigational Information

.4 **Advise VHF channel on which the broadcast will be made**
The phrase to be used is: *Switch to VHF Channel ...*

e.g.

> Switch to VHF channel one-four.

.5 **Over**
Example of an Initial Call:

> All ships in Malacca Straits;
> all ships in Malacca Straits.
> This is
> China Star, November Alfa Alfa Alfa;
> China Star, November Alfa Alfa Alfa.
> Weather report.
> Switch to VHF channel one-two.
> Over.

| 2.6.2 |

1
2
3
4

Switch-Over Rules (Step 2)

.1 These cover the conduct of all involved stations whilst the CS is switching over to the working VHF channel.

.2 If the calling and working VHF channels are different:

(a) the CS will listen on the calling VHF channel for a short period. The purpose of this listening period is to allow other stations to ask for a repeat of the VHF channel that the broadcast is going to be made on;

(b) all stations will switch their VHF sets to the working VHF channel (see Training Note to 2.6.2);

(c) the CS will ensure that the working VHF channel is free before transmitting on it. If necessary, the CS may employ the interruption rules at this stage (Section 2.2.3.3).

.3 If the calling and working VHF channels are the same:

(a) The Initial Call transmission (2.6.1) must still be made, in order to warn other stations that the broadcast is about to take place.

(b) After making the Initial Call transmission, the CS will listen for a short period before commencing the message, in order to allow other stations to prepare to receive the broadcast.

TRAINING NOTE to 2.6.2: Switch-Over Rules

Clearly, if the calling VHF Channel and the working VHF Channel are the same then there is no need to switch channels. However, the other rules, for example the listening period, still apply. There can be a period of up to 40 seconds between the end of the Initial Call and the beginning of the Message Broadcast.

When the broadcast is made in a scheduled service at published broadcasting times (e.g. the Channel navigation Information Service broadcasts), listeners will be ready for the broadcast. In these circumstances it may be reasonable to halve the length of the Switch-Over listening and waiting periods. However, these periods should never be less than:

(a) In the case of Initial Call and Broadcast Transmission being made on different VHF Channels, 10 seconds each.

(b) In the case of Initial Call and Broadcast Transmission being made of the same VHF Channel, 20 seconds.

| 2.6.3 |

Broadcast Message (Step 3)

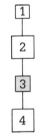

TRAINING INTRODUCTION to 2.6.3: Broadcast Message (Step 3)

This is the step during which the Message is sent. This transmission need contain only five items:

1. the proper form of ADDRESS
2. the proper form of IDENTIFICATION
3. an indication of the CONTENT of the broadcast
4. the MESSAGE
5. the return word 'OVER'

When transmitting the Broadcast Message remember that receiving stations may wish to write the contents down therefore speak slowly (see 1.1.1.3 and 1.1.1.4).

Remember, too, that Broadcasts should be made from a carefully-prepared written script.

If VHF propagation conditions are poor (see Introduction) it is advisable to repeat each content section of the broadcast. This may save you having to respond to questions or requests for repeats from other stations later.

TRAINING NOTE to 2.6.3:
Broadcast message

This acts as a confirmation of the message content of the broadcast, and also indicates that the next words to be transmitted will be the broadcast message itself.

.1   This is the transmission during which the message will be broadcast.

.2   **Address and identify**
These will be transmitted in the same way as in the Initial Call (2.6.1.2).

.3   **Indicate content of the broadcast** (See Training Note to 2.6.3.)
The same phrase is to be used as was used in the Initial Call (2.6.1.3).

.4   **Transmit content of the message**
The content of the broadcast as indicated at .3 above is to be transmitted at this stage. The rules concerning the construction of broadcast messages are given in Section 4. If it becomes necessary to make a broadcast about a subject that was not indicated in the Initial Call and at .3 above then the broadcasting station must finish the current broadcast first and then initiate a new broadcast for the new subject.

.5   **Out**
Saying this word at the end of the Message Transmission indicates that the broadcast message has been transmitted and that the station that made the broadcast will shortly be switching back to the appropriate watchkeeping VHF channel.

2.6.4   End Procedure (Step 4)

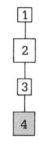

.1   This is designed to allow other stations time to request repeats of all or part of the broadcast, message, before the station making the broadcast switches back to the watchkeeping VHF channel. (See Training Notes to 2.6.4.)

.2   After saying *Out* the station making the broadcast will listen for a short period. (See Training Notes to 2.6.4.)

.3   If any of the stations wish for a repeat of all or part of the broadcast message, then they should request it now. (See standard phrases, Section 4.1.) (See Training Notes to 2.6.4.)

.4   If a repeat is requested, the broadcast becomes an exchange. (See Training Notes to 2.6.4.)

.5   If no request for a repeat is received within a reasonable time, the station that made the broadcast will switch his VHF set back to the appropriate watchkeeping VHF channel.

TRAINING NOTES to 2.6.4: End Procedure

Note 1 **Listening Period**
This does not allow for complicated communications (e.g. discussions on the content of the broadcast message, or challenges as to its accuracy). If the desired communication is anything other than a simple request for a repetition, then the station wishing to make the communication must wait until the broadcasting station has switched back to the watchkeeping VHF channel; it can then initiate an exchange.

Note 2 **Listening Period**
The length of time will depend on prevailing circumstances, but it is unlikely to be more than 20 seconds.

Note 3 **Requests for Repetition**
The request for repetition should be made using Standard Phrases (see Section 4).

     e.g. 'Say again. . .'
        This phrase may be followed by an indication of which part of the message was not heard clearly.

     e.g. 'Say again after. . . 'or' Say again before. . .'

Example (see example of a broadcast as given below)

> *China Star*;
> this is *Rattler*.
> Say again all after visibility.
> Over.

to which the response would be:

> *Rattler*;
> this is *China Star*.
> I say again,
> visibility: five miles,
> pressure: nine-seven-two falling.
> Over.

Note 4. **Broadcast Becomes an Exchange**
In the example given above the ship *Rattler* has requested a repeat of all of the broadcast message after the word visibility. The broadcast has therefore become an exchange and will be continued and terminated in accordance with the Exchange Procedure Rules.

2.6.5 Example of a broadcast

Step 1

> All ships in Malacca Straits;
> all ships in Malacca Straits.
> This is
> China Star, November Alfa Alfa Alfa;
> China Star, November Alfa Alfa Alfa.
> Weather report.
> Switch to VHF channel one-three.
> Over.

Step 2

> China Star listens on the VHF channel.
> No station requests a repeat of the working VHF channel.
> China Star and all interested stations switch on VHF channel 13.
> China Star listens on VHF channel 13 for a short period.
>
> For the purpose of this example VHF channel 13 is assumed to be free.

Step 3

> All ships in Malacca Straits;
> all ships in Malacca Straits.
> This is
> China Star, November Alfa Alfa Alfa;
> China Star, November Alfa Alfa Alfa.
> Weather report for Malacca Straits,
> time: one-two-zero-zero GMT.
> INFORMATION: wind: South, force: eight,
> sea: rough, weather: rain showers,
> visibility: five miles, pressure:
> nine-seven-two falling.
> Out.

Step 4

> China Star listens on VHF channel 13.
> No request for a repeat is received.
> China Star switches her VHF set back to the appropriate watchkeeping VHF channel.

SECTION 2.
EXERCISES

> GENERAL NOTES
> 1. Two kinds of exercises are provided:
>   (i) exercises which practise factual knowledge about the most important training points in Section 2;
>   (ii) practical exercises, in which the student is expected to simulate the various elements of a VHF exchange.
> 2. Exercises based on the practical tasks of a VHF broadcast are also supplied: the authors recommend that these should be undertaken later, *after* the student has worked through Section 4 (Messages) and then Section 3 (Distress, Urgency and Safety Procedures).
> 3. Exercises have the same number as the most relevant section in the text of the *Training Manual*.

Exercises on Factual Knowledge

A. Construct your own check-list of important principles. On a separate sheet, write down the answers to the following 4 questions. (The numbers indicate where you will find the answers.)

Check with the model answers on p. 54.

A.1 How many types of VHF procedures are there? (2.1)

A.2 What is (a) an exchange? (2.1.1)
           (b) a broadcast? (2.1.2)

A.3 Which three types of communication have the highest priority? (2.2.1)

A.4 What is the main responsibility of the CS (Controlling Station)? (2.2.2)

B. Using the Readability Code (2.2.4) write down how you would say the following:

(a) Your signal is so poor that it is unusable.
(b) I am receiving an excellent signal from you.

C. The following 4 stages in a VHF exchange (2.3) are in the wrong order. Write down the letters of the correct sequence.

A AGREE A WORKING VHF CHANNEL
B EXCHANGE MESSAGES
C TERMINATE
D MAKE CONTACT

D. The following sets of elements each make up a particular kind of call (2.4). Name the types of call.

(a) Address — Identify — State VHF calling channel — Over
(b) Address — Identify — Out
(c) Address — Identify — Over

E. A station may say *Nothing more* before ending a transmission, if it has no further messages to transmit. What will it say if it does wish to pass on further messages?

(*NB*: Model answers are printed at the end of the Exercises to Section 2.)

Practical exercises

> INTRODUCTORY NOTES TO THE PRACTICAL EXERCISES
> 1. There are six sets of practical exercises. They begin with a reminder of the 4 stages of a conversation, and of the nine steps in practical procedure. Then follow 4 sets of exercises introducing the various steps appropriate to Stages 1–4. Finally, there is a set of exercises which practice whole conversations.
> 2. Students should work in pairs when possible, one taking the part of Ship Station A, the other taking Ship Station B, since the exercises are laid out in that way.
> 3. It is desirable that students should be able to record their transmissions and to learn from replaying their efforts. If the tape recorder can simulate VHF equipment, so much the better.
> 4. Students should be encouraged to make a clear distinction between the *speaking* state and the *listening* state, for example by maintaining a finger to the lips when not speaking. Some simple device to simulate channel switching is also helpful: for instance, to prepare cards with the numbers of the channels, and to physically move an object from one card to another. These activities are intended to teach and remind the students that VHF simplex working is not like the telephone, and makes special demands on the user.

Set A
Exercise A. 1

Study the diagram below: It represents the nine steps that are involved in a VHF conversation between Ship Stations A and B, including a switch-over from one VHF channel to another.
  Make your own copy of the diagram. Refer to the text (Section 2.3) and write the name of the Step in each box.
  Remember that the calling ship is Ship A in each case.
  Work with a partner. Make sure that you are each familiar with the sequence of steps, both as A and as B.

Ship Station A   *Ship Station B*

Step 1

                          Step 2

Step 3

                          Step 4

Step 5

Step 6

                          Step 7

Step 8

Step 9

Exercise A. 2

Recall the 4 stages of each conversation. Write them down (if necessary, refer to the text, Section 2.3).

Set B. Stage 1: Make Contact

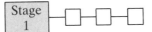

STEPS

Exercise B. 1

Working with a partner as A and B respectively, and if possible with a tape recorder, make the correct Call and Respond to Call for ships listed below.

Example:

Ship A	VHF Channel on which the initial call is being made
Captain Stefanos (SZYH)	16

> *Rose Maru*, Juliett Alpha Alpha Alpha
> *Rose Maru*, Juliett Alpha Alpha Alpha
> This is *Captain Stefanos*, Sierra
> Zulu Yankee Hotel
> *Captain Stefanos*, Sierra Zulu
> Yankee Hotel
> On VHF channel one-six
> Over

Ship B

Rose Maru
(JAAA)

> *Captain Stefanos*,
> Sierra
> Zulu Yankee Hotel
> This is *Rose Maru*,
> Juliett
> Alpha Alpha Alpha
> Over

Follow this example with these names and callsigns:

Group 1 (Name and callsign known)

(a)	*Veniamis* (SXTE)	*Vincent Gann* (WZR8)	16
(b)	*Kyriakou* (P3UT)	*Rattler* (GXXX)	16
(c)	*Spyros* (C4B1)	*Vincent Gann* (WZR8)	16
(d)	*Harriet* (GBOI)	*Olivia* (PBXQ)	
(e)	*Star Vega* (AYLD)	*Northport Voyager* (M2ZO)	

Now exchange roles (A becomes B, B becomes A) and repeat the exercise on Group 1.

Exercise B. 2

Use the same technique with the next group. Notice that Ship A does not know the name of ship B, in each case, and addresses an unknown ship in the position given. Ship B responds with her name and callsign, as given.

Group 2 (Calling unknown ships)

(a)	*Lady Alice* (GB01)	Unknown ship, bearing 250°: five miles from Cap Monares (reply: *Olivia Queen* (TX3B))	16
(b)	*Cormorant Alpha* (ZXQF)	Unknown ship, in position six miles from Mow Point, steering a course of 151°, at a speed of approximately 5 knots (reply: *Packer* (P3XQ))	16
(c)	*Jupiter* (D6GT)	Unknown ship, tanker: hull colour white with black funnel steering 85°, at a speed of 10 knots (reply: *Sarah* (GX11))	16
(d)	*Walnut* (SQR6)	Unknown ship, passenger ferry, white hull with green funnels. 2 miles from Southport harbour entrance, steering North (reply: *Zandar* (L1X2))	16
(e)	*Eva* (AIST)	Unknown ship, LASH type, steering a course of 50°, at a speed of 15 knots, sea area Masekar. (reply *Ingrid* (NXQP))	16

Now exchange roles (A becomes B, B becomes A) and repeat the exercise on Group 2.

Set C. Stage 2: Agree working VHF Channel and Switch to it

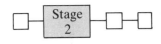

Exercise C. 1

STEPS

Practise making the correct 'Indicate Working Channel' (step 3) and the correct 'Agree, Disagree or Ask Working VHF Channel' (step 4). As each of these pairs of transmission are performed, finish up the sequence by simulating the Switch-over (step 5). This involves:

(a) listening for a short time on the calling VHF channel;

(b) switching or simulating a switch to a working VHF channel;

(c) listening for a short time on the working VHF channel.

Example:

| *Oscar* (BXQ3) | *Elin Star* (NQRS) | 04 |

> *Elin Star*, this is *Oscar*
> Switch to VHF channel
> zero-four.
> Over

> *Oscar*, this is *Elin Star*
> Agree VHF channel zero-four
> Over

Then: — Wait —
          — Switch —
          — Wait —

Follow this example with these names and callsigns. Notice that items (d) and (e) present additional problems.

(a) *Veniamis* (SXTE) *Vincent Gann* (WZR8)   08

(b) *Kyriakou* (P3UT) *Rattler* (GXXX)   12

(c) *Spyros* (C4B1)   *Vincent Gann* (WZR8)   09

(d) *Harriet* (GBO1)   *Olivia* (PBXQ)   04
                        (*Olivia* does not have 04 but
                        does have 08 to 12)

(e) *Star Vega* (AYLD) *Northport Voyager* (M2ZO) 12
                        (*Northport Voyager* does
                        not hear *Star Vega* indicate
                        a working channel)

NB: *(d) and (e) above involve 2 more transmissions.*

Now exchange roles (A becomes B, B becomes A) and repeat the exercise with the same list of names and callsigns.

Set D. Stage 3: Exchange Messages

STEPS

1
2
3
4
5
6
7
8
9

Exercise D. 1

This exercise does not ask the student to construct messages: the rules for doing so are presented in Section 4. But it is useful to be able to practise not only with callsigns and names. The following pair of simple messages, consisting of a question and its answer, are used throughout this exercise:

QUESTION: What is your destination?
ANSWER: My destination is Buenos Aires.

Practise making the correct Message transmission (step 6) and the correct respond to Message (step 7) as in this example:

Example:

Oscar (BXQ3)

> *Elin Star*, this is Oscar.
> Question: What is your destination?
> Over.

                              Elin Star (NQRS)

                              > *Oscar*, this is *Elin Star*.
                              > Answer: My destination is Buenos Aires.
                              > Over

Follow this example with these names and callsigns. Notice that items (d) and (e) present additional problems

(a) *Veniamis* (SZTE)   *Vincent Gann* (WZR8)

(b) *Kyriakou* (P3UT)   *Rattler* (GXXX)

(c) *Spyros* (C4B1)   *Vincent Gann* (WZR8)

(d) *Harriet* (GBO1)   *Olivia* (PBXQ)
     (This ship asks   (This ship reads 5)
     'How do you
     read?' before
     making the neces-
     sary transmission)

(e) *Star Vega* (AYLD)   *Northport Voyager* (M2ZO)
     (*Star Vega* does   (After hearing *Star Vega's*
     not hear the last   'say again' transmission,
     two words of   *Northport Voyager* trans-
     Northport Voya-   mits once more and says 'I
     ger's reply. She   say again — *Buenos Aires*')
     therefore asks
     Northport Voya-
     ger to 'say again'
     her destination)

NB: *(d) and (e) above require 2 extra transmissions.*

Now exchange roles (A becomes B, B becomes A) and repeat the exercise.

Set E. Stage 4: Terminate the Exchange

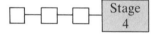

Exercise E. 1

STEPS

1
2
3
4
5
6
7
8
9

This exercise gives practice in making the End Transmission (step 8) followed by the End Procedure (step 9).

Instructions for this exercise:

(i)   respond to a previous message.

(ii)   terminate the exchange, using the word Out.

(iii) listen for a short period on the working VHF channel.

(iv)   switch back to the VHF watchkeeping channel (or simulate doing this).

Notice that it is necessary to repeat the response to the previous message to make sure that it has been received correctly. The word 'Understood' is used, followed by a brief readback. The polite term 'Thank you' is optional.

Example:

Oscar (BXQ3)   *Elin Star* (NQRS)

> *Elin Star*, this is *Oscar*.
> Understood: destination:
> Buenos Aires.   (Listening only)
> Thank you. Out.

                    Then: — Wait —
                              — Switch —

Now practise this with each of the pairs of names (a), (b), (c), (d) and (e) in exercise D 1 (callsigns are not necessary when terminating).

Exchange roles (A become B, B becomes A) and repeat the exercise.

Set F. Complete Conversations

CON-TACT	CHAN-NELS	MESSA-GES	TERMI-NATE

ALL
STEPS

Exercise F. 1

When the student can deal with each of the steps on its own, he is ready to practise complete conversations. Work with a partner and a tape recorder.

Here again are the names and callsigns of the ships mentioned in previous exercises, but in a different order:

Ship Station A	*Ship Station B*
Sarah (GX11)	Zandar (L1X2)
Elin Star (NQRS)	Captain Stefanos (SZYH)
Rose Maru (JAAA)	Packer (P3QX)
Vincent Gann (WZR8)	Jupiter (D6GT)
Ingrid (NXQB)	Cormorant Alpha (ZXQF)
Star Vega (AYLD)	Kyriakou (P3UT)
Veniamis (SXTE)	Rattler (GXXX)
Olivia (PBXQ)	Walnut (SQR6)
Northport Voyager (M2ZO)	Oscar (BXQ3)
Eva (AIST)	Harriet (GBO1)
Spyros (C4B1)	Olivia Queen (TX3B)

Working with a partner and with a tape recorder, practise giving complete conversations for successive pairs of ships. Keep to the simple message, QUESTION: *What is your destination?* in each case. In the reply, use a variety of ports, e.g.: ANSWER: *My destination is Mombasa*. Remember also that the words QUESTION and ANSWER must be spoken. They form part of the message (see Section 4).

It will be helpful if the student initiating the call (i.e. acting as CS) writes down in advance:
(i)   the name and callsign of his own ship;
(ii) the name and callsign of the ship he is calling (or the information about its type and position, if he does not know the name);
(iii) the proposed working VHF channel;
(iv) the message.

Similarly, the student taking the part of Ship B should write down in advance the name and callsign of his ship, and a destination.

When the students feel confident in handling the routine of a complete VHF exchange in its simplest form, variations can be introduced.
E.g.: (1)   Practise making, the initial call on to a working VHF channel that has been previously arranged.

(2)   Practise dealing with an interruption (2.2.3.5).

(3)   Assume that one ship is producing a weak signal, so use the readability code (2.2.4).

(4)   Simulate loss of radio contact at the channel switching step (2.2.5).

(5)   Make the receiving station a coast or shore station, which becomes CS and then must nominate the working VHF channel in step 2.

To increase the variety of exercises, to maintain interest, and to give both partners experience as CS, reverse the roles, so that A becomes B, B becomes A.

When the student is thoroughly familiar with all the procedures in Exercise F 1 above, the authors recommend that he should next work on the content of Section 4 **Messages**, then moving to Section 3 **Distress, Urgency and Safety**, and then to Section 2.6 **Broadcasts** (which he will then find very simple to grasp). The exercises that follow here (Exercise G) relate to Broadcasts and are thus best to return to at a later stage.

Set G. Broadcasts

Exercise G. 1

The following diagram represents the sequence to be followed in making a Broadcast. Refer to the text for the names of the 4 steps involved (2.5.2).

Step 1

Step 2

Step 3

Step 4

Make you own copy of the diagram. Write the name of the step in each box.

Practise step 1 (Initial Call, Broadcast) using the following information:

BROADCAST

1
2
3
4

(a)   *Kotka Radio* is about to make a broadcast to ships in the Gulf of Riga. The content of the broadcast will be *Ice Information* and the VHF channel to be used will be 68.

(b)   *Eastport Radio* is about to make a broadcast to ships in the Shannon area. The content of the broadcast will be a *Weather Forecast* and the VHF channel to be used will be 11.

After each transmission simulate the activities of step 2, i.e. listen — switch — listen.

Exercise G. 2

Practise step 3 (Broadcast Message) using the information below. Remember to read slowly, so that listeners have time to write down what you are saying.

BROADCAST

1
2
3
4

(a)   *Kotka Radio* broadcasts to ships in the Gulf of Riga some *Ice Information*, the text of which is as follows:

Information: The ice type is: thick sea ice
Ice change: no change
Ice navigation: ice-breaker assistance is necessary

Repeat the broadcast immediately, preceded by the Standard Phrase *I say again*.

(b)   *Eastport Radio* broadcasts a *Weather Forecast* to ships in the Shannon area, the text of which is as follows:

page 53

Information: Wind: North, Force 7. Sea: Rough. Weather: Rain showers. Visibility: six miles except in showers. Pressure: nine-nine-five millibars, falling.

Repeat the broadcast immediately, preceded by the standard phrase *I say again*.

After each repeat message transmission, simulate the activities of step 4, i.e. listen and wait, then switch back to the VHF calling channel.

Exercise G. 3

BROADCAST

Work with one or more partners, who act as listeners to the broadcast. The 'shore station' making the broadcast should write down a text in advance. After making the broadcast (including immediate repeat) all participants should check that they have correctly written down the broadcast message.

Practise the same exercise, but arrange for one of the listeners to call back and ask for a repeat of a particular part of the broadcast (See Training Notes to End Procedure, Section 2.6.4).

ANSWERS

Exercises on Factual Knowledge:

A.1 Three: exchange procedure
broadcast procedure
distress and safety communications

A.2 (a) See 2.1.1.

(b) See 2.1.2.

A.3 See 2.2.1.

A.4 The Controlling Station is responsible for making and maintaining contact

B. (a) I read one

(b) I read five

C. Correct sequence is D, A, B, C

D. (a) Initial Call

(b) End Transmission

(c) Respond to call

E. Stay on

Practical Exercises:

Set A

A.1 Oral. No answers

A.2 Oral. No answers

Set B

B.1 Oral. No answers

B.2 Group 2

(a) 1. All ships, All ships. Calling unknown ship in position: bearing two-five-zero degrees from Cap Monares distance five miles. This is Lady Alice, Gulf Bravo Oscar India, Lady Alice, Gulf Bravo Oscar India. Over.

2. Lady Alice, Gulf Bravo Oscar India. This is Olivia Queen, Tango Xray Three Bravo, in position: bearing two-five-zero degrees true from Cap Monares distance five miles. Over.

(b) 1. All ships, All ships. Calling unknown ship in position: Mow Point distance six miles, course: one-five-one degrees, speed: five knots. This is Cormorant Alpha, Zulu Xray Quebec Foxtrot, Cormorant Alpha, Zulu Xray Quebec Foxtrot. Over.

2. Cormorant Alpha, Zulu Xray Quebec Foxtrot. This is Packer, Papa Three Xray Quebec, in position: Mow Point distance six miles. Over.

(c) 1. All ships, All ships. Calling unknown ship. Type: Tanker: hull colour: white. Funnel: black. Course: zero-eight-five degrees. Speed: one-zero knots. This is Jupiter, Delta Six Gulf Tango, Jupiter, Delta Six Gulf Tango. Over.

2. Jupiter, Delta Six Gulf Tango. This is Sarah, Gulf Xray One One. Tanker: hull colour: white. Funnel colour: black. Course: zero-eight-five degrees. Speed: one-zero knots. Over.

(d) 1. All ships, All ships. Calling unknown ship. Type: Passenger ferry: hull colour: white. Funnels: quantity: two, colour: green. Position: Southport harbour entrance distance two miles. Course: North. This is Walnut, Sierra Quebec Romeo Six, Walnut, Sierra Quebec Romeo Six. Over.

2. Walnut, Sierra Quebec Romeo Six. This is Zandar, Lima One Xray Two. Passenger ferry: hull colour: white. Funnels: quantity: two, colour: green. Position: Southport harbour entrance distance two miles. Course: North. Over.

(e) 1. All ships in sea area Masekar. All ships in sea area Masekar. Calling unknown ship. Type: LASH. Course: zero-five-zero degrees. Speed: one-five knots. This is Eva, Alpha India Sierra Tango, Eva, Alpha India Sierra Tango. Over.

2. Eva, Alpha India Sierra Tango. This is Ingrid, November Xray Quebec Papa. Type: LASH. Course: zero-five-zero degrees. Speed: one-five knots. Over.

Set C

C.1 (a) See example

(b) See example

(c) See example

(d) 1. Olivia. This is Harriet. Switch to VHF channel zero-four. Over.

2. Harriet. This is Olivia. VHF channel zero-four Unable. VHF channels available zero-eight through one-two. Over.

3. Olivia. This is Harriet. Switch to VHF channel zero-eight. Over.

4. Harriet. This is Olivia. Agree VHF channel zero-eight. Over.

(e) 1. Northport Voyager. This is Star Vega. Switch to VHF channel one-two. Over.

2. Star Vega. This is Northport Voyager. Question: Which VHF channel. Over.

3. Northport Voyager. This is Star Vega. Answer: Switch to VHF channel one-two. Over.

4. Star Vega. This is Northport Voyager. Agree VHF channel one-two. Over.

Set D

D.1 (a) See example

(b) See example

(c) See example

(d)
1. Olivia. This is Harriet. Question: How do you read. Over.
2. Harriet. This is Olivia. Answer: I read five. Over.
3. As example
4. As example

(e)
1. Northport Voyager. This is Star Vega. Question: What is your destination. Over.
2. Star Vega. This is Northport Voyager. Answer: My destination is Buenos Aires. Over.
3. Northport Voyager. This is Star Vega. Say again your destination. Over.
4. Star Vega. This is Northport Voyager. I say again my destination is Buenos Aires. Bravo Uniform Echo November Oscar Sierra Alpha India Romeo Echo Sierra. Over.

Set E

Oral. No answers

Set F

Oral. No answers

Set G

G.1. (a)
1. All ships in Gulf of Riga. All ships in Gulf of Riga. This is Kotka Radio, Kotka Radio. Ice Information. Switch to VHF channel six-eight. Over.

(b)
1. All ships in sea area Shannon. All ships in sea area Shannon. This is Eastport Radio, Eastport Radio. Weather forecast. Switch to VHF channel one-one. Over.

G.2.

(a) [Precede message by message in G.1.(a) 1.]
2. All ships in Gulf of Riga. All ships in Gulf of Riga. This is Kotka Radio, Kotka Radio. On VHF channel six-eight. Ice information.
Information: Ice type: Thick sea ice
Ice change: No change
Ice navigation: Icebreaker assistance is necessary.
I say again.
Information: Ice type: Thick sea ice
Ice change: No change
Ice Navigation: Icebreaker assistance is necessary.
Out.

(b) [Precede message by message in G1 (b) 1]

2. All ships in sea area Shannon. All ships in sea area Shannon. This is Eastport Radio, Eastport Radio. On VHF channel one-one. Weather forecast.
Information:
Wind: North, force seven
Sea: Rough
Weather: Rain showers
Visibility: six miles except in showers
Pressure: nine-nine-five millibars, falling.
I say again.
Information:
Wind: North, force seven
Sea: Rough
Weather: Rain showers
Visibility: six miles except in showers
Pressure: nine-nine-five millibars, falling
Out.

G.3

Oral. No answers

SECTION 3

Distress, urgency and safety procedures

3.1 GENERAL RULES

3.1.1 When to use distress, urgency and safety procedure

Type of procedure	Marker word	To be used when:
Distress	*Mayday*	a ship or aircraft is threatened by grave and imminent danger, and requests immediate assistance.
Urgency	*Pan-Pan*	the station sending it has a very urgent message to transmit concerning the safety of a ship, aircraft or other vehicle, or the safety of a person.
Safety	*Sécurité* (pronounced Say-cure-e-tay)	the station sending it has a message to transmit containing an important navigational or meteorological warning.

3.1.2 General instructions which must be applied when using any of the procedures in this section.

.1 Before using any of the procedures in this section check carefully from the above diagram to make sure that you use the correct procedure and marker word. (See Training Notes to 3.1.2.)

.2 The situations are given in order of radio priority. An initial distress message from a ship or aircraft in distress has absolute priority over all other radio transmissions. (See Training Notes to 3.1.2.)

.3 The procedures are designed to ensure accurate communication and the rapid provision of assistance. Always observe them when communicating in one of the above situations.

.4 Where no standard phraseology exists, use SEASPEAK. (See Training Notes to 3.1.2.)

.5 Never abuse these marker words, procedures or any automatic alarm systems. It is dangerous to do so, as it will lead to the necessity for any distress call to be checked for authenticity before action is taken to effect a rescue (possibly yours).

.6 Before making any transmission under these procedure rules, consider carefully what you want to say. When making the transmission, ensure that you are transmitting on VHF channel 16 (when required to do so), that the VHF set is switched to maximum power, and that you do not speak too quickly. (See Training Notes to 3.1.2.)

.7 Your attention is drawn to Section 1.0.2 concerning the authority of the Master or person in charge.

TRAINING NOTES to 3.1.2: General Instructions.

1. A properly trained student should know the contents of the diagram 3.2.1. so well that he can immediately use the correct procedure.

2. If you hear an initial distress message being transmitted you must immediately stop transmitting. Do not transmit again until distress traffic is finished. (See 3.2.4.8). You may resume transmitting provided that:

   (a) you use a different VHF channel to the one on which distress communications are being conducted;

   (b) you keep yourself up-to-date with the distress situation, by listening on the appropriate VHF channel as frequently as possible, in case your assistance is required.

3. Where more information is required it should be transmitted in the most simple and straightforward manner possible, using the SEASPEAK principles set out in Section 4.

4. Write down your message before speaking. Speak in a calm, slow, deliberate voice.

3.2 DISTRESS — *MAYDAY*

3.2.1 Outline diagram of distress communications

Each transmission is explained in detail in Section 3.2.3.

Ship in Distress	Other Stations
All transmissions on VHF channel 16	
.1 **Initial Distress Message** *Mayday Mayday Mayday.* Identify (three times). *Mayday.* Ship's name + callsign. Position. What is wrong. What assistance is required. *Over.*	

Note:
Do not reply to Acknowledgement at this stage. Allow time for other stations to acknowledge unless your situation is too desperate to spare time for this.

.4 **Acknowledge Response**
Mayday.
Address and identify.
Understood.
Repeat his position.
Repeat his speed.
Repeat his ETA.
Out.

.2 **Acknowledgement**
Mayday.
Name of station in distress.
(Three times).
Callsign of station in distress.
Identify.
Received Mayday
Over.

Note;
Obtain up-to-date position, speed and ETA at the distressed ship's position.

.3 **Assistance Information**
Mayday.
Name of station in distress.
Identify.
Own position.
Own speed.
Own ETA at position given in Initial Distress Message.
Over.

Note:
If you do not hear any other stations acknowledge the Initial Distress Message make a **Mayday-Relay** transmission.

.5 **Mayday-Relay Transmission**
Mayday-relay, Mayday-relay, Mayday-relay.
Identify.
Mayday.
Name of ship in distress and its callsign.
Following received from Name of ship in distress.
Time (time of receipt) *GMT.*
Mayday.
Name of ship in distress.
Repeat of position, problem and assistance required elements of Initial Distress Message.
Identify.
Over.

Notes:
(i) The remainder of the distress communication is to be conducted in accordance with the rules in Sections 1 and 2. All transmissions in distress communications are to be prefaced by the word *Mayday*.

(ii) In addition to the rules from Sections 1 and 2 **certain special rules apply during distress communications.** They are explained in Section 3.2.4. Control of Distress communications.

3.2.2 General rules applicable to distress communications

.1 An Initial Distress Message is only to be transmitted with the section authorisation of the Master or person responsible for the ship or aircraft. (See Section 3.1.2.7 and Section 1.0.2.)

.2 One station will take control of the conduct of the distress communications and assume the duties of Controlling Station.

.3 The CS will either be:
   (a) the vessel in distress;
   (b) a shore or coast radio station;
   (c) the one scene commander (OSC)*;
   (d) the co-ordinator surface search (CSS)*.

   *N.B. Definitions of these terms will be found in the MERSAR manual. (See Training Notes to 3.2.2.)

.4 Once a station has become CS it must continue until:
   (a) the distress situation has been resolved;
   (b) a positive arrangement has been made with another station for it to assume the duties of CS. (See Training Notes to 3.2.2.)

.5 All stations have a legal obligation to acknowledge an Initial Distress Message, and to provide assistance where it is needed to save life. If it is not possible or necessary to go to the assistance of a vessel in distress, then entries detailing the circumstances must be made in official log-books.

3.2.3 How to conduct distress communications

.1 **Initial Distress Message.**

(a) *Mayday Mayday Mayday*
An Initial Distress Message is always prefixed by the distress marker word, given three times. It gives this transmission absolute priority over all other communications.

(b) **Identify**
The phrase *This is* followed, by own ship's name spoken three times. (See Training Notes to 3.2.3.1.)

e.g | This is
Rattler Rattler Rattler.

(c) *Mayday*
The marker word is used on its own to indicate that the information part of the Initial Distress Message is about to commence.

(d) **Ship's name and Callsign** (See Training Notes to 3.2.3.1)

e.g. | Rattler, Golf Xray Xray Xray.

(e) **Position** (See Training Notes 3.2.3.1)
Position is to be expressed in the method by which it was obtained, i.e. do not convert a range and bearing into latitude and longitude or vice-versa. The stations receiving the Initial Distress Message have the leisure to make any such conversions themselves, and are less likely to make mistakes. If they require further positional information they will ask for it once contact has been established.

e.g. Position taken off an open waters chart by dead reckoning:

Position: latitude: five-zero degrees three-zero minutes North, longitude: zero-three-nine degrees two-zero minutes West.

TRAINING NOTES to 3.2.2:
General rules

Note 1.
MERSAR (MERchant ship Search and Rescue) manual. This is an IMO publication dealing with the operational side of distress at sea and Search and Rescue, as conducted by merchant ships. Every bridge watchkeeping officer should be familiar with its contents.

Note 2.
In addition to the normal duties of a controlling station (see Section 2), certain other specific duties are imposed in the case of distress communications. These are given in Section 3.2.4 Control of Distress communications.

SECTION

Distress, urgency and safety procedures

TRAINING INTRODUCTION to 3.2.3.1: Initial Distress Message

This is the transmission used by a ship or aircraft in distress to inform other stations about the situation. It is only used in this form until an acknowledgement is received. The complete sequence of items to be spoken is as follows:

— Mayday Mayday Mayday
— Identify (3 times)
— Mayday
— Ship's name and callsign
— Position
— What is wrong
— What is assistance is required
— Over.

(See Training Note 3.2.3.1.5. Distress Card)

(f) **Problem**
Problem is to be expressed simply. Details can be given once contact has been established.

e.g. 'I have a lube-oil fire at the port for'd end of the main engine room', should be given at this stage as:

> fire in engine room

(g) **What assistance is required**
Assistance is to be expressed simply. Details can be given once contact has been established. If the type of assistance required cannot be specified then the phrase:

> request: immediate assistance

is to be used.

e.g 'I am going to have to abandon ship soon so please send a lifeboat', should be given at this stage as:

> request: lifeboat

(h) *Over*
This serves the same purpose as in any other communications.

(i) This transmission is only to be made on the authority of the Master or person responsible, and only if the ship or aircraft is threatened by grave and imminent danger and requests immediate assistance.

(j) Example of an Initial Distress Message: (See Training Notes to 3.2.3.1.)

> Mayday Mayday Mayday
> This is
> Rattler Rattler Rattler.
> Mayday.
> Rattler, Golf Xray Xray Xray.
> Position: latitude: five-zero degrees three-zero minutes North, longitude: zero-three-nine degrees two-zero minutes West.
> Collision with iceberg, sinking.
> Request: immediate assistance.
> Over.

TRAINING NOTES to 3.2.3.1: Initial Distress Message

1. **Identify:**
   There is no need to give the ship's callsign at this stage because it comes later in the transmission.

2. **Ship's name and callsign:**
   This is the first information element of the message.
   In the case of an Initial Distress Message, the Message Markers given in Section 4 are not used, because the Initial Distress Message is constructed to an established fixed format.
   It is particularly important that the Ship's name and callsign are spoken clearly.

3. **Position**
   The position element should always be constructed in accordance with the instructions given in Section 1.8 entitled 'Position'.

4. It is a requirement that other stations hearing your Initial Distress Message must acknowledge it. Before repeating your Initial Distress Message, allow sufficient time for all stations that hear it to acknowledge it.
   If it is not acknowledged, repeat the Initial Distress Message until you have to abandon ship.

TRAINING INTRODUCTION to 3.2.3.2: Acknowledge
The sequence of points in this transmission is as follows:
   Mayday (once only;
   Name of station in distress (three times)
   Call sign of station in distress
   Identify
   Mayday received
   Over

5.   **Distress Card Suggestion**
   Card to make out for each ship you join

(Distress Message Contents:

Mayday Mayday Mayday

This is

_____ (ship's name 3 times)*[1]

Mayday

_____ (ship's name and callsign)*[1]

Position _____*[2]
_____ (what is wrong*[2]
_____ (what assistance is required)*[2]

Over

Notes: The words inside the brackets are not to be spoken
   *[1] = fill these in when you first join the ship
   *[2] = fill these in immediately before transmitting.

.2 Acknowledge

(a) *Mayday*
   All transmissions during distress communications are to be prefaced with the marker word Mayday.

(b) **Name of station in distress (three times)**
   Callsign of station in distress

   e.g. | Rattler Rattler Rattler, Golf Xray Xray Xray. |

(c) **Identify**
   The phrase *This is* followed by own ship's name and callsign.

   e.g. | This is Rose Maru, Juliett Alfa Alfa Alfa. |

(d) *Mayday received*
   This is to inform the station in distress that you have heard his transmission and understand that it was an Initial Distress Message.

(e) *Over*

(f) Example of an Acknowledgement:

> Mayday.
> Rattler Rattler Rattler.
> Golf Xray Xray Xray.
> This is
> Rose Maru, Juliett Alfa Alfa Alfa.
> Mayday received.
> Over.

(g) Every Initial Distress Message must be acknowledged. If you are a large distance from the position given in the Initial Distress Message, allow time for a station which is closer to acknowledge before doing so yourself. (See Training Notes to 3.2.3.2.)

(h) In coastal waters, allow time for the appropriate search and rescue authorities to acknowledge before doing so yourself. (See Training Notes to 3.2.3.2.)

.3 Assistance Information Message

This is the transmission by which either the ship in distress or the search and rescuc (SAR) authorities obtain the information which enables them to decide who is in a position to assist. It will be made either unsolicited, to the ship in distress after Acknowledgements have ceased, or in reply to a request from the SAR authorities or the ship in distress. (See Training Note to 3.2.3.3.)

(a) *Mayday*

(b) **Name of station in distress**

e.g. | Rattler |

(c) **Identify**

e.g. | This is
Rose Maru |

(d) **Own position**
Own ship's position, as up-to-date as possible, given with the time at which it applies. This and the speed and ETA elements are transmitted in order to help the responsible person to decide who is best suited to help. When possible, a position given to a ship in distress should be given in the same method as the Initial Distress Message position. (See Training Notes to 3.2.3.3.)

e.g | position: time: one-four-three-zero GMT,
latitude: five-zero degrees two-zero minutes North,
longitude; zero-three-nine degrees one-five minutes West. |

(e) **Own speed**
Own ship's speed, at which the ETA for the distress position was calculated. (See Training Notes to 3.2.3.3.)

e.g. | speed: one-eight knots |

(f) **Own ETA at distress position**
Own ship's ETA at the distress position, calculated at the speed given in the previous element.

e.g. | ETA: one-five-three-zero GMT. |

(g) **Over**

SECTION

3

Distress, urgency and safety procedures

(h) Example of Assistance Information Transmission

> Mayday.
> Rattler. This is Rose Maru.
> position: time: one-four-three-zero GMT,
> latitude: five-zero degrees two-zero minutes North,
> longitude: zero-three-nine degrees one-five minutes West.
> speed; one-eight knots.
> ETA: one-five-three-zero GMT.
> Over.

TRAINING NOTES to 3.2.3.3: Assistance Information Message

Training Note 1. **Diagrammatic summary of the use of an Assistance Information Transmission**

where it is used as part of the acknowledgement of an Initial Distress Message.

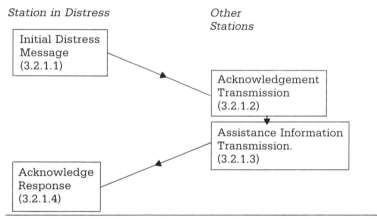

Continuation of Distress Communications

In the case where it is used in response to a request by another station.

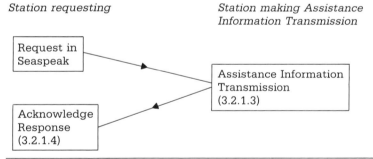

Continuation of Distress Communications (Stage 3)

Training Note 2.

Own position
For example, if the ship in distress used Latitude and Longitude, then Latitude and Longitude should also be used in this transmission. If bearing and distance from a point of land was used, then bearing and distance from the same point of land should be used.

e.g.
> position: time: now;
> bearing: zero-nine five degrees;
> from Masirah.
> distance: two-zero-miles.

Training Note 3. **Own Speed**

The method of expression is taken from the Standard Units of Measurement and the method of expressing quantities given in Section 1.

SECTION

3

Distress, urgency and safety procedures

TRAINING INTRODUCTION
to 3.2.3.4: Acknowledge
Response

The sequence of information in this transmission is as follows:
— *Mayday*
— Address and Identify
— Understood
— Repeat his position ⎫
— Repeat his speed ⎬readback
— Repeat his ETA ⎭
— Over

.4 **Acknowledge Response**

This is the transmission by which the ship in distress or the SAR authorities will acknowledge receipt of the Assistance Information Transmission. (See Training Note below.)

(a) *Mayday*

(b) **Address and identify**

All further transmissions in distress procedure will be addressed and identified in the normal manner except in the case of a Mayday-Relay transmission (3.2.1.5 & 3.2.2.5).

e.g. | Rose Maru. This is Rattler. |

(c) *Understood + Readback*

In order to indicate that it has correctly received the Assistance Information Transmission, the station which is making this transmission will read back the message content.

e.g.
> Understood,
> position: time: one-four-three-zero GMT,
> latitude: five-zero degrees two-zero minutes North,
> longitude: zero-three-nine degrees one-five minutes West,
> speed: one-eight knots,
> ETA: one-five-three-zero GMT.
> Over.

(d) Example of Acknowledge Response transmission

> Mayday.
> Rose Maru. This is Rattler.
> Understood,
> position: time: one-four-three-zero GMT,
> latitude: five-zero degrees two-zero minutes North,
> longitude: zero-three-nine degrees one-five minutes West.
> speed: one-eight knots.
> ETA; one-five-three-zero GMT.
> Over.

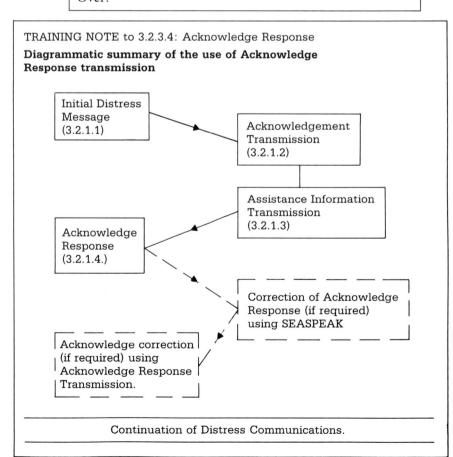

TRAINING NOTE to 3.2.3.4: Acknowledge Response

Diagrammatic summary of the use of Acknowledge Response transmission

Continuation of Distress Communications.

SECTION 3

Distress, urgency and safety procedures

TRAINING INTRODUCTION to 3.2.3.5: Mayday Relay Transmission

The sequence of items of information in this transmission is as follows:

— *Mayday-Relay, Mayday-Relay, Mayday-Relay*
— Identify
— *Mayday*
— Name of ship in distress and its call sign
— Following received from
— Name of ship in distress
— Time (time of receipt of Initial Distress Message) GMT/UTC
— Mayday
— Name of ship in distress
— The position, what is wrong and what assistance is required (parts of the Initial Distress Message)
— Identify
— Over

.5 **Mayday Relay Transmission**

If no other station makes an Acknowledgement transmission you must make a Mayday Relay transmission. If a shore or coast station makes the Acknowledgement transmission, it will then make a Mayday Relay transmission. If a shore or coast station makes an Acknowledgement transmission, it will assume the duties of CS. (See Training Notes to 3.2.3.5).

(a) *Mayday relay Mayday relay Mayday relay*
The marker phrase for a Mayday Relay transmission. It gives this transmission priority over all other communications except an Initial Distress Message. (See Training Notes to 3.2.3.5.)

(b) **Identify**
The phrase *This is*, followed by own ship's name (three times)

> e.g. This is
> Rose Maru Rose Maru Rose Maru.

(c) *Mayday*
The distress marker word is given here to indicate that a repeat of the Initial Distress Message is about to be made.

(d) **Name of ship in distress and its callsign**
The identity of the ship in distress is given here.

> e.g Rattler, Golf Xray Xray Xray.

(e) *Following received from*
This phrase is used in order to clearly differentiate the procedure from the actual repeat of the Initial Distress Message. Any information given between now and the end of this transmission is to be a strictly accurate repeat of the Initial Distress Message. No personal interpretations are to be given in a Mayday Relay transmission.

(f) **Name of ship in distress**

> e.g. Rattler.

(g) *Time* **(time of receipt)** *GMT* **or** *UTC*
This is the time that you received the Initial Distress Message.

> e.g. time: one-four-one-five GMT.

(h) *Mayday*
The distress marker is to be followed by a repeat of the Initial Distress Message.
i.e. Name and callsign of the ship in distress. (See Training Notes to 3.2.3.5.)

> e.g. Rattler, Golf Xray Xray Xray.

Position of the ship in distress:

> e.g. position: latitude: five-zero degrees three-zero minutes North, longitude: zero-three-nine-degrees two-zero minutes West.

What is wrong with ship in distress:

> e.g. collision with iceberg, sinking.

What assistance is required by ship in distress:

> e.g. request: immediate assistance.

page 65

(i) **Identify**

The phrase *This is*, followed by own ship's name.

(j) **Over**

(k) Example of Mayday-Relay transmission:

> Mayday-relay Mayday-relay Mayday-relay.
> This is
> Rose Maru Rose Maru Rose Maru.
> Mayday.
> Rattler, Golf Xray Xray Xray.
> Following received from,
> Rattler,
> time: one-four-one-five GMT
> Mayday.
> Rattler, Golf Xray Xray Xray,
> position: latitude: five-zero degrees three-zero minutes North,
> longitude: zero-three-nine degrees two-zero minutes West.
> Collision with iceberg, sinking.
> Request immediate assistance.
> This is Rose Maru.
> Over.

TRAINING NOTES to 3.2.3.5: Mayday Relay Transmission

1. **Diagrammatic summary of the use of a Mayday-Relay transmission**

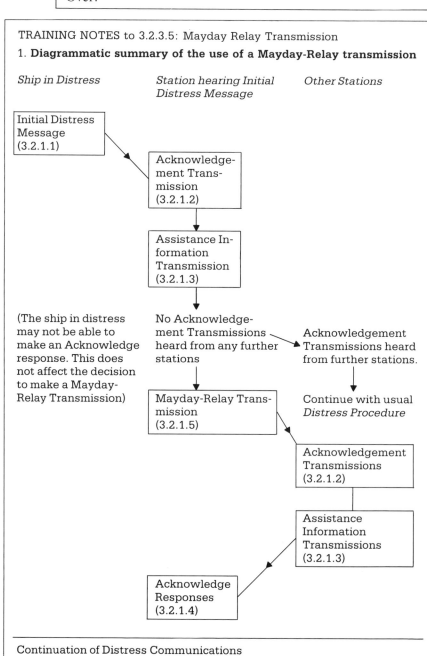

Continuation of Distress Communications

CONTD.

Distress, urgency and safety procedures

N.B. The procedure to be adopted after transmission of a Mayday-Relay transmission is the same as that after an Initial Distress Message. The only difference is that the station receiving the Acknowlegement Transmissions and the Assistance Information Transmissions is not the ship in distress.

2. **Mayday-Relay**
This phrase also indicates to other stations that the station making the transmission is not the ship which is in distress.

3. Any acknowledgements or other responses to a Mayday Relay should be addressed to the station that has sent the Relay, and not to the ship in distress.

3.2.4 Control of distress communications

.1 Distress communications will be conducted primarily on VHF channel 16. Other VHF channels may be employed as necessary and silence imposed on them (Section 1.2.2.1). It should be remembered that greatest range will normally be obtained on VHF channel 16.

.2 No station is permitted to make transmissions which are unrelated to the resolution of the distress situation, on VHF channels which are being used for distress communications. (See Training Notes to 3.2.4.)

.3 To stop a station which is interfering with distress communications, the CS will make the following transmission:

> Interruption,
> Seelonce Mayday,
> Stop transmitting,
> Seelonce Mayday,
> Out.

.4 During SAR operations the ship, aircraft, shore or coast station in control of the SAR operations will make Information Broadcasts. These broadcasts will give:
information on SAR activities in progress;
requests for specific types of assistance;
translations of the position given in the initial distress message into other forms, and guidance on its believed accuracy.

.5 Information broadcasts will be consecutively numbered. They will be transmitted at regular intervals, and when there is a change in the distress situation.

.6 Information broadcasts will be constructed and handled in accordance with the rules for broadcast procedure, except that:
(a) they will be made on VHF channel 16;
(b) they will be prefaced with the word *Mayday*.

> e.g. Mayday,
> All ships.
> This is Land's End Radio.
> Mayday Rattler.
> Information number ...
> message element of
> broadcast.
> This is Land's End Radio.
> Out.

.7 Only the ship in distress, or the station controlling the SAR activities, has the authority to indicate completion of distress communications. (See Training Notes to 3.2.4.)

.8 It will do so by making the following transmission:

> Mayday.
> All ships.
> This is Land's End Radio,
> time: (of this broadcast)
> (name of ship in distress and its callsign)
> Seelonce fee nee.
> Out.

.9 This transmission will be made on each VHF channel on which silence was imposed.

.10 Receipt of this transmission indicates that distress communications and their associated restrictions are terminated. Normal working may now be resumed on VHF.

3.3 URGENCY — *PAN-PAN*

> TRAINING INTRODUCTION to 3.3: URGENCY — PAN-PAN
>
> This type of procedure is used when a station has to transmit a message concerning the safety of a ship, aircraft or other vehicle, or the safety of a person.

3.3.1 Outline diagram of urgency communications

> TRAINING NOTES to 3.2.4:
> Control of distress communications
>
> *Note 1*
> All distress communications transmissions must be prefaced by the distress marker word *Mayday* so that their priority is made clear to all stations.
>
> *Note 2*
> Note that it has to be the *station controlling SAR activities* and not the station controlling distress communications. These two functions will not always be conducted by the same station.

Each transmission is explained in detail in Section 3.3.3

Ship making an Urgency transmission	Other stations
.1 **Initial Urgency Message** *Pan-Pan Pan-Pan Pan-Pan.* Identify (three times), *Pan-Pan,* Ship's name and callsign. Position. What is wrong. What assistance is required. *Over.*	.2 **Acknowledgement** *Pan-Pan,* Address, Identify. *Pan-Pan received.* *Over.*

All subsequent urgency communications will be conducted in accordance with the exchange and broadcast rules.

3.3.2 General Rules

.1 Urgency exchanges will be conducted on VHF channel 16, unless a distress is in progress on VHF channel 16, or they are expected to take a long time to complete.

.2 All transmissions will be prefaced with the urgency marker *Pan-Pan*.

.3 Urgency transmissions have priority over all the other transmissions except those connected with distress situations.

.4 Control of urgency communications will follow the rules for exchange and broadcast.

.5 An urgency transmission is only to be made with the authorisation of the Master or person responsible for the ship or aircraft.

SECTION

3

Distress, urgency and safety procedures

TRAINING INTRODUCTION
to 3.3.3.1: Initial Urgency
message

The sequence of the items in this transmission is as follows:

— Pan-Pan (3 times)
— Identify (3 times)
— Pan-Pan
— Ship's name and callsign
— Position
— What is wrong
— What assistance is required
— Over

TRAINING NOTES to 3.3.3.1: Initial Urgency message

Note 1
Note the similarity in format between the Initial Urgency Message and the Initial Distress Message. The only difference is the use of different marker words for urgency and distress communications.

Note 2
There is no equivalent of a Mayday-Relay transmission in urgency procedure.

Note 3
Note that in the example the position is given as 15 miles off-shore. Although *Vega* has lost her propellor and therefore her ability to move, she is not in grave and imminent danger, and distress procedure is not applicable.

TRAINING INTRODUCTION to 3.3.3.2: Acknowledgement

The sequence of items in an acknowlegement transmission is as follows:
— *Pan-Pan*
— Address
— Identify
— *Pan-Pan* received.
— Over.

3.3.3 | How to conduct urgency communications

.1 **Initial Urgency message**

(a) *Pan-Pan Pan-Pan Pan-Pan*
The urgency marker, which is given three times to indicate that this is the Initial Urgency message. (See Training Notes to 3.3.3.)

(b) **Identify (three times)**
The phrase *This is* followed by own ship's name given three times.

> e.g. | This is
> Vega Vega Vega

(c) *Pan-Pan*
The urgency marker repeated to indicate that the urgency message is about to be given.

(d) **Ship's name + callsign** (See Training Notes to 3.3.3.)

> e.g. | Vega, Seven Victor Alfa Tango

(e) **Position**
Give the position in the way it was obtained. Let the other stations at their leisure convert latitude and longitude to distance and bearing etc, if they wish to do so.

(f) **What is wrong**
Problem, i.e. what is wrong, is to be expressed as simply as possible. Details can be given once contact has been established.

> e.g. | lost propeller

(g) **What assistance is required**
Type of assistance required is to be expressed simply. Details can be given once contact has been established.

> e.g. | require tow

(h) *Over*

(i) Example of an Initial Urgency Message. (See Training Notes to 3.3.3.)

> Pan-Pan Pan-Pan Pan-Pan
> This is
> Vega Vega Vega,
> Pan-Pan,
> Vega, Seven Victor Alfa Tango
> position: bearing zero-nine-zero degrees true, from Ras Sarkan.
> distance: one-five miles
> Lost propeller,
> Require tow.
> Over.

(j) When you have made the transmission allow adequate time for a reply before repeating it.

.2 **Acknowledgement**

(a) *Pan-Pan*
The urgency marker, which must prefix all further transmissions in the exchange.

(b) **Address**
This is to consist of name and callsign of the station that gave the Initial Urgency Message.

e.g. | Vega, Seven Victor Alfa Tango

(c) **Identify**
The phrase *This is* followed by own ship's name and callsign.

e.g. | This is
Rose Maru, Juliett Alfa Alfa Alfa.

(d) ***Pan-Pan received***
This phrase indicates that you have received the Initial Urgency Message. No readback of the content of that message is required at this stage.

(e) ***Over***

(f) Example of Acknowledgement

> Pan-Pan
> Vega, Seven Victor Alfa Tango.
> This is
> Rose Maru, Juliett Alfa Alfa Alfa.
> Pan-Pan received.
> Over.

3.3.4 | Medical communications

> TRAINING INTRODUCTION to 3.3.4: Medical communications
>
> These are a specific type of urgency communications. They employ urgency procedures, modified and added to as described in this subsection.
>
> In order to study urgent medical communications procedure you will require a copy of the International Code of Signals. This is an IMO publication and is usually referred to as 'Interco'. You should make sure that the copy is up-to-date as amendments are issued from time to time.
>
> It is not expected that non-medical personnel will be required to transmit messages about complex medical matters in SEASPEAK. Instead, such messages are to be spoken in accordance with the standard phrases given in the International Code.

.1 Urgent requests for medical assistance are not to be made under distress procedure, since by definition (Section 3.1.1) Mayday procedure only covers situations where a whole **ship** or **aircraft** is threatened. Requests for assistance where a **person** is threatened are to be handled by the use of the urgency procedure.

.2 Urgent medical communications are those where medical assistance or evacuation is urgently needed to save life or limb.

.3 The initial description of the medical problem should be simple and in plain language.

.4 If, during the course of an exchange, it becomes necessary to use medical terms (e.g. drugs, symptoms, physiology) the medical section of the **International Code of Signals** is to be used.

.5 The following method is to be employed when using the medical section of the **International Code of Signals:**

(a) Prefix any codes used with the words:

> Interco Medical.

(b) spell the code group using the phonetic alphabet;

(c) suffix the code groups with the words:

> end of Interco.

.6   Example of a transmission in an exchange concerning medical advice.

> Pan-Pan.
> Rose Maru.
> This is Papeete Radio.
> Information.
> Interco Medical,
> mike tango delta three-two,
> End of interco.
> Over.

Translated, this transmission reads:

'Rose Maru, this is Papeete Radio,
you should give aspirin tablet,
over,'

3.4   SAFETY—SÉCURITÉ (pronounced *Say-cure-e-tay*)

3.4.1   Outline diagram of safety communications

Each transmission is explained in detail in Section 3.4.3

Ship making safety transmission	Other stations
.1 **Initial Safety Transmission** *Sécurité Sécurité Sécurité.* All ships (or all ships in a particular area) *This is* Ship's name (three times) *Sécurité.* Ship's name and callsign. Phrase indicating content of safety message to follow. *Switch to VHF channel* *Over.*	(which will be on VHF channel 16)

Broadcast procedure switch-over rules to be used.
Any subsequent communications to be conducted on working VHF channel

.2 **Safety Message** *Sécurité Sécurité Sécurité* All ships. (or all ships in a particular area) *This is* Ship's name (three times). *Sécurité.* Phrase indicating content of safety message to follow. Content of safety message. Out.	

All subsequent safety communications will be conducted in accordance with
the exchange and broadcast rules.

SECTION

3

Distress, urgency and safety procedures

3.4.2 General rules applicable to safety communications

.1 All transmissions will be prefaced with the safety marker *Sécurité* pronounced Say-cure-e-tay.

.2 Safety exchanges will be conducted on a working VHF channel unless it is impossible to do so.

.3 Safety transmissions have priority over all other transmissions except those connected with distress and urgency situations.

.4 A safety transmission is only to be made with the authorisation of the Master or person responsible for the ship or aircraft.

3.4.3 How to conduct safety communications

.1 **Initial Safety Transmission**

This is the transmission by which other stations are warned that a safety message is about to be transmitted, what its content will be and on which VHF channel it will be made.

(a) *Sécurité (pronounced say-cure-e-tay)*
This is the safety marker word. At the beginning of the initial safety transmission and at the beginning of the safety message it is to be given three times. Elsewhere in an exchange concerning safety it is to be given once only at the beginning of each transmission. (See Training Notes to 3.4.3.)

(b) **Address of a particular station(s)**
In most cases a safety message will be addressed to 'all ships'. If it is desired to address safety communications to a particular ship or group of ships, then an appropriate address(es) should be formulated from the exchange and broadcast rules and used here.

(c) *This is* + **ship's name (three times)**
This is the identification element of the transmission.

> e.g. | This is
> Arcadia Arcadia Arcadia

(d) **Sécurité (pronounced say-cure-e-tay)**
The safety marker is spoken here to indicate that the call has been completed, and that information is about to be transmitted. (See Training Notes to 3.4.3.)

(e) **Ship's name and callsign**
This is given again at this stage.

> e.g. | Arcadia, Charlie Alfa Alfa Alfa

(f) **Phrase indicating content of safety message to follow**
This phrase is used to inform receiving stations of the content of the safety message to come, so that they can decide if it will be of value for them to listen to it. The phrase is to be taken from the list of Major Communication Subjects given in Section 5. A few words may be appended to the phrase in order to expand upon it. (See Training Notes to 3.4.3.)

> e.g. | Navigational information: Decca warning.

(g) **Switch to VHF channel**
This is the Advise Working VHF Channel element of the transmission, and is treated in the same way as in broadcast procedure. (See Training Notes to 3.4.3.)

(h) *Over*

(i) Example of an Initial Safety Transmission:

> Sécurité Sécurité Sécurité.
> All ships (*may be repeated if thought necessary*)
> This is
> Arcadia Arcadia Arcadia.
> Sécurité.
> Arcadia, Charlie Alfa Alfa Alfa.
> Navigational information; Decca warning.
> Switch to VHF channel zero-six.
> Over.

TRAINING NOTES to 3.4.3: How to conduct safety communications

1. **Address**
In most cases a safety message will be addressed to 'All Ships' or 'All Stations'. This of course implies all ships within VHF range.
If it is desired to address a geographically larger group of ships, then a medium of communication such as MF or HF, which have a greater range, should be used.
If it is desired to address, a geographically smaller group of ships, then the phrase 'All ships' should be appropriately modified. e.g. 'All ships in Cook Straits'.
If it is desired to address Safety communications to a particular ship or group of ships, then an appropriate address(es) should be formulated from the exchange and broadcast rules and used here. If a single ship is addressed the word 'Warning' may be used instead of Sécurité (See Section 4.2).
e.g. 'All tankers in Lyme Bay'
The address may be repeated if necessary up to 3 times in order to attract attention. The most usual form of address used in safety communications is the following:-

> All ships

2. **Sécurité**
The safety marker is spoken here to indicate that the call has been completed and that information is about to be given.

3. **Phrase indicating content**
The definition of safety communications says that the Safety Message will contain an important navigational or meteorological warning. This therefore implies that the phrase indicating content of safety message to follow must always start with either.

> NAVIGATIONAL INFORMATION
> OR
> METEOROLOGICAL INFORMATION

4. **Switch**
When making a choice of working VHF channels, the contents of Section 1.2 (Use of VHF channels) should be borne in mind; particularly 1.2.1.4, which permits the use of VHF channel 16 for certain short transmissions concerning the safety of navigation.

TRAINING INTRODUCTION to 3.4.3.2: Safety message

The sequence of items to be spoken in this transmission is as follows:
— *Sécurité* (3 times)
— Address
— Identify (3 times)
— *Sécurité*
— Phrase indicating content of safety message to follow
— Safety Message
— Out.

.2 Safety message

This is the transmission during which the safety message itself will be given.

(a) It is to be transmitted on the working VHF channel (Section 1.2.2) which has been nominated in the Initial Safety Transmission. (See Training Introduction to 3.4.3.1)

(b) *Sécurité* (**pronounced Say-cure-e-tay**) **three times**
The safety marker is given three times at the beginning of the safety message. *page 73*

(c) **Address of a particular stations(s)**
This will be the same address that was used in the Initial Safety Transmission.

e.g. | All ships, all ships, all ships |

(d) ***This is* + ship's name (three times)**
Identification, conducted exactly the same way as in the initial safety transmission.

e.g. | This is
Arcadia Arcadia Arcadia. |

(e) **Phrase prefixed by the word Sécurité indicating content of safety message to follow**
This phrase is used to inform receiving stations of the content of the safety message to come so that they can decide if it will be of value for them to listen to it. The phrase is to be taken from the list of Major Communication Subjects given in Section 5. A few words may be appended to the phrase in order to expand upon it.

e.g. | Sécurité Navigational information; Decca warning. |

(f) **Content of safety message**
The safety message itself is transmitted at this stage and is to be constructed using the message section of the manual, Section 4. The content of the safety message may be repeated if it is thought necessary to do so.

e.g. | Decca chain two bravo is not working. |

(g) ***Out***

(h) Example of a safety message

| Sécurité Sécurité Sécurité.
All ships all ships.
This is
Arcadia Arcadia Arcadia.
Sécurité.
Navigational information; Decca warning.
Decca chain two bravo is not working.
I say again.
Decca chain two bravo is not working.
Out. |

.3 **Procedure**
Broadcast and exchange procedure rules will be utilised in safety procedure. This includes the end procedure rules which give the other stations time to request repeats. (Section 2.4.9) (See Training Note below.)

TRAINING NOTE to 3.4.3.3: Procedure

There is one special case in safety procedure which requires slightly different handling from normal safety procedure. The rules concerning the use of VHF Channel 16 state:

'An exchange less than one minute in length concerning the safety of navigation may be made on VHF channel 16 if it is important that all ships within range hear it. (see subsection 1.2.1.4)'

This can be achieved by omitting the Initial Safety Transmission and making the Safety Message transmission (3.4.3.2) only, and doing so on VHF channel 16.

The above concession is likely to be of particular use in the case of a 'not-under-command' ship in a constrained fairway, who wishes to inform the other ships of her predicament so that they will keep clear.

That is not the only case in which this concession will be of use, but it should be remembered that it is only a concession and should not be abused. Generally the normal full safety procedure should be utilised.

SECTION 3.
EXERCISES

TRAINING INTRODUCTION:
EXERCISES FOR SECTION 3

Distress, Urgency and Safety Communications are
subject to rigid rules. Very little flexibility is permitted in the sequence and content of transmissions
made in the early stages of such communications.

The learning task therefore involves becoming
word-perfect in the standard transmissions and the
rules which govern their use. In order to assist with
this task, a number of direct factual questions have
been included alongside the practice exercises.
Correct answers to both those and the exercises are
given at the end of this section.

Ex. 3.A

It is important to know which procedure is relevant to any
given circumstance. If you do not know which to use, the
communication may be confused by your choice of the
wrong one. Delay and loss of life may result.

In the questions below, choose the correct procedure to
use from the multiple choice answers. Each one must be
answered correctly before going to the next exercise.
Write down the answers on a separate sheet of paper.

1. Your ship is sinking and you need a lifeboat to come
   to your rescue.
   (a) *Distress* procedure
   (b) *Urgency* procedure
   (c) *Safety* procedure

2. A crew member has been badly injured in an
   accident and you want him taken ashore.
   (a) *Distress* procedure
   (b) *Urgency* procedure
   (c) *Safety* procedure

3. Your propeller has dropped off in a gale two miles
   off Cape Guardafui with an onshore wind.
   (a) *Distress* procedure
   (b) *Urgency* procedure
   (c) *Safety* procedure

4. Your propeller has dropped off, one hundred miles
   from Cape Guardafui, with an off-shore wind.
   (a) *Distress* procedure
   (b) *Urgency* procedure
   (c) *Safety* procedure

5. Your propeller has dropped off in N.E. bound lane
   off, CAP GRIS NEZ, Dover Strait.
   (a) *Distress* procedure
   (b) *Urgency* procedure
   (c) *Safety* procedure

6. You are Not Under Command (as defined in Colregs)
   and you wish to warn other shipping to keep clear.
   (a) *Distress* procedure
   (b) *Urgency* procedure
   (c) *Safety* procedure

7. You have a small fire on board a passenger ship, and
   you wish to make preparations for the event of
   evacuating the passengers. This is solely a precau-
   tion — you do not think it likely to be necessary.
   (a) *Distress* procedure
   (b) *Urgency* procedure
   (c) *Safety* procedure

8. You have urgent information that you wish to
   convey to another ship of the same company,
   regarding a stevedores' strike.
   (a) *Distress* procedure
   (b) *Urgency* procedure
   (c) *Safety* procedure

9. You sight a container floating in the Malacca Strait,
   and you wish to warn other vessels.
   (a) *Distress* procedure
   (b) *Urgency* procedure
   (c) *Safety* procedure

10. You see a ship sinking, and you wish to advise the
    appropriate SAR authorities.
    (a) *Distress* procedure
    (b) *Urgency* procedure
    (c) *Safety* procedure

11. You see an aircraft ditching, and you wish to advise
    the appropriate SAR authorities.
    (a) *Distress* procedure
    (b) *Urgency* procedure
    (c) *Safety* procedure

12. You hear a *Mayday* transmission which is not
    acknowledged, and you wish to advise the appropri-
    ate SAR authorities.
    (a) *Distress* procedure
    (b) *Urgency* procedure
    (c) *Safety* procedure

Ex. 3.B Form of the Transmissions

It is imperative to know by heart a few of
these transmissions.

These are: **Initial Distress Message**
            Initial Urgency Message
            Safety Message

What they have in common is that they may have to be
transmitted under pressure, without time to refer to a
bridge book or other manual, and it is important that they
are correctly handled.

1. (i) Write out the appropriate message for the
       following circumstances:

       You are sinking, due to collision with a sub-
       merged object, which has punctured the hull in
       the area of nos. 4 and 5 and double bottom
       tanks. The ballast line non-return valves have
       failed, probably due to grit in the valve seat-
       ings. It is now 15:00 ship's time, and you are
       keeping zone + 11. Your dead reckoning
       position is twenty-five degrees and ten min-
       utes south, one-hundred-and-sixty and a half
       degrees west.

   (ii) Which VHF channel would you transmit on?

2. (i)   Write out the appropriate message for the following circumstances:

    Your chief engineer has fallen down an engine room ladder. He has broken both legs and is bleeding from the mouth. It is three-twenty in the afternoon and Ouessant lighthouse is eight miles bearing one-nine-five from your ship. There is no doctor or proper medical facility on board.

    (ii) Who will you show the message to for approval before you transmit it?

3. (i)   Write out the appropriate message for the following circumstances:

    You have to stop your main engine for a while to replace a cooling water pipe. Just to the north of you, one mile away, is the South East Ridens light buoy. The time is 01:30 GMT.

    (ii) If you have to repeat this message due to repairs taking longer than expected, at what time would you make the next transmission and why would you choose that time to do it?

Ex. 3.C As you are more likely to have to respond to more of other people's problems than you are to have problems of your own during your career at sea, knowing how to respond to communications is as important as knowing how to make them.

The following exercise presents an incoming communication. Name the transmission that should be made in response. Make your own copy of the diagram, and fill in the appropriate names.

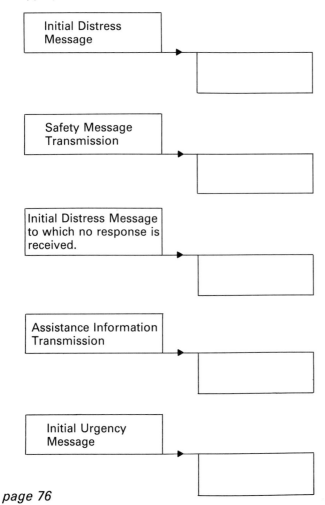

Ex. 3.D It is important to know what priority applies to the different types of procedure.

Arrange the items in order of priority, in each of the following sets:

1. (a)   Initial Urgency Transmission
    (b)   Initial Safety Transmission
    (c)   Initial Distress Transmission

2. (a)   Safety Message Transmission
    (b)   Urgency communications
    (c)   Initial Safety Transmission
    (d)   Distress communications

3. (a)   Distress communications
    (b)   Safety Message Transmission
    (c)   Mayday Relay Transmission
    (d)   Urgency communications

4. (a)   A transmission prefixed by 'Mayday'.
    (b)   A transmission prefixed by 'Pan-Pan'.
    (c)   A transmission prefixed by 'Mayday-Relay'. 'Mayday-Relay' 'Mayday-Relay'.
    (d)   A transmission prefixed by 'Sécurité-Sécurité-Sécurité'.
    (e)   A transmission prefixed by 'Mayday, Mayday, Mayday'.

5. (a)   A communication concerning containers afloat in the North Sea.
    (b)   A communication concerning a sinking ship.
    (c)   A communication concerning a very serious medical problem.
    (d)   A broadcast updating information about a search and rescue exercise.
    (e)   A broadcast warning shipping about the closure of a port due to an industrial dispute.

Ex. 3.E Test Questions

1. What is the order of priority of the 3 main types of procedure covered in this section?

2. In what circumstances should distress procedure be used?

3. What is the distress marker word?

4. What is the urgency marker word?

5. In what circumstances should urgency procedure be used?

6. Which VHF channel should distress communications be conducted on?

7. Which control on your VHF set (apart from the channel selector) must you check before making an *Initial Distress Message* transmission?

8. If you hear an unanswered *Initial Distress Message* transmission, what must you do?

9. In what circumstances are you legally required to assist another ship?

10. In a case where these circumstances referred to in Question 9 apply, and you do not go to the assistance of the other ship, what action must be taken?

11. Who has responsibility for how a ship's VHF set is operated?

12. If you make an *Acknowledge Transmission* in response to an *Initial Distress Message* transmission, what information should you be collecting together in order to be ready for your next transmission?

13. What is the address element of an *Initial Distress Message* transmission?

14. Who must authorise the sending of an *Initial Distress Message*?

15. What type of danger must you be in in order to justify the sending of an *Initial Distress Message* transmission?

16. What kind of assistance must you require in order to justify the sending of an *Initial Distress Message* transmission?

17. What is MERSAR?

18. Where should you find MERSAR?

19. What is the difference between a CSS and an OSC?

20. If you are talking to another station and you hear a transmission prefixed by the word *Mayday*, what must you do?

21. Who would you expect to make a distress information broadcast?

22. During the course of a distress situation, how would you know if you had missed a distress information broadcast?

23. What information would you expect to get in a distress information broadcast?

24. You are involved in distress communications. A station interrupts, with lower priority traffic. Write out the transmission that you would use in order to tell that station to be quiet.

25. Your VHF aerial is 100 feet above sea level. You know that the VHF station in a port is 64 feet above sea level. At what maximum range would you expect the port VHF station to be able to hear your Initial Distress Message transmission in conditions of normal propagation?
(If you prefer, use a VHF aerial height of 36m and a port VHF station height of 25m.)

26. In what circumstances should urgency procedure be used?

27. Which transmission is prefixed by the urgency marker spoken three times?

28. To which stations may an *Initial Urgency Transmission* be addressed?

29. In *Initial Urgency Transmissions* and *Initial Distress Message* transmissions, of what should the 'what is wrong' element be composed, and how should it be expressed?

30. In the message part of an *Initial Urgency* (or *Distress Message*) transmission there are three elements of information. What are they?

31. How would you know if distress communications had been completed?

32. What method would you use to describe medical symptoms, during a VHF communication?

33. What is the qualification which you must apply to medical communications, to decide whether or not to conduct them using *Urgency Procedure*?

34. Is it legally permitted to use *Distress Procedure* for medical communications?

35. Explain your answer to question 34.

36. When giving a position by bearing and distance, should the bearing given be the bearing of a navigation mark from your ship, or the reciprocal of that bearing?

37. When giving your position in an *Initial Distress* and *Urgency message*, in what form should it be expressed?

38. When giving times, particularly in relation to position, which would be used: GMT, UTC or local?

39. In which publication are the medical codes to be found?

40. What does UTC stand for, and what is its relationship to GMT?

41. What response should you make to a *Safety Message* transmission?

42. What transmissions are prefixed by the safety marker word spoken three times?

43. Safety communications must be concerned with which two subjects?

44. What kind of messages about safety communications are permissible when using safety procedures?

45. Under what circumstances can you use VHF channel 16 to conduct safety communications?

46. Are message markers required to be used in a *Safety Message*?

47. If you required a repeat of all or part of a safety message, when would you ask for it?

48. Generally speaking, what type of procedure do safety communications employ?

49. What is the largest single cause of delay in SAR operations?

50. Can you initiate an *Initial Distress Message* for another ship?

ANSWERS

Ex. 3.A

1 (a)
2 (b)
3 (a)
4 (b)
5 (b)
6 (c)
7 (b)
8 none of these
9 (c)
10 (a)
11 (a)
12 (a)

Ex. 3.B

1. (i) (a) Mayday Mayday Mayday. This is Arcadia Arcadia Arcadia. Mayday. Arcadia, Charlie Alpha Alpha Alpha. (b) (c) Position, Time: zero-two-zero-zero UTC. Latitude two-five degrees one-zero minutes South; Longitude one-six-zero degrees three-zero minutes West. (d) We are sinking. Request immediate assistance. Over.

Main points to note in answer:

(a) use of correct, i.e. distress, marker word;

(b) position given in the correct format;

(c) time of position converted to UTC (or GMT);

(d) simple expression of the problem.

(ii) VHF channel 16

2. (i) (a) Pan-Pan Pan-Pan Pan-Pan. This is Arcadia Arcadia Arcadia. Pan-Pan. Arcadia, Charlie Alpha Alpha Alpha. (b) Position, (c) Time: one-five-two-zero GMT. (d) Bearing zero-one-five from Oeussant light distance eight miles. (e) We have a badly injured man. (f) Request medical evacuation (or assistance). Over.

Main Points to note in answer:

(a) use of correct, i.e. urgency, marker word;

(b) position marker word;

(c) time given in the correct format, (i.e. twenty four hour clock;

(d) position given as bearing converted to reciprocal, i.e. *from* the lighthouse;

(e) simple expression of problem;

(f) simple expression of type of assistance required.

(ii) The Master or person in charge of the ship.

3. (i) (a) Securite Securite Securite. All ships All ships All ships. This is Arcadia Arcadia Arcadia. Securite. Arcadia, Charlie Alpha Alpha Alpha. (b) Navigation warning time: zero-one-three-zero GMT. (c) Arcadia position: bearing one-eight-zero degrees true from South East Ridens light buoy, distance one mile. Not under command. Reason: engine repairs. (d) Request all ships keep clear of me. (e) Out.

Main points to note in answer:

(a) Use of correct, i.e. safety marker word.

(b) A safety message, not an initial safety transmission, and made on VHF channel 16 as it is important to all ships in the area. Note that this transmission takes about 40–45 seconds to transmit and therefore is also inside the time limit of 1 minute on VHF channel 16.

(c) Position and time correctly handled.

(d) This request would be the reason for making such a transmission.

(e) Use of 'out' as is required at the end of a safety message and not 'over'.

(ii) Between 02.00 and 02.03 GMT if using MF radio, because this is at end of silence period. If using VHF, any time as may be thought suitable.

Ex. 3.C

1. Acknowledgement transmission followed by Assistance Information.

2. None, listen only.

3. Mayday Relay Transmission.

4. Acknowledge Response.

5. Acknowledge transmission.

Ex. 3.D

1. (c)

(a)

(b)

2. (d)

(b)

(c)

(a)

3. (c)

(a)

(d)

(b)

4. (e)

(c)

(a)

(b)

(d)

5. (b)

(d)

(c)

(a)

(e)

Ex. 3.E

Test Answers

1. Distress

Urgency

Safety

2. When a ship is threatened by grave and imminent danger and requests immediate assistance.

3. Mayday

4. Pan-Pan

5. When a station has a very urgent message to transmit concerning the safety of a ship, aircraft or other vehicle or the safety of a person.

6. VHF channel 16

7. The power switch to ensure that you are using maximum power.

8. Acknowledge it then make a Mayday-Relay transmission.

9. In order to save life when it is endangered.

10. An entry detailing the circumstances and the reasons why you did not go to the assistance of the other ship must be made in the official log book.

11. The Master or person responsible for the ship or aircraft.

12. Your position, speed and ETA at the position given in the Initial Distress Message at that speed.

13. There is no separate address element. The distress marker word spoken three times is automatically assumed to be an address to all ships hearing it.

14. The Master or person responsible for the ship or aircraft in distress.

15. Grave and imminent danger.

16. Immediate assistance.

17. The MERchant ship search and rescue manual published by IMO.

18. On the bridge.

19. These are definitions from MERSAR:
    CSS is the Co-ordinator Surface Search, usually a merchant ship. If a ship or aircraft of the SAR or military services arrives on the scene, it will become: OSC, On Scene Commander.

20. Cease transmitting immediately until distress communications are finished. Note that it would be permissible to continue talking to the other ship on another VHF channel not being utilised for the distress communications provided that a listening watch on the distress communications is maintained.

21. The ship, aircraft, shore or coast station in control of the SAR operations.

22. They are consecutively numbered.

23. SAR activities in progress, requests for specific types of assistance, translations of the position given in the Initial Distress Message into other forms and guidance on its believed accuracy, a general update on the distress situation.

24. Interruption
    Seelonce Mayday
    Stop transmitting
    Seelonce Mayday
    Out.

25. Using feet — 22.5nm (22 or 23 nm)
    Using metres — 24.8nm (25nm)
    Answer to nearest miles is sufficiently accurate.

26. When there is a very urgent message to transmit concerning the safety of a ship, aircraft or other vehicle or the safety of a person.

27. Initial Urgency Transmission.

28. The urgency marker spoken three times automatically addresses the Initial Urgency Transmission to any station that can hear it.

29. A description of the nature of the problem that caused the transmission to be made. As simply as possible.

30. Position, Problem (or What is wrong) and What assistance is required.

31. On completion of distress communication, the station controlling the SAR activities (or the station controlling distress communications and acting on the instructions of the station controlling SAR activities) will make a transmission containing the words Mayday-fee nee.

32. Codes from the medical section of the International Code of Signals.

33. Is medical assistance or evacuation urgently needed to save life or limb?

34. No, unless all persons, or the whole ship, is threatened.

35. The definition of distress procedure states 'a *ship* is threatened by grave and imminent danger'. It makes no mention of the safety of a person as does the definition of urgency procedure.

36. The reciprocal, i.e. the bearing of your ship from the navigation mark.

37. The same form as it was taken, i.e. don't try to convert a position expressed in latitude and longitude (star sight, DR position etc.) into a bearing and range or vice versa.

38. GMT or UTC outside port limits. Local inside port limits.

39. The International Code of Signals.

40. Universal Co-ordinated Time. For practical purposes only it is the same as GMT.

41. None. The only 'response' is to note and take into account the safety message itself.

42. Initial Safety Transmissions and Safety Message Transmission.

43. Navigation and Meteorology.

44. They must contain important warnings.

45. When you have a warning concerning the safety of navigation, it is important for all ships within range to hear it and it will take less than 1 minute to transmit.

46. No.

47. After the station transmitting the Safety Message had finished its transmission (marked by the use of the word out), and before it switched back to the appropriate VHF watchkeeping channel.

48. Broadcast procedure.

49. Inaccurate or wrong positional information given in the Initial Distress Message.

50. Yes, but only when the ship in distress is not able to do so herself.

SECTION 4

VHF standard phrases and messages

This is an important section. It contains (i) the recommendations for the use of the full set of SEASPEAK **Standard Phrases**, (ii) guidance on the construction of SEASPEAK **Messages**, and (iii) the **Checks** used to ensure that messages are correctly received.

(i)   A number of **Standard Phrases** are used in the examples in Section 2 where it is shown that very little language is needed for making contact, maintaining contact and terminating; so little in fact, that **Standard Phrases** are quite adequate for the purpose. That section does not, however, give the *full* list of SEASPEAK **Standard Phrases** which are available to the VHF user. The list given in Section 4.1 is complete and comprises not only those phrases used in fixed positions in every conversation but also those which may be used at a variety of points in the conversation to cope with other commonly occurring circumstances.

It is essential to realise that **Standard Phrases** are used for a limited number of purposes. They are only available for the types of statements which are transmitted over and over again during VHF conversations, and furthermore, are almost totally concerned with the process of establishing and maintaining radio contact. They are 'radio phrases' or 'conversation management phrases'. They are *not*, primarily, maritime phrases.

It must be noted that there are two classes of maritime communication which are subject to special rules of transmission. The first class, *Distress and Safety*, is covered in Section 3 and the second, *Fixed Format Messages*, such as MAREP, in Section 5. Both of these classes contain a few, long established, fixed words and phrases such as *Mayday, Sécurité Seelonce Fee Nee Surnav Avaries* which are applicable in certain maritime contexts. Such phrases are a form of maritime 'shorthand' and as such do not appear in the list below. Their use must be learned separately under the operational headings indicated. It is also worth noting at this point that endeavours will be made shortly to regularise and standardise operations in large busy ports operating Vessel Traffic Systems (VTS). In order to achieve this, it is likely that a small number of additional maritime phrases (suitable for mandatory fixed format reports) will come into general use. Such phrases will be selected from English using SEASPEAK principles and will, consequently, be simple in construction.

(ii)   The language structures necessary for communicating maritime information are explained in Sections 4.2 and 4.3. These are not based on the principle of standard *phrases* because no list of standard phrases could ever be made which would contain all that a mariner might wish to say and, even if such a listing were available, it would be so enormous as to be impossible to learn. Instead, SEASPEAK recommends a small group of simple and standard message *patterns*. This means that such things as *questions* are always framed in the same way, *commands* in another way, *warnings* in yet another way and so on. By this means, complicated and ambiguous language is excluded from SEASPEAK.

(iii)   It is not sufficient merely to transmit information in an easily-understood manner. It is just as important to be sure that the information so transmitted has been correctly received. To ensure, therefore, that there is mutual agreement on what has been said, recommendations for the routine reading-back of information as the conversation progresses are given in Section 4.4.

There are further points to be learned in this section, but provided that the three major areas listed above are considered carefully, the remaining points should pose no problems.

In Section 2.3, a simple diagram based on the minimum number of steps in a straightforward VHF radio exchange was used to explain routine procedure.

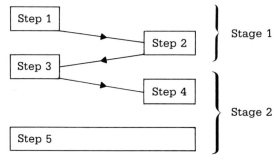

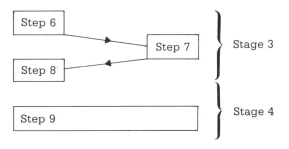

The same type of presentation is used here in Section 4. In this section, however, the number of *steps* is not restricted to the minimum; other Standard Phrases are introduced, which sometimes require extra transmissions; and longer, more complex exchanges of messages are considered, which also extend the conversation. The number of stages, however, remains the same.

Thus, whereas in Section 2 the exchange of messages (stage 3) is accomplished in just two transmissions, in the examples in this section four or more transmissions may be required to complete it.

This section is best approached by first revising the sequence of transmissions given in Section 2 and the few Standard Phrases which are used there. Having done that, the student is advised to examine the full list of Standard Phrases and their definitions and to practice using them as directed in the various training introductions, notes and exercises provided. The next stage is to learn how to construct SEASPEAK Messages as introduced in Section 4.2 (Message Markers). It is probably easier, at that point, to ignore stages 1, 2 and 4 and to concentrate exclusively on stage 3. The purpose in doing this is to achieve full competence in constructing and exchanging SEASPEAK Messages (stage 3), without having constantly to go through the routines for the establishment and termination of contact (stages 1, 2 and 4). Once the learning of message construction has been accomplished, the whole sequence of stages should be practised.

Points for Special Attention

Standard Phrases	(4.1)
Message Markers	(4.2)
Message Patterns	(4.3)
Message Checks	(4.4)

4.0 GENERAL INTRODUCTION

SEASPEAK by definition is in the English language, subject to certain rules, restrictions and precise definitions for the needs of maritime communications, particularly for use on VHF radio.

In Sections 1, 2 and 3 the necessary VHF procedures have been described. This section deals with the following additional features of essential maritime English, which enable the mariner to organise the structure of messages:

— Standard phrases
— Message and reply markers
— Message patterns
— Message checks
— Information content

There are in existence a small group of standard message formats (fixed formats) including MAREP, which have been recommended for particular purposes. These are covered in detail in Section 5.

4.1 STANDARD PHRASES

The preceding Sections have concentrated on the VHF Conventions and Procedures themselves rather than on the language commonly used, but the examples given have included a number of words or phrases which are in widespread customary use, such as This is ..., calling, I say again, over, out, etc. This Section gives the full list of such recommended standard phrases, broadly grouped into six types.

page 81

SECTION

4

VHF standard phrases and messages

TRAINING INTRODUCTION to 4.1.1: List of standard Phrases

Almost half of the **standard phrases** in the following list are marked with asterisks(*). This indicates: (i) that they are heavily used in maritime VHF and (ii) that they have already been introduced in Section 2. The majority of the phrases marked in this way are essential to the establishment and maintenance of contact, and should be thoroughly practised.

The list of phrases is broadly classified under six headings. The headings give the student an indication of the function of groups of phrases in a VHF exchange. Thus, for example, all the phrases which are generally used by participants to make transmitted information clearer to each other, are listed under the heading 'clarification'. Similarly, all those used for reaching agreement about VHF channels to be used during exchanges are listed together, under the heading 'Channel Switching'.

The purpose of using standard phrases is to avoid the large number of paraphrases or alternative ways of expressing the same meaning which are available in everyday English. Thus the meaning 'I did not hear your last message: please repeat it.' might be expressed by 'Say that again, will you?', or 'Do you mind repeating what you have just said?', or 'What did you say?', or in many other ways. In SEASPEAK this request for clarification is to be expressed by say again, and not by any paraphrase of the type quoted.

The thirty-nine standard phrases recommended for SEASPEAK are listed below; in the following sub-section their meaning is defined, with indications where appropriate of the usual response and its meaning.

4.1.1 List of standard phrases

1	*All ships (in … area)	
2	Calling …	
3	*How do you read	
4	*I read … (1–5)	
5	*Interruption.	
6	*Out.	Making and
7	*Over.	maintaining
8	Stand by on VHF channel …	contact.
9	Standing by on VHF channel …	
10	Stop transmitting	
11	*This is …	
12	Unknown ship …	
13	Wait … minutes.	
14	Break.	
15	*Nothing more.	
16	Please acknowledge.	
17	Please read back.	Conversation
18	Read back	controls.
19	*Stay on	
20	*Understood	
21	Readback is correct	
22	Correction	
23	Mistake	
24	Please speak in full.	
25	Please speak slowly.	
26	Please spell …	Clarification.
27	I spell …	
28	Please use SEASPEAK	
29	*Say again …	
30	*I say again …	
31	Final call.	
32	Message for you.	Announcements.
33	Pass your message.	
34	Reference …	
35	Sorry	Polite statements.
36	*Thank you	
37	*On VHF channel …	
38	*Switch to VHF channel …	
39	*Agree VHF channel …	
40	*VHF channels …, …, … available.	Channel switching.
41	VHF channels …, …, … unable.	
42	*Which VHF channel?	

4.1.2 | Standard phrases defined by use and response

	Standard phrase	Meaning	Response (phrase/action)	Meaning
(1)	All ships in … area ('in … area' is optional)	I request that all ships receiving this transmission (or those receiving in the sea area specified) listen to what follows	All ships, or just those in the area specified, listen. (If what follows is an attempt to make contact with an unknown ship, then the ship so addressed should respond in the normal way)	
(2)	Calling … (optional)	I wish to speak to …	Respondent replies using name, callsign …	
(3)	How do you read?	How well are you receiving me?	(4) I read … (1–5)	Reception is … (unusable-excellent)
(5)	Interruption.	I am being interrupted. I will take action to deal with it.	Respondent waits on same channel while the interruption is dealt with.	
(6)	Out.	I am terminating the conversation.	Respondent switches back to normal watch channel.	
(7)	Over.	I have completed my transmission and am ready to receive yours.	Respondent transmits.	
(8)	Stand by VHF channel … (Note 1)	Remain on VHF channel …	(9) Standing by VHF …	I agree to keep watch on VHF channel …
(10)	Stop transmitting.	Stop transmitting on this VHF channel.	Respondent ceases to transmit on that channel.	
(11)	This is …	My name (or callsign) is …		
(12)	Unknown ship … (details) … (always preceded by 'All ships …')	I wish to make contact with the ship described. I do not know its name or callsign.	Respondent replies using name, callsign	
(13)	Wait … minutes.	Wait for … minutes and do not terminate	Respondent waits for … minutes.	

Standard phrase	Meaning	Response (phrase/action)	Meaning
(14) Break.	I must break into this conversation for urgent reasons.	Respondent allows user of the word break to change subject or to terminate prematurely.	
(15) Nothing more.	I have finished my messages. You are free to change subject or terminate.	Respondent changes subject or terminates the conversation.	
(16) Please acknowledge (Note 2)	Indicate that you have received what I have just said.	Respondent gives the appropriate reply marker or says understood.	I received the following information.
(17) Please read back.	Read back to me the information I have just given.	(18) Read back.	I shall now read back the information you gave.
(19) Stay on.	Do not terminate this conversation or change the subject because I have more to say.	Respondent replies to the message, then says over.	You may continue the conversation.
(20) Understood.	I received the following information which I shall now read back to you.	(21) Readback is correct. (optional)	You have received my information correctly.
(22) Correction ...	I have just made a mistake in this transmission. The information should be ...		
(23) Mistake. ... (Note 3)	There is a mistake in your last transmission. The information should be ...	Correction. ...	You indicated a mistake in my transmission. I understand that the following is correct ...
(24) Please speak in full.	Do not abbreviate your messages.	Respondent ceases to abbreviate.	
(25) Please speak slowly.	Speak slowly. I am having difficulty in following or understanding.	Respondent speaks more slowly.	

Standard phrase	Meaning	Response (phrase/action)	Meaning
(26) Please spell ... (Note 4)	Spell ... using the phonetic alphabet.	(27) I spell ...	Respondent spells ... using the phonetic alphabet
(28) Please use SEASPEAK.	Use SEASPEAK during this conversation.	Respondent uses SEASPEAK	
(29) Say again ... (Note 5)	Repeat your message.	(30) I say again ...	I will repeat ...
(31) Final call.	I have completed my operation and wish to cease communicating.		
(32) Message for you.	I have a long/important message for you which I intend to read. Please indicate if you are ready to receive it.	(33) Pass your message.	I am ready to receive your message.
(34) Reference ... (Note 6)	I wish to refer to ...		
(35) Sorry	Polite statement of apology.		
(36) Thank you	Polite statement of gratitude.		
(37) On VHF channel ... (Note 7 — channel switching.)	I am calling on channel ...	Respondent answers on same channel.	
(38) Switch to VHF channel ... (Note 8)	I suggest that we switch to channel ... (to use as our working channel.)	(39) Agree VHF channel ...	I agree to switch to channel ... (to use as our working channel.)
(40) VHF channel ... unable.	I cannot switch to channel ...		
(41) VHF channels ..., ..., ... available.	I can transmit on these VHF channels. ..., ..., ...		
(42) Which VHF channel?	Which channel do you suggest that we use?	Switch to VHF channel ...	I suggest that we switch to channel ...

4.1.3 Notes

1. **Stand by VHF channel** ... This phrase should be followed by a number to designate the channel, and in appropriate cases by a time period e.g. Stand by VHF channel one-four, period; two hours.

2. **Please acknowledge**. This phrase may be followed by a reference to a particular item e.g. Please acknowledge this broadcast.

3. **Mistake**. This phrase may be followed by a corrected version e.g. Mistake. My ETA is time: one-five-zero-zero GMT. Where convenient a complete message can be repeated e.g. Mistake. QUESTION: What is your ETA at the harbour entrance?

4. **Please spell** ... This phrase should be followed by the word which requires spelling. If this cannot be stated it may be referred to e.g. Please spell ship's name or Please spell last port of call.

5. **Say again** ... This phrase may be followed by an indication of which part of the message was not heard clearly e.g. Say again after ... or Say again before ...

6. **Reference** ... This phrase will be followed by references to particular topics e.g. Reference, your manifest ..., Reference, your request for bunkers ..., Reference, berthing charges.

7. **Channel Switching**. Please refer to Section 2.4 — How to conduct an exchange — for a full explanation of the six standard phrases connected with channel switching.

8. **Switch to VHF channel** ... This phrase is also used in announcing a broadcast, in which case no response is expected.

4.1.4 Example of standard phrases in a typical conversation

The following is an example of a short SEASPEAK conversation in which the standard phrases used have been italicised.

VHF Station A The port, Stowbridge   VHF Station B The Ship, Gammon

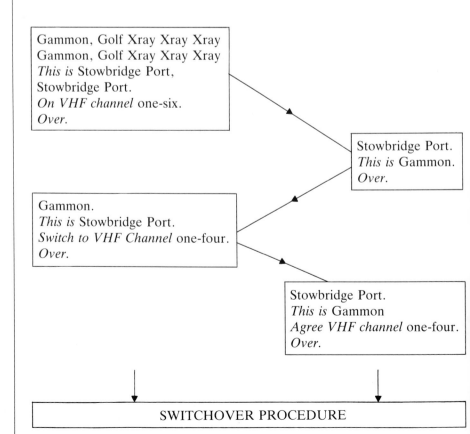

4

VHF standard phrases and messages

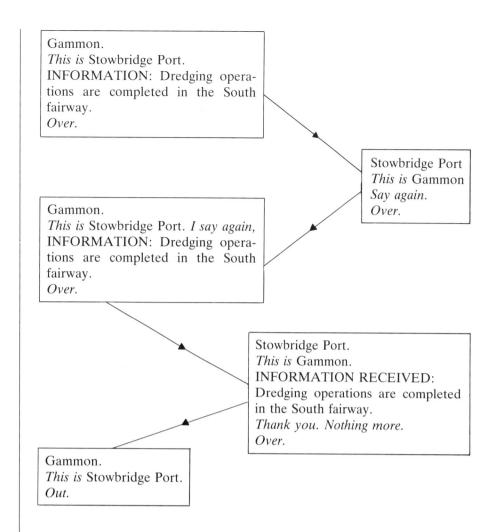

Gammon.
This is Stowbridge Port.
INFORMATION: Dredging operations are completed in the South fairway.
Over.

Stowbridge Port
This is Gammon
Say again.
Over.

Gammon.
This is Stowbridge Port. *I say again,* INFORMATION: Dredging operations are completed in the South fairway.
Over.

Stowbridge Port.
This is Gammon.
INFORMATION RECEIVED:
Dredging operations are completed in the South fairway.
Thank you. Nothing more.
Over.

Gammon.
This is Stowbridge Port.
Out.

END PROCEDURE

TRAINING NOTES to 4.1.4: Standard phrases in a typical conversation

Examples are given here of the use of the Standard Phrases which are not exemplified in great detail in earlier sections of this manual. In most of the examples, two VHF stations are represented. The boxes on the left represent one station and those on the right, the other. The presence of boxes containing dots (...) indicates that other transmissions precede or follow the transmissions given in the examples.

(1)   *All ships (in ... area)*   — used here to announce an imminent traffic information broadcast.

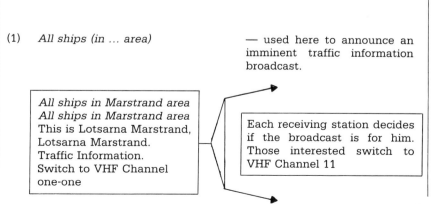

All ships in Marstrand area
All ships in Marstrand area
This is Lotsarna Marstrand, Lotsarna Marstrand.
Traffic Information.
Switch to VHF Channel one-one

Each receiving station decides if the broadcast is for him. Those interested switch to VHF Channel 11

(2) *Calling (optional)*

Calling Karata, Delta Alfa Kilo Sierra.
Calling Karata, Delta Alfa Kilo Sierra.
This is Karang Raya, Papa Kilo Lima Uniform.
This is Karang Raya, Papa Kilo Lima Uniform.
On VHF Channel one-six.
Over.

Karang Raya, Papa Kilo Lima Uniform.
This is Karata, Delta Alfa Kilo Sierra.
Over.

...

(3) *How do you read?*

(4) *I read ... (1–5).*

...

South Wind. This is Southern Ace.
How do you read?
Over.

Southern Ace.
This is South Wind.
I read four.
Over.

...

(5) *Interruption* (see 2.2.3)

(6)&(7) *Out and Over* (Many examples in Section 2 and elsewhere)

(8) *Stand by VHF channel*

(9) *Standing by VHF channel*

Uganda, Golf Foxtrot Romeo Quebec.
This is Southport Harbour.
Understood, ETA at Sierra Bravo Buoy; time: zero-five-zero-zero GMT.
Stand by VHF channel:
one-four, period: one hour.
Over.

Southport Harbour.
This is Uganda.
Standing by VHF channel one-four
period: one-hour.
Over.

...

(10) *Stop transmitting* (see *2.2.3* Interruptions).

(11) *This is* (numerous examples in Section 2 and elsewhere).

(12) *Unknown ship ... (details) ...*

*All ships in Duck Bay area.
Calling Unknown ship, position:
bearing one-two-six degrees true; from
Duck Rock: distance: ten miles Calling
Unknown ship, position: bearing one-two-six degrees true, from
Duck Rock: Distance:
Ten miles.*
This is Urdarnik, Uniform Papa Kilo Kilo, Urdarnik, Uniform Papa Kilo Kilo.
On VHF Channel one-six.
Over.

Urdarnik, Uniform Papa Kilo Kilo.
Urdarnik, Uniform Papa Kilo Kilo.
This is Udang, Yankee Charlie November Uniform. Udang, Yankee Charlie November Uniform.
Position: Bearing: one-two-seven degrees true, from Duck Rock. Distance nine-decimal six miles.
Over.

...

(13) *Wait ... minutes*

...

Uganda Carrier.
This is Grandport.
Question: How many tugs are
required? Over.

Grandport.
This is Uganda Carrier.
Wait five minutes.
Thank you.
Over.

Grandport.
This is Uganda Carrier.
Reference: Tugs.
Answer: quantity: two
tugs are required.
Over.

Uganda Carrier
This is Grandport.
Understood: Quantity:
two tugs.
Thank you.
Out.

(14) *Break*

...

Nissos Chios.
This is Talara.
Warning: Buoy number three-
six and buoy number:
three-seven are off position.
Over.

Talara.
This is Nissos Chios.
Break.
Out.

Note: presumably the warning from Talara has required some urgent
action aboard Nisson Chios causing the abrupt termination of
the exchange.

or

...

Petit Port.
This is Talara.
Question: What is the depth at
berth number:
four-six?
Over.

Talara.
This is Petit Port.
Break.
Warning:
The Leading Lights are not lit.
Over.

Petit Port.
This is Talara.
Warning Received: the leading
lights are not lit.
Question: What is the depth at
berth number one-six?
Over.

..

SECTION

VHF
standard
phrases and
messages

(15) *Nothing more*

> ...

> Southdale Hotel.
> This is Ugland Carrier.
> Understood: delays at Bergen.
> *Nothing more.*
> Over.

> Ugland Carrier.
> This is Southdale Hotel.
> Thank you.
> Out.

(see also the standard phrase 'stay on' and Section 2.4.10 — training note 1.)

(16) *Please acknowledge*

> ...

> Udzhary, Uniform
> Quebec Kilo India.
> This is Malosta Harbour.
> Information: There are no pilots until time: one-five-zero-zero GMT.
> Over.

> Malosta Harbour.
> This is Udzhary.
> Question: What is the berth number?
> Over.

> Udzhary.
> This is Malosta Harbour.
> Information: There are no pilots until time:
> one-five zero zero GMT
> *Please acknowledge.*
> Over.

> Malosta Harbour.
> This is Udzhary.
> Information Received:
> There are no pilots until time:
> one-five zero zero GMT.
> Question: What is the berth number?
> Over.

> ...

(17) *Please read back*   (18) *Read back*

> ...

> Star Vega.
> This is Maritime.
> Advice: Slow down to speed: four knots before buoy number: one-two.
> Over

> Maritime.
> This is Star vega.
> Advice Received:
> Buoy one-two.
> Over.

> Star Vega.
> This is Maritime.
> Advice: Slow down to speed: four knots before buoy number: one two.
> *Please read back.*
> Over.

> Maritime.
> This is Star Vega.
> *Read back.*
> Advice: Slow down to speed four knots before buoy number: one two.
> Over.

> ...

(19) *Stay on*

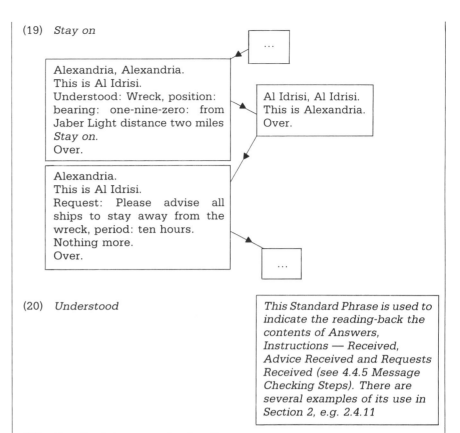

Alexandria, Alexandria.
This is Al Idrisi.
Understood: Wreck, position: bearing: one-nine-zero: from Jaber Light distance two miles *Stay on.*
Over.

Al Idrisi, Al Idrisi.
This is Alexandria.
Over.

...

Alexandria.
This is Al Idrisi.
Request: Please advise all ships to stay away from the wreck, period: ten hours.
Nothing more.
Over.

...

(20) *Understood*

> *This Standard Phrase is used to indicate the reading-back the contents of Answers, Instructions — Received, Advice Received and Requests Received (see 4.4.5 Message Checking Steps). There are several examples of its use in Section 2, e.g. 2.4.11*

(21) *Readback is correct* (optional)

This Standard Phrase may be used on very rare occasions where one participant in the conversation feels that it is necessary to reassure the other that the information which has been read back as part of a normal reply (Information Received, Warning Received or Intention Received) is in fact correct.

It may also be used in response to information which is read back in statements beginning with the standard phrases 'Understood' or 'Read back'. Under normal circumstances, no verbal confirmation of the correctness of such information is given. Instead, only those statements which are *wrong* are brought to the attention of the speaker with the standard phrase 'Mistake'. Thus, if the other speaker does not say 'mistake' the the readback is assumed to be correct. (See also Section 4.4.5.)

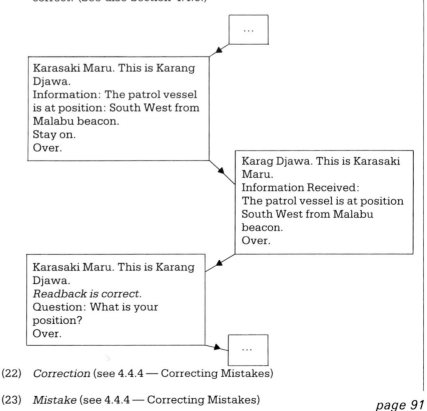

...

Karasaki Maru. This is Karang Djawa.
Information: The patrol vessel is at position: South West from Malabu beacon.
Stay on.
Over.

Karag Djawa. This is Karasaki Maru.
Information Received:
The patrol vessel is at position South West from Malabu beacon.
Over.

Karasaki Maru. This is Karang Djawa.
Readback is correct.
Question: What is your position?
Over.

...

(22) *Correction* (see 4.4.4 — Correcting Mistakes)

(23) *Mistake* (see 4.4.4 — Correcting Mistakes)

(24) *Please speak in full*

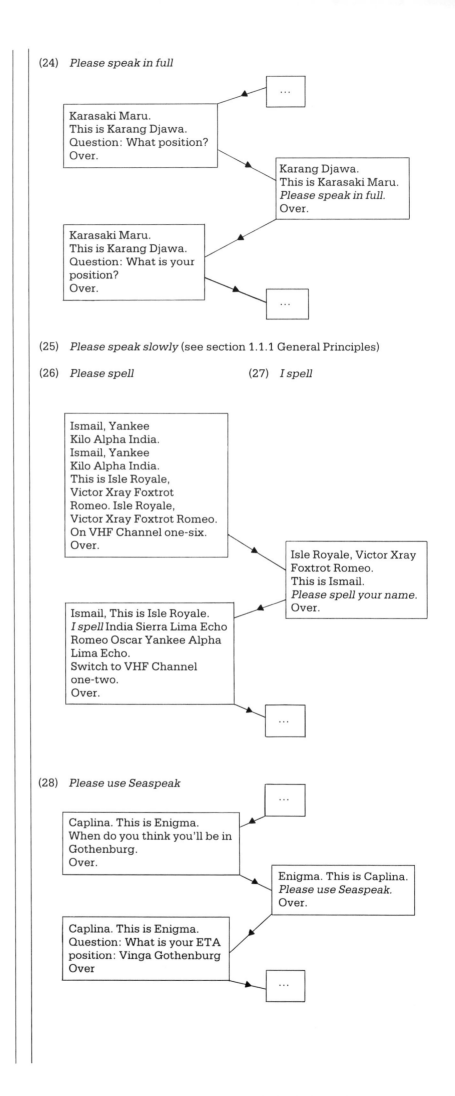

```
                                              ┌───────┐
                                              │  ...  │
                                              └───────┘
                                                  ▲
┌─────────────────────────┐                       │
│ Karasaki Maru.          │──────────────────────┘
│ This is Karang Djawa.   │
│ Question: What position?│                  ┌──────────────────────────┐
│ Over.                   │─────────────────▶│ Karang Djawa.            │
└─────────────────────────┘                  │ This is Karasaki Maru.   │
                                              │ *Please speak in full.*  │
                                              │ Over.                    │
                                              └──────────────────────────┘
┌─────────────────────────┐                       ▲
│ Karasaki Maru.          │──────────────────────┘
│ This is Karang Djawa.   │
│ Question: What is your  │                  ┌───────┐
│ position?               │─────────────────▶│  ...  │
│ Over.                   │                  └───────┘
└─────────────────────────┘
```

(25) *Please speak slowly* (see section 1.1.1 General Principles)

(26) *Please spell*   (27) *I spell*

```
┌─────────────────────────┐
│ Ismail, Yankee          │
│ Kilo Alpha India.       │
│ Ismail, Yankee          │
│ Kilo Alpha India.       │
│ This is Isle Royale,    │
│ Victor Xray Foxtrot     │
│ Romeo. Isle Royale,     │
│ Victor Xray Foxtrot Romeo.│                ┌──────────────────────────┐
│ On VHF Channel one-six. │─────────────────▶│ Isle Royale, Victor Xray │
│ Over.                   │                  │ Foxtrot Romeo.           │
└─────────────────────────┘                  │ This is Ismail.          │
                                              │ *Please spell your name.*│
┌─────────────────────────┐                  │ Over.                    │
│ Ismail, This is Isle Royale.│              └──────────────────────────┘
│ *I spell* India Sierra Lima Echo│               ▲
│ Romeo Oscar Yankee Alpha│──────────────────────┘
│ Lima Echo.              │
│ Switch to VHF Channel   │                  ┌───────┐
│ one-two.                │─────────────────▶│  ...  │
│ Over.                   │                  └───────┘
└─────────────────────────┘
```

(28) *Please use Seaspeak*

```
                                              ┌───────┐
                                              │  ...  │
                                              └───────┘
                                                  ▲
┌─────────────────────────┐                       │
│ Caplina. This is Enigma.│──────────────────────┘
│ When do you think you'll be in│
│ Gothenburg.             │                  ┌──────────────────────────┐
│ Over.                   │─────────────────▶│ Enigma. This is Caplina. │
└─────────────────────────┘                  │ *Please use Seaspeak.*   │
                                              │ Over.                    │
                                              └──────────────────────────┘
┌─────────────────────────┐                       ▲
│ Caplina. This is Enigma.│──────────────────────┘
│ Question: What is your ETA│
│ position: Vinga Gothenburg│                ┌───────┐
│ Over                    │─────────────────▶│  ...  │
└─────────────────────────┘                  └───────┘
```

**VHF
standard
phrases and
messages**

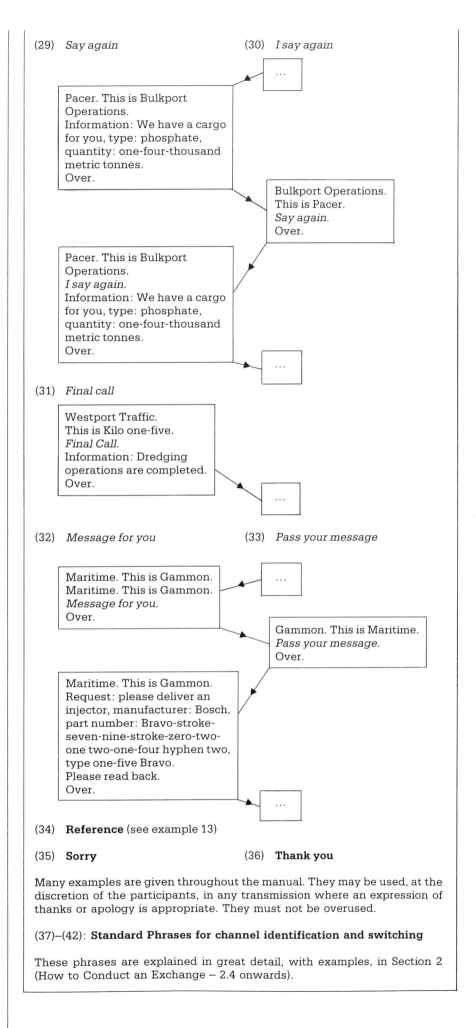

(29) *Say again*   (30) *I say again*

> ...

> Pacer. This is Bulkport
> Operations.
> Information: We have a cargo
> for you, type: phosphate,
> quantity: one-four-thousand
> metric tonnes.
> Over.

> Bulkport Operations.
> This is Pacer.
> *Say again.*
> Over.

> Pacer. This is Bulkport
> Operations.
> *I say again.*
> Information: We have a cargo
> for you, type: phosphate,
> quantity: one-four-thousand
> metric tonnes.
> Over.

> ...

(31) *Final call*

> Westport Traffic.
> This is Kilo one-five.
> *Final Call.*
> Information: Dredging
> operations are completed.
> Over.

> ...

(32) *Message for you*   (33) *Pass your message*

> ...

> Maritime. This is Gammon.
> Maritime. This is Gammon.
> *Message for you.*
> Over.

> Gammon. This is Maritime.
> *Pass your message.*
> Over.

> Maritime. This is Gammon.
> Request: please deliver an
> injector, manufacturer: Bosch,
> part number: Bravo-stroke-
> seven-nine-stroke-zero-two-
> one two-one-four hyphen two,
> type one-five Bravo.
> Please read back.
> Over.

> ...

(34) **Reference** (see example 13)

(35) **Sorry**   (36) **Thank you**

Many examples are given throughout the manual. They may be used, at the
discretion of the participants, in any transmission where an expression of
thanks or apology is appropriate. They must not be overused.

(37)–(42): **Standard Phrases for channel identification and switching**

These phrases are explained in great detail, with examples, in Section 2
(How to Conduct an Exchange – 2.4 onwards).

SECTION

VHF standard phrases and messages

TRAINING EXPLANATION: MESSAGE CONSTRUCTION

1. The pattern of the total VHF radio conversation is explained in detail in Section 2 (VHF Procedures). In that section, emphasis is given to the stages of the exchange concerned with making and terminating radio contact: stages 1, 2 and 4.

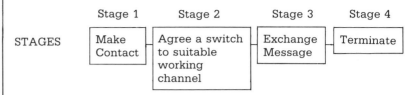

2. Stage 3 is mentioned briefly but is kept to a simple minimum of just two transmissions (steps 6 and 7 of the following diagram):

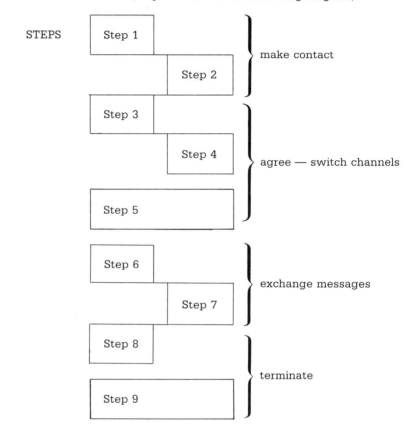

3. Generally, however, more than two transmissions are required to complete the exchange of messages necessary to achieve the purpose of the call. The organisation and contents of such transmissions is the subject of the subsections which follow.

4. The most important point to grasp is that to achieve mutual understanding the content and organisation of the message transmissions needs to be as precise as the content and organisation of the transmissions required to achieve contact. However, such precision is more difficult in message transmissions because of the great variety of possible messages. It would be impossible to make a list, like the list of Standard Phrases, of all the things which a mariner might wish to say. Instead, other recommendations are made, the adoption of which will permit an orderly exchange of messages with a minimum of misunderstandings.

5. SEASPEAK messages are best explained by looking at a particular example. Imagine that a shore station (in this case Singapore Port Operations) wishes to know the time of arrival of the ship Western Sky. After contact has been made on a suitable working VHF channel the first message transmission (step 6) might be:

> Western Sky, this is Singapore Port Operations.
> Question: What is your ETA, position: East Johore pilot station?
> Over.

Within this transmission the actual message is:

> Question: What is your ETA, position: East Johore pilot station?

6. Various recommendations to ensure accuracy and simplicity have been used here, most important of which are the *MESSAGE MARKER*, (Question) and the *PATTERN* of the message which follows it.

Thus:

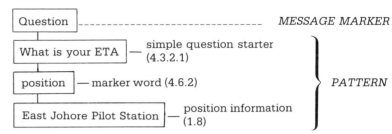

7. The message marker indicates what sort of message is to follow, and the message pattern is a simple one which will pose no problems for either native English speakers or non-native speakers of the language.

8. Within the message in this example, a 'marker word' *position* is used to indicate that maritime positional information will follow. Other possibly confusing alternatives such as *by, at,* and *for* are not recommended. 'Marker words': *position, time, quantity* etc., are always transmitted in advance of the position times and quantities which they announce.

9. The reply transmission to the above message (step 7) might be:

> Singapore Port Operations. This is Western Sky.
> Answer: My ETA, position: East Johore Pilot station is, time: one-three-four-five UTC.
> Over.

Within this transmission the actual message is:

> Answer: My ETA, position: East Johore pilot station, is time: one-three-four-five UTC

10. The message recommendations in use are as follows:

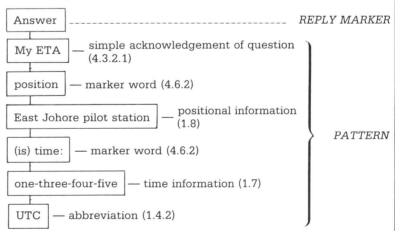

11. This breakdown indicates the importance of Reply Markers (4.2.5) Message Patterns for replies (4.3), the marking of quantities etc. (4.6.2) and the conventions for the transmission of such things as time and position (1.7 and 1.8).

12. To ensure mutual understanding, any fresh information received (for example the *time* in the above reply) must be read back to the issuing station using, as an introduction, the standard phrase 'understood'. Cf. (step 8):

> Western Sky. This is Singapore Port Operations.
> Understood: ETA: one-three-four-five UTC.
> Out.

13. Here the message read back is restricted to the fresh information only and is consequently abbreviated. This process of *making sure* is very important and recommendations are given in Section 4.4 (Message Checks).

14. The purpose of this brief introduction is to demonstrate the way in which the various recommendations come into use. It will be clear that Message Markers (4.2), Message Patterns (4.3), marker words (4.6.2) and the recommendations for the transmission of certain types of information such as time and position (1.7, 1.8) are important first considerations in learning SEASPEAK message constructions.

4.2 MESSAGE MARKERS

TRAINING INTRODUCTION to 4.2: MESSAGE MARKERS

Maritime messages transmitted over VHF radio should be short, accurate, and relevant. Furthermore, messages should be transmitted in language simple enough for a non-native speaker of English to comprehend without difficulty.

One useful means of making the language simpler is to indicate, at the beginning of a message, what sort of message it is going to be. Thus, if a question is going to be asked, the speaker simply says the word 'QUESTION' before the question itself. Similarly, if a piece of advice is going to be given, the speaker says the word 'ADVICE' in advance of his message. There are just seven of these *Message Markers* and after a little practice, learners should experience no difficulty in using them.

These *Message Markers* have another function: that of imposing order on the conversation, since each message marked in this way requires a reply correspondingly marked (even if that reply is nothing more than an acknowledgement of the message received). This procedure helps to ensure that :

1. messages do not become confused with each other
2. each message is dealt with in turn
3. a participant receiving a reply knows which message is being replied to.

The best strategy for learning to use the *Message Markers* is to do the exercises relating to them immediately after reading through the relevant Section 4.3 and before going on to consider the actual patterns of messages in Section 4.3.

4.2.1 Standard phrases are used only for the specific and routine purposes detailed in the preceding subsection. They cannot be used to convey maritime messages. Maritime messages should be transmitted in clear uncomplicated English according to the guidelines given in this section. The first recommendation is that a message should always be initiated by a **message marker** to indicate its message type. All messages belong to one of only seven types, or the responses thereto. The seven types identified by their **message markers** are listed below. The succeeding sub-sections give examples of each.

N.B. The message and reply markers (shown in capitals in the examples, **are to be spoken**. The effect of this is to greatly increase the probability of the message being properly heard and understood.

4.2.2
   a. **QUESTION**

   b. **INSTRUCTION**

   c. **ADVICE**

   d. **REQUEST**

   e. **INFORMATION**

   f. **WARNING**

   g. **INTENTION**

4.2.3

a. The word QUESTION will be used to signal all questions, e.g.

> **QUESTION: What is your ETA at the dock entrance?**

b. The word INSTRUCTION will be used to signal commands, e.g.

> **INSTRUCTION: Go to berth number: two-five.**

c. The word ADVICE will be used to signal suggestions, e.g.

> **ADVICE: Anchor, position: bearing: one-nine-four degrees true, from Keel Point distance: one mile.**

Note: **ADVICE** may be followed by the word **please**.

d. The word **REQUEST** will be used to signal messages which mean 'I want something to be arranged or provided' as in ships' stores requirements, bunkering, permission, ... It is commonly accompanied by the word **Please.** e.g.

> **REQUEST: Please send, quantity: five acetylene cylinders.**

e. The word **INFORMATION** will be used to signal messages which simply contain information e.g.

> **INFORMATION: The pilot is waiting now, position: near buoy number: two-six.**

f. The word **WARNING** will be used to signal messages which contain information of critical importance to the safety of vessels, e.g.

> **WARNING: Buoy number: two-five and buoy number: two-six are unlit.**

g. The word **INTENTION** will be used to signal messages which contain information about immediate operational intentions, e.g.

> **INTENTION: I intend to reduce speed, new speed: six knots.**

But in critical situations the marker **WARNING** will be used.

4.2.4 Each marked message received must be acknowledged and a response given, if appropriate.

4.2.5 There are seven reply markers to match the seven message markers as follows:

message markers	*reply markers*
a. QUESTION	a. **ANSWER**
b. INSTRUCTION	b. **INSTRUCTION-RECEIVED**
c. ADVICE	c. **ADVICE-RECEIVED**
d. REQUEST	d. **REQUEST-RECEIVED**
e. INFORMATION	e. **INFORMATION-RECEIVED**
f. WARNING	f. **WARNING-RECEIVED**
g. INTENTION	g. **INTENTION-RECEIVED**

SECTION

VHF standard phrases and messages

TRAINING INTRODUCTION to 4.3: MESSAGE PATTERNS

Another way of ensuring that VHF radio messages are comprehensible in the multi-lingual environment of international shipping is to avoid the use of complex language. However, it is not always easy for a speaker of a particular language to know when he is using complex language.

To avoid such problems, all maritime VHF communicators are advised to transmit all operational messages using the straightforward English patterns detailed below.

There are seven types of message: questions, instructions, pieces of advice, requests, pieces of information, warnings and expressions of intention. In the following section, recommendations are made of simple and standard ways of phrasing each of them. Colloquial expression and complex constructions are not recommended. By this means the learning load for the non-native speaker of English for maritime VHF purposes is reduced and the native speaker is made aware of language constructions which will be understood in this particular operational context.

We recommend that you work the pattern exercises provided at the end of Section 3 before going on to Section 4.3.3.

a. The word **ANSWER** will be used to signal **messages** in reply to **QUESTION**, e.g.

> QUESTION: What is your ETA at the dock entrance?
> ANSWER: My ETA at the dock entrance is: time: one-six-zero-zero GMT.

b. The words INSTRUCTION-RECEIVED will be used to signal messages in reply to INSTRUCTION, e.g.

> INSTRUCTION: Go to berth number: two-five.
> INSTRUCTION RECEIVED: Go to berth number: two-five, positive.

c. The words **ADVICE-RECEIVED** will be used to signal messages in reply to **ADVICE,** e.g.

> ADVICE: Please anchor, position: bearing: one-nine-four degrees true, from Keel Point: distance one mile.
> ADVICE RECEIVED: Anchor, position: bearing: one-nine-four degrees true, from Keel Point. Distance one mile.

d. The words **REQUEST-RECEIVED** will be used to signal messages in reply to **REQUEST**, e.g.

> REQUEST: Please send, quantity: five acetylene cylinders.
> REQUEST-RECEIVED: Send, quantity: five acetylene cylinders, positive.

e. The words **INFORMATION-RECEIVED** will be used to signal messages in reply to **INFORMATION**, e.g.

> INFORMATION: The pilot is waiting now at position: near buoy number: two-six.
> INFORMATION-RECEIVED: The pilot is waiting now at position: buoy number: two-six.

f. The words **WARNING-RECEIVED** will be used to signal **messages** in replay to **WARNING,** e.g.

> WARNING: Buoy number: two-five and buoy number: two-six are unlit.
> WARNING-RECEIVED: Buoy number: two-five and buoy number: two-six are unlit.

g. The words **INTENTION-RECEIVED** will be used to signal messages in reply to **INTENTION**, e.g.

> INTENTION: I intend to reduce speed, new speed: six knots.
> INTENTION-RECEIVED: You intend to reduce speed, new speed: six knots.

4.3 MESSAGE PATTERNS

4.3.1

The preceding sections have dealt with the **standard phrases** and the use of **message markers.** In this section the pattern of the messages which

follow the markers is illustrated. SEASPEAK uses messages and message replies constructed strictly in accordance with these patterns.

4.3.2 Examples of message patterns

.1 **QUESTION**

The use is recommended of only the three following types of question: (See Note 1.)

a. Questions beginning with the words **when, what, where, why, which, who, how, how many** ... (these are referred to as **Wh-**Questions) e.g.

> **QUESTION: What is your position?**
>
> **QUESTION: How many tugs are required?**

b. Questions which give alternatives (X or Y) e.g.

> **QUESTION: Is the vessel loading or unloading?**

c. Questions requiring a **Yes** or **No** answer e.g.

> **QUESTION: Do you intend to pass ahead of me?**
>
> **QUESTION: Is the beacon operating normally?**

It is recommended that the replies to (a) Wh- Questions and (b) X or Y questions take the same pattern, e.g.

Wh- reply

> **QUESTION: What is your ETA, position: buoy number: two-three?**
>
> **ANSWER: My ETA, position: buoy number: two-three is: time: one-six-zero-zero GMT.**
>
> **OR**
>
> **I do not know my ETA, position: buoy number: two-three.**

X or Y reply

> **QUESTION: Is the vessel loading or unloading?**
>
> **ANSWER: The vessel is loading.**
>
> **OR**
>
> **I do not know if the vessel is loading or unloading.**

Yes or **No** replies (question type (c) above) should take the following pattern:

— The words **positive** or **negative** or I **do not know** immediately follow the reply marker e.g.

> **QUESTION: Is buoy number: two-three in the correct position?**
>
> **ANSWER: Positive, buoy number: two-three is in the correct position.**
>
> **OR**
>
> **ANSWER: Negative, buoy number: two-three is not in the correct position.**
>
> **OR**
>
> **ANSWER: I do not know if buoy number: two-three is in the correct position.**

Note 1: The English language possesses several other types of question, e.g. questions formed by tone of voice alone, statements followed by "isn't it?" "won't they?" etc. It is strongly recommended that SEASPEAK messages use only the types outlined in this section. Similar principles of selection have been applied to the other message types.

.2 **INSTRUCTION**

Statements after the message marker **INSTRUCTION** should follow the pattern: **turn** ..., **anchor** ..., **stop** ..., or: **do not turn** ..., **do not anchor** ..., **do not stop** ... e.g.

> **INSTRUCTION: Stop your engines.**
> OR
> **INSTRUCTION: Do not anchor in the fairway.**

Replies to instructions will be as follows:

— The respondent indicates agreement to an instruction by the word **positive** after quoting the command, e.g.

> **INSTRUCTION-RECEIVED: Do not anchor in the fair-way, positive.**

— The respondent indicates disagreement by the word negative e.g.

> **INSTRUCTION-RECEIVED: Stop my engines, negative.**

— A reason should be given for this inability to carry out an instruction. This will be marked by the word **reason** (Section 4.3.3), e.g.

> **INSTRUCTION-RECEIVED: Stop my engines, negative, reason: the tide is too strong.**

.3 **ADVICE**

The message pattern for this marker which signals suggestions is the same as for **INSTRUCTION** (except that the word **please** is sometimes used). e.g.

> **ADVICE: Turn to starboard.**
> **ADVICE-RECEIVED: Turn to starboard, positive.**
> OR
> **ADVICE-RECEIVED: Turn to starboard, negative, reason: another vessel is aproaching.**

.4 **REQUEST**

Requests for items to be delivered should follow the pattern: **Please, supply, Please deliver** ... e.g.

> **REQUEST: Please deliver: quantity: one thousand metric tonnes, fresh water to berth number: two-six.**

The reply to a **REQUEST** will be as follows:
e.g.

> **REQUEST-RECEIVED: Please deliver: quantity: one thousand metric tonnes fresh water to berth number: two-six, positive.**
> **OR**
> **REQUEST-RECEIVED: Deliver, quantity: one thousand metric tonnes fresh water to berth number: two-six, negative.**

— In many cases the respondent will wish to give a reason, eg..

> **REQUEST-RECEIVED: Deliver, quantity: one thousand metric tonnes fresh water to berth number: two-six, negative, reason: the barge is busy now.**

— The **REQUEST** marker may also be used when seeking confirmation of information. In this case the marker will be followed by the words **Please confirm,** e.g.

> **REQUEST: Please confirm that your length is: two-six-zero metres.**

.5 **INFORMATION AND WARNING**
These types of message may take several forms e.g.

> **INFORMATION: No vessels are at the anchorage.**
>
> **INFORMATION: My ETA at the West pier is: time: one-six-three-zero GMT.**
>
> **INFORMATION: The icebreaker intends to assemble the convoy at time: zero-five-three-zero GMT.**
>
> **INFORMATION: The casualty is approximately, position: North distance: three miles from you.**
>
> **WARNING: A vessel is adrift, position: near the Foreland light.**
>
> **WARNING: A strong South-Westerly wind is blowing now at the berth.**
>
> **WARNING: Buoy number: three-five is off position.**

Replies to **INFORMATION** and **WARNING** are simply acknowledgements e.g.

> **INFORMATION-RECEIVED: The icebreaker intends to assemble the convoy at time: zero-five-three-zero GMT.**
>
> **WARNING-RECEIVED: A vessel is adrift, position: near the Foreland light.**

.6 **INTENTION**
The message pattern for this marker is as follows:

> **INTENTION: I intend to anchor now, and I will proceed to the berth at time: zero-six-zero-zero GMT.**
>
> **INTENTION: I intend to unload hold number: five.**
>
> **INTENTION: I intend to reduce speed, new speed: seven knots.**

4.3.3 Giving Reasons

In section 4.3.2 it was recommended that only three types of question should be used for SEASPEAK messages, although the English language possesses several other types of question. Similarly with **reasons.** Among the many alternative ways of indicating cause of reason are the following: **so that, in order to, since, because, as, due to,** etc. In

TRAINING INTRODUCTION to 4.3.3 continued

like 'Because of the bad weather I intend to return to Eagle Bay' (which is quite acceptable in general English) would be spoken in Seaspeak as INTENTION: I intend to return to Eagle Bay, reason: bad weather. The reason itself is always introduced by the word **reason**. The alternative ways of introducing reasons or causes listed below should be avoided during maritime VHF exchanges.

SEASPEAK it is recommended that only the single word **reason** should be used. e.g.

> **INTENTION: I intend to enter the berth stern first, reason: my starboard thruster is damaged.**
>
> **INSTRUCTION-RECEIVED: Stop immediately, negative, reason: I am towing now.**

The reading back of reasons is optional.

4.3.4 Clarifying Messages

It may sometimes be impossible to respond to a message without first seeking further clarification. Such a clarification message may result in the response to a QUESTION being another QUESTION e.g.

1st message	1st speaker	QUESTION: What is your ETA at Dover?
Clarification message	2nd speaker	QUESTION: Do you want my ETA at the East entrance or the West entrance?
Clarification provided	1st speaker	ANSWER: I want your ETA at the East entrance.
Response to 1st message	2nd speaker	ANSWER: My ETA at the East entrance is: time: one-five-three-zero GMT

4.4 MESSAGE CHECKS

TRAINING INTRODUCTION to 4.4: MESSAGE CHECKS

To help prevent wastage of time and unnecessary use of VHF channels, participants in VHF radio conversations should keep to an orderly sequence of relevant transmissions from start to finish. Thus, the discipline necessary for establishing contact in the most efficient manner (stages 1 and 2) needs to be maintained throughout that part of the conversation where messages are exchanged (stage 3).

The use of Message Markers, described in the preceding section, is important in this respect; these markers help the speaker and the listener to divide up what is being said into manageable units, which can be organised.

The term **Message Checks** refers to this organisation; it covers both the **sequence** which should be followed in an exchange of messages, replies and confirmations (see Section 4.4.5 table: Message Checking Steps), and also the various recommendations which ensure that all parties in a conversation have mutual understanding. Thus, under normal circumstances if speaker A makes a request then speaker B must reply to that request by acknowledging and quoting it, and responding to it either positively or negatively. e.g.

Speaker A

> Shell Southport. This is Paisano.
> REQUEST: Please supply bunkers: quantity: two thousand metric tonnes.
> Over.

Speaker B

> Paisano. This is Shell Southport.
> REQUEST RECEIVED: Supply bunkers: quantity: two thousand metric tonnes, positive.
> Over.

Furthermore, Speaker A must read back the fresh information contained in B's reply, using the Standard Phrase 'Understood'.

> Shell Southport. This is Paisano
> Understood: supply bunkers, positive.
> Out.

A similar sequence applies to all messages. However, where no fresh information is transmitted in the reply, as would be the case if the reply was merely an acknowledgement, no further reference to the message is required.

> Shell Southport. This is Paisano.
> Information: bunkering is completed.
> Nothing more.
> Over.

> Paisano. This is Shell Southport.
> Information Received; bunkering is completed.
> Out.

Naturally, if the reply contains an *incorrect* acknowledgement.

> Paisano. This is Shell Southport.
> Information Received: *berthing* is completed.
> Out.

Then this must be remedied by a further transmission using the Standard Phrase 'mistake'.

> Shell Southport. This is Paisano
> Mistake.
> Information: bunkering is completed.
> Over.

Message checks are described in the following four subsections and exercises are provided at the end of the section.

4.4.1   The object of the SEASPEAK procedures, standard phrases and message markers is to produce clear, unambiguous exchanges. A correct message can easily be mis-heard, however, without either speaker realising that this has happened. Message checks are therefore essential.

4.4.2   Message checks are a system for ensuring that both speakers agree on what has actually been said, in order to detect mistakes and correct them at once. The checks include techniques for **confirmation** and **correction. Confirmation** involves the reading back of information (i.e. repetition by the hearer of what he believes the salient information to be); either as part of a reply or by the use of the standard phrase **understood** (meaning 'I received the following information which I shall now read back to you ...'). Correction of the other speaker uses the standard phrase **mistake**.

4.4.3   Confirmation

Reading back and the use of **understood** are illustrated in the following example. The salient information is underlined.

1st Speaker:	**QUESTION: What is your ETA at the dock entrance?**
2nd Speaker:	**ANSWER: My ETA at the dock entrance is time: one-six-zero-zero GMT.**
1st Speaker:	**Understood, time: one-six-zero-zero GMT.**

The use of the word **understood** in the third transmission in the above example is an indication that something is being read back. This word has no other meaning than 'I received the following information'. The word **understood** by itself is insufficient: it must be followed by the reading back of salient information, as a form of confirmation of mutual understanding.

4.4.4 Correcting Mistakes

If a mistake or discrepancy is detected in a previous transmission this will be signalled by the word **mistake.** E.g. the word **berth** in the second transmission in the following example is not a reply to the question. The use of **mistake** in the next transmission enables the speaker concerned to point out the mistake and to repeat the original question.

E.g. (the error is indicated by asterisks)

1st speaker:	**QUESTION: What is your ETA at the dock entrance?**
2nd speaker:	**ANSWER: My ETA at the *berth* is time: one-six-zero-zero GMT.**
1st speaker	**Mistake:** **QUESTION: What is your ETA at the dock entrance?**
2nd speaker:	**Correction.** **ANSWER: My ETA at the dock entrance is time: one-five-zero-zero GMT**
1st speaker:	**Understood, time; one-five-zero-zero GMT**

If a mistake is detected in the final readback. i.e. in the **understood** transmission, then this must be signalled by the other speaker; similarly in the case of the number six in the following example:

2nd speaker:	**ANSWER: My ETA at the dock entrance is: time: one-five-zero-zero GMT.**
1st speaker:	**Understood, time: *one-six-zero-zero* GMT.**
2nd speaker:	**Mistake.** **Time: one-five-zero-zero GMT.**
1st speaker:	**Correction. Time: one-five-zero-zero GMT**

Note: It is acceptable to abbreviate message which begin with the standard phrases **understood** so as to include only the critical information. However, words should not be left out in this way in messages prefixed by message markers.

4.4.5

The system of message checks applies to all types of message. The following diagram shows how the steps operate for all message types. Where, for example:

— Speaker A asks a question (Step 1.)

— Speaker B gives an answer which will include a reference to the question (Step 2.)

— Speaker A acknowledges the answer by reading back the information provided (Step 3.) using the standard phrase **understood** ...

Step 1	Step 2	Step 3
QUESTION	... **ANSWER** ... (followed by response which includes a readback)	**Understood** + readback
INSTRUCTION	... **INSTRUCTION-RECEIVED** ... (followed by response which includes a readback).	**Understood** + readback.
REQUEST	... **REQUEST-RECEIVED** ... (followed by response which includes a readback).	**Understood** + readback.

INFORMATION ...	**INFORMATION-RECEIVED** ... (followed by readback)	Say nothing unless a mistake has been detected.
WARNING	... **WARNING-RECEIVED** ... (followed by readback)	Say nothing unless a mistake has been detected.
INTENTION	... **INTENTION-RECEIVED** ... (followed by readback)	Say nothing unless a mistake has been detected.

N.B. Where a fresh piece of information is transmitted in Step 2, such as an answer to a question or a response to an instruction, a further Step, 3, is necessary to confirm it.

Step 3 is not necessary where the information transmitted in Step 2 is a direct readback of Step 1. Any mistakes detected will be signalled by the standard phrase **mistake**.

4.4.6

The standard phrases: "Stay on" and "Nothing more"

TRAINING INTRODUCTION to 4.4.6: 'Stay on' and 'Nothing more'

Unnecessary transmissions often result from neither participant knowing when the other has finished talking. It is therefore important to indicate when you have finished, so that the other station may terminate the exchange without having to **ask** if you have finished. The Standard Phrase **Nothing more** is used for this purpose. Just as important is to indicate when you have **more** to say so that the other station will not break contact too soon. This is done by using the phrase **Stay on**.

This phrase is particularly useful when one participant wishes to change the subject since, whenever possible, participants should avoid speaking about different subjects in the same transmission. Therefore if a participant is concluding one subject in a particular transmission and requires to go on to another in the next, the use of the Standard Phrase **Stay on** will prevent premature termination by the other speaker.

.1 **Stay on**
Premature termination of a conversation is prevented by the use of the standard phrase Stay on, e.g.

1st speaker:	X. **This is Y. Understood, time: one-six-zero-zero GMT. Stay on. Over**
2nd speaker:	Y. **This is X. Over.**

.2 **Nothing more**
Alternatively, if a participant has nothing more to say he may signal this with the standard phrase **Nothing more**, e.g.

1st speaker:	X. **This is Y. Understood, time: one-six-zero-zero GMT. Nothing more. Over.**
2nd speaker:	Y. **This is X. Out.**

SECTION

VHF standard phrases and messages

TRAINING INTRODUCTION to 4.5:
INFORMATION CONTENT

The sections which follow contain guidance on controlling the type, presentation and amount of information which any single transmission may hold.

Clearly, if a listener is sitting down with a pencil and paper to listen to a weather forecast he is able to receive a very large amount of information. However, in many maritime conversations the listener is not so relaxed, neither is he sure of the type of messages he is going to receive. Therefore, to avoid over loading such a listener with more information than he can reasonably be expected to deal with, it is essential to restrict the length and complexity of transmissions.

Section 4.5.1 recommends that no more than two marked messages be transmitted in a single transmission: section 4.5.2 shows that even within one message, a large amount of information can be transmitted if properly organised; section 4.5.3 recommends a method of increasing a listener's expectancy through the use of announcements at the beginnings of transmissions; section 4.5.4 simply states that, wherever possible, participants should not change the subject in the middle of a transmission, but should wait until the subject under discussion has been dealt with by both speakers.

4.5 INFORMATION CONTENT

It is important not to overload a single transmission with too much information content. Very long transmissions often lead to confusion which results in longer conversations. The participants should restrict their transmissions in the following way.

4.5.1 Number of marked messages

A message-bearing transmission should not contain more than two marked messages, e.g.

(Call)	**Paisano. This is Kotka Harbour.**
(Message 1)	**QUESTION: What is your ETA at the harbour entrance?**
(Message 2)	**INFORMATION: There will be no tugs until time: one-six-three-zero GMT.**
(I have more to say)	**Stay on.**
(Return)	**Over.**

4.5.2 Message length

Messages should be short, to the point, and constructed according to the guidelines given in Section 4.3. However, in some cases, several items of information can be put together under, a single marker e.g.

> **QUESTION: What is your ship description:**
> **ANSWER: My ship description is:**
> **ship type: tanker,**
> **length: two-zero-zero metres,**
> **beam: four-eight metres,**
> **tonnage: one-five-zero thousand tonnes.**

4.5.3 Announcements in a transmission

It is sometimes mandatory and frequently very useful to indicate, at the beginning of a message-bearing transmission, after addressing and identifying, what the subject of the transmission is to be. Examples of familiar announcements of this sort are **Mayday, Pan-Pan, Sécurité, Met. report, Ice information.** However, it is acceptable to construct short announcements like this at the beginning of conversations and broadcasts and wherever a new subject is introduced. For example, **boarding arrangements, cargo handling, bunkering charges,** etc.

4.5.4 Communication Subjects

It is strongly recommended that different subjects of communication (listed in Section 5) are kept separate during the VHF conversation. For example, it is not recommended that messages concerning pilot **arrangements** be intermingled with messages about **commercial and cargo matters.** Instead they should be dealt with subject by subject.

4.6 FURTHER GUIDANCE FOR THE CONSTRUCTION OF MESSAGES

4.6.1 Summary

It will be clear that **standard phrases** are used for important *routine* purposes within the VHF conversations. The process of making, maintaining and terminating contact is handled entirely by them. In addition, standard phrases like **nothing more, break,** and **stay on** are used for the control of the

SECTION 4

VHF standard phrases and messages

conversation. Other standard phrases like **mistake, please spell,** and **I say again** and for the clarification of the messages.

SEASPEAK **messages** themselves are not standardised in the same way as the standard phrases. Instead, the messages are controlled by the use of the message and reply markers described in Section 4.2, the recommended message patterns described in Section 4.3 and the rules for the transmission of particular items of information such as course and position given in Section 1.

The **message checking system** detailed in Section 4.4 calls for confirmation of all messages to reduce the possibility of misunderstanding occurring in the conversation.

The **amount** of **information** in a transmission is controlled by the number of marked messages permitted in a single transmission (Section 4.5.1) and examples are given throughout this manual of ideal length messages. In addition, Section 4.5.2 and the examples in Section 5 demonstrate the arrangement of several items of information within a single message.

Finally, the different subjects of communication, listed in Section 5 are kept separate during the VHF conversation.

Further guidance on the following aspects of message construction is given below:
— the marking of quantities, codes, etc.;
— lists;
— responding;
— two messages in one;
— message markers in broadcasts.

4.6.2 The marking of quantities, codes etc.

> TRAINING INTRODUCTION to 4.6.2: The marking of quantities, codes, etc.
>
> Most maritime VHF messages contain a great deal of numerical information, information expressed according to established maritime convention, abbreviated information and so on. The same is true of VHF messages used by other professions, for example, the police. However, mariners, unlike the police, frequently operate in a very special professional community in which the professionals involved come from a large number of different language groups. During radio contact between mariners, therefore, extra care must be taken about the transmission of numerical, coded and abbreviated information. The rule is that *before* a piece of such information is transmitted, the speaker must state what it is that the numbers, codes, abbreviations refer to. Thus, it is not sufficient to say one-one-zero-zero GMT, two-zero metres or two-five-two-five-six deadweight tonnes. Instead, such measurements should be prefixed by marker words thus: time: one-one-zero-zero GMT; length; two-zero metres (or depth: two-zero metres); tonnage: two-five-two-five-six deadweight tonnes. By using such marker words the speaker makes it quite clear to the listener what is being referred to.
>
> In the following example marker words are not used and the meaning is therefore not clear:
>
> "This is Astra on one-six. There is a floating wreck. One-zero degrees zero-six minutes North zero-two-zero degrees two-five minutes East."
>
> The addition of the marker words *Securite, VHF channel, information, position, Latitude, Longitude* would make the message much clearer, as shown below:
>
> "Securite, Securite, Securite. This is Astra on VHF channel one-six Information: There is a floating wreck in position: Latitude one-zero degrees zero-six minutes North; Longitude zero-two-zero degrees two-five minutes East."
>
> The most common marker words are given in the table below and an exercise to practise each item is given at the end of the section.

The examples given throughout this manual incorporate marker words such as course:, speed:, name:, time:, which are used *within* the message. Their purpose is to indicate to the listener exactly what it is that a group of numbers, a set of letters, a name, etc., refers to. Without such a system these things are easily confused. The most common words used for this purpose are listed below:

Word	Specialised uses and examples of variations
area:	
bearing:	
cargo:	followed by **type:**, and **quantity:**
code:	
condition:	**ice condition:, condition of cargo:**
course:	
year/month/day.	
depth:	
destination:	
direction:	**approach direction:, relative wind direction:,** etc.
draught:	
ETA:	
ETD:	
first:	ordering or items e.g. **first:, second:, third:**
flash:	relating to characteristics of lights only.
force:	relating to wind only.
height:	
interval:	regular time periods.
length:	
letter:	**track letter:**
name:	
new ...:	**new course:, new speed:,** etc.
number:	**buoy number:, berth number:, hatch number:, place number:** (in convoy), etc.
period:	
position:	
quantity:	
range:	
reason:	
shows:	characteristics of lights only
spacing:	**track spacing:** e.g. in search and rescue.
speed:	
swell:	
through:	amount of change on a scale e.g. **change course through: two zero degrees.**
time:	
tonnage:	
trend:	present indications of change e.g. **decreasing/increasing.**
VHF channel:	
via:	
visibility:	
wind:	
zone ...:	**zone plus:, zone minus:**

4.6.3 Lists

Some lists of items in a message, such as search instructions and ship's stores requests, will contain a list of more than two pieces of information. These pieces of information should not be transmitted as independent messages because that would be too complicated and cumbersome. Instead, they should be stated as if each were joined to the preceding one with the word **and**.

The message should be clearly punctuated by slight pauses between each item of information and clear transmission of the marker words like **time:, speed:, quantity:,** etc

For example, in the search and rescue pattern instruction given in Section 5.4 which contains four items of information that must be transmitted together, the message comes out as follows:

> **INSTRUCTION: Search Mersar pattern number: two, start time: one-zero-two-zero GMT, initial course: two-four-zero degrees true, search speed: six knots.**

Again, the ship's stores examples given in Section 5.29 is organised in a similar way. However, in this case, the marker word quantity: is the same but

SECTION 4

VHF standard phrases and messages

its repetition still provides the essential punctuation, e.g.

> REQUEST: Please deliver,
> quantity: two metric tonnes potatoes,
> quantity: four sides beef,
> quantity: two-zero-zero litres deck paint, colour: green,
> etc.

4.6.4 Responding

All messages must be *replied to* even if they require nothing more than an acknowledgement. Certain messages like questions, instructions, and requests also require a *response* within the reply which indicates agreement, disagreement, yes, no, or ignorance. The words **positive, negative** or **I do not know** are used to reinforce responses of this sort. It is important to note, however, that these words should not be used in isolation. They must always be accompanied by a full quotation of the message being replied to, e.g.

> INSTRUCTION: Turn starboard immediately.
> INSTRUCTION-RECEIVED: Turn starboard immediately, negative.

The position of the words positive and negative is important. They should *follow* the full quotation in INSTRUCTION-RECEIVED, ADVICE-RECEIVED and REQUEST-RECEIVED as in the example above, and *precede* the full quotation in answers to yes/no questions.

e.g.

> ANSWER: positive, I am able to see the wreck.

Naturally, in third stage confirmations, beginning with the word understood, the quotation will be abbreviated. (See Section 4.4.5.)

4.6.5 Two messages in one

It is possible to transmit the equivalent of two messages after one marker where separation would be artificial. In such cases the two messages should be linked with the word and, e.g.

> ADVICE: Please alter course to port and slow down to your minimum safe speed.

> INFORMATION: The complete crew is on board and there are no injuries.

In case of questions which are of the same type, for example, **What is the relative wind direction and wind speed across your deck?** the question words (**What is**) may be omitted for the second question.

4.6.6 Message markers in broadcasts

The use of message markers is not confined to two-way conversations; they are also used in broadcasts. However, in broadcasts, the amount of information which follows a single marker is likely to be greater than in a two-way conversation. A long broadcast may contain, for example, just a single **INFORMATION** message marker.

The usefulness of message markers in broadcasts lies in the possibility of a change in sense taking place during the course of the broadcast. For example, some information may well lead to some important warnings which may in turn lead to some suggestions or instructions emphasised by the **ADVICE** or **INSTRUCTION** markers.

SECTION 4. EXERCISES

Ex. 4.A Standard Phrases

1. Insert or complete the appropriate Standard Phrase in the blank spaces (____) in the conversation given below. Then practice speaking the conversation with a partner.

   Note: Unlike earlier diagrams in this manual, this diagram does not represent a simplified conversation and steps are not marked. Instead, the transmissions are simply numbered from 1–9 for reference purposes.

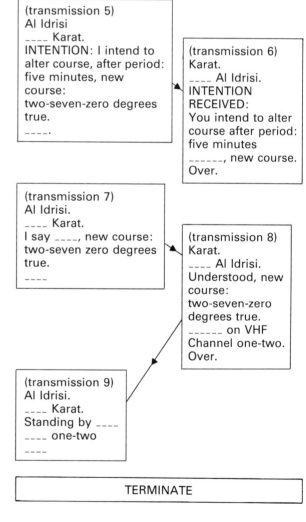

(transmission)
Al Idrisi, Sierra Uniform Sierra Whiskey. Al Idrisi, Sierra Uniform Sierra Whiskey. ____ Karat, Delta Alfa Kilo Sierra. Karat, Delta Alfa Kilo Sierra ____ one-six.
____

(transmission 2)
Karat,
____ Al Idrisi.
Over.

(transmission 3)
Al Idrisi.
____ Karat.
_____ one-two.
____.

(transmission 4)
Karat.
____ Al Idrisi
Agree _____
Over.

SWITCHOVER

(transmission 5)
Al Idrisi
____ Karat.
INTENTION: I intend to alter course, after period: five minutes, new course:
two-seven-zero degrees true.
____.

(transmission 6)
Karat.
____ Al Idrisi.
INTENTION RECEIVED:
You intend to alter course after period: five minutes
_____, new course.
Over.

(transmission 7)
Al Idrisi.
____ Karat.
I say ____, new course:
two-seven zero degrees true.
____

(transmission 8)
Karat.
____ Al Idrisi.
Understood, new course:
two-seven-zero degrees true.
_____ on VHF Channel one-two.
Over.

(transmission 9)
Al Idrisi.
____ Karat.
Standing by ____
____ one-two
____

TERMINATE

2. In the above conversation, the speaker aboard Karat is suddenly interrupted by an emergency on board. This occurs just after he has repeated his new course. He is unable to continue with the conversation. Repeat the conversation but terminate the exchange in the seventh transmission using the correct Standard Phrase.

3. Imagine that Al Idrisi fails to respond properly in transmission six. He says, for example:

> Karat
> This is Al Idrisi.
> Message received.
> Over.

Karat does not know if the information has been received correctly and therefore has to ask for it to be repeated. Using the correct Standard Phrase, repeat the conversation as suggested.

4. Imagine that Al Idrisi read back the information incorrectly in transmission 8. He says:

> Karat,
> This is Al Idrisi,
> Understood, new course:
> one-seven-zero degrees true.
> Stand by on VHF Channel one-two.
> Over.

Using the appropriate Standard Phrases repeat the conversation so that *Karat* corrects the error made by *Al Idrisi*.

5. Imagine other variations of this conversation which involve the following Standard Phrases.

— How do you read?
— Wait _ _ minutes.
— Please spell
— Please use SEASPEAK
— Sorry
— Thank you
— VHF channel _ _ unable.

In each case, go through a complete conversation.

Ex. 4.B Message Markers

Put a suitable message marker in the blank spaces (____) in the messages below.

1. _____ Stop immediately.
2. _____ steer course: one-seven-zero degrees true.
3. _____ The ship ahead of you is not under command.
4. _____ The leading lights are not lit.
5. _____ The cargo is phosphate.
6. _____ Please send a doctor immediately.
7. _____ The wind direction is: North East force: six
8. _____ The visibility is very poor.
9. _____ What is the depth in the outer fairway?
10. _____ What time will the pilot come aboard?
11. _____ I intend to change course. New course: two-two-zero degrees true.
12. _____ Berthing is completed at berth number: two Bravo, time: one-one-zero-zero local.
13. _____ Please give me a weather report.

14. _____ Please permit me to enter the restricted zone: reason: steering gear breakdown.
15. _____ The ore carrier Zulu is next.
16. _____ Please arrange the documents before we arrive.
17. _____ Proceed to the nearest safe anchorage.
18. _____ What is her cargo, wheat or maize?
19. _____ Do not anchor near South point; reason; diving operations will begin at time: one-two-three-zero local.
20. _____ I intend to leave via: Orford gap.

Read the completed messages to a partner and ask him to give the appropriate reply marker.

Ex. 4.C Message Patterns

Construct complete SEASPEAK messages using the information provided.

(a) **Questions**

Example   Ask a ship to give you her position.
Question: What is your position?

1. Ask if buoy maintenance operations are completed in fairway A.

2. Ask ship for her E.T.A. at the harbour entrance.

3. Ask a shore station for your berth number.

4. Ask the pilot which side he wants the pilot ladder.

5. Ask if the pilot service is operating normally.

6. Ask how many cranes are operational at berth thirty.

7. Ask for the depth in the main fairway.

8. Ask a ship if she intends to leave via the North or the South fairway.

9. Ask a shore station for the position of the bunkering terminal.

10. Ask a ship if she requires radar assistance to navigation.

(b) **Instructions and Advice**

Example: Instruct or advise a vessel to reduce speed before waypoint number three.

Instruction: reduce speed before waypoint number: three.

Or: Advice: reduce speed before waypoint number: three.

1. Instruct or advise a vessel to stop her engines immediately.

2. Instruct or advise a vessel to change course to a new course of one-three-three degrees true.

3. Instruct or advise a vessel to make fast to the lock tail.

4. Instruct or advise a helicopter to keep clear for five minutes.

5. Instruct or advise a tug to push your port bow.

(c) **Requests**

Example: Ask the chandler to deliver the stores before two-thirty this afternoon.

Request: please deliver the stores before time: one-four-three-zero local.

1. Ask for permission to enter sector two.

2. Make a request for fresh water (2,000 tonnes).

3. Ask a ship to confirm that her tonnage is one hundred and ten thousand gross tonnes.

4. Make a request for the following stores: one metric tonne of rice, ten frozen lambs and 200 litres of lube oil.

5. Ask for a doctor.

(d) **Pieces of Information and Warnings**

Example: Inform or Warn a ship that buoy number 33 is off position.

Warning: buoy number: three — three is off position.

1. Inform or Warn ships that the icebreaker is aground.

2. Tell a shore station that your ETA at the pilot station is eleven o'clock in the morning (local time).

3. Tell a vessel that the wind direction is South West force four.

4. Warn the coastguard that you are not under command.

5. Inform ships that the pilot service is suspended.

(e) **Intentions**

Example: Tell the ship behind you that you intend to reduce speed to five knots.

Intention: I intend to reduce speed. New speed: five knots.

1. Tell the shore station that you will proceed to the anchorage.

2. Tell the harbour station that you intend to close down (radio) now.

3. Announce that you intend to change course to a new course of 210° true.

4. Tell the shore station that you do not intend to sail today.

5. Tell the shore station you intend to be under way within an hour.

Ex. 4.D Responding to Messages

Respond to the messages completed in Exercise 4.C (a) *Questions*, using the information given below.

(a) **Answers**

Example: give your position as bearing 270° true, from West Cape, distance 6 miles.

Answer: My position is bearing: two-seven-zero degrees true, from West Cape distance six miles.

1. Buoy maintenance operations *are* completed. (begin the message pattern with the word 'positive').

2. ETA is 12:00 GMT.

3. berth number is 14A.

4. starboard side.

5. the service is operating normally.

6. three cranes are operational.

7. 35 metres.

8. the South fairway.

9. the bunkering terminal is at the entrance to dock number 2.

10. no assistance is required.

(b) **Responses to Instructions or Advice**

Respond to the messages in Exercise 4.C (b) *Instructions and Advice,* as below.

Example: Agree to comply with the instruction.

'Instruction Received reduce speed before waypoint number: three, positive.'

1. agree

2. disagree.

3. agree

4. agree

5. agree

(c) **Responses to Requests**

Respond to the messages in Exercise 4.C (c) *Requests,* as below.

Example: State that you are unable to deliver the supplies at that time.

'Request — Received: deliver the supplies before time: one-four-three-zero local, negative.'

1. agree to request (begin 'you are permitted to')

2. agree to supply

3. state that your tonnage is not 110,000 GRT

4. agree to supply

5. agree to send a doctor

(d) **Responses to pieces of Information and Warnings**
Respond to the messages in Exercise 4C (d) *Information and Warnings,* as below.

Example: acknowledge the warning.

                 Warning Received: buoy number three-three is off position

1.   acknowledge this warning

2.   acknowledge this information

3.   acknowledge this information

4.   acknowledge this warning

5.   acknowledge this information

(e) **Responses to Intentions**
Respond to the messages in Exercise 4.C (e) Intentions, as below.

Example: acknowledge the message.

                 Intention Received: you intend to reduce speed, new speed: five knots.

1.   acknowledge this message

2.   acknowledge this message

3.   acknowledge this message

4.   acknowledge this message

5.   acknowledge this message

Ex. 4.E Giving Reasons

Construct complete SEASPEAK messages using the information provided.

Example: Tell ships that the pilot service is suspended due to bad weather.

                 'Information: the pilot service is suspended, reason: bad weather.'

1.   Reply to the following instruction stating that you cannot leave because you have an engine breakdown.

       'Instruction: leave berth number one-six immediately.'

2.   Ask for a doctor because a crewman has severe stomach pains.

3.   Inform the harbour master that you are not able to leave at 07:30 local because bunkering is delayed.

4.   Warn another ship (Eros) that you are unable to stop because of engine breakdown. Own ship name Spartan.

5.   Warn ships to proceed with extreme caution because a dredger is operating in fairway.

Ex. 4.F Message Checks

Insert the correct text in the blank transmissions boxes below, then read the transmission aloud. Work with a partner.

Example:

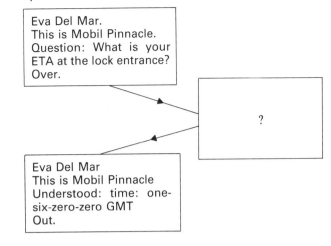

The missing transmission should be:

> Mobil Pinnacle
> This is Eva Del Mar
> Answer: My ETA at the lock entrance is time: one-six-zero-zero GMT.
> Over.

Now work the following 5 transmissions;

1.

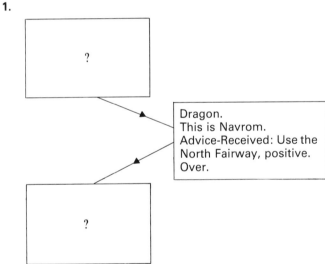

2.

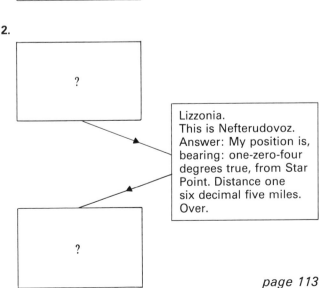

page 113

3.

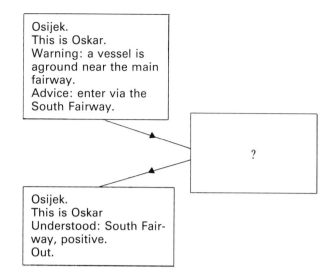

Osijek.
This is Oskar.
Warning: a vessel is aground near the main fairway.
Advice: enter via the South Fairway.

?

Osijek.
This is Oskar
Understood: South Fair-way, positive.
Out.

4.

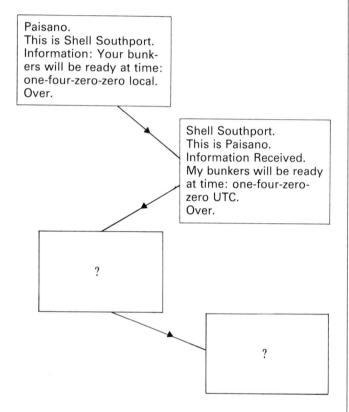

Paisano.
This is Shell Southport.
Information: Your bunkers will be ready at time: one-four-zero-zero local.
Over.

Shell Southport.
This is Paisano.
Information Received.
My bunkers will be ready at time: one-four-zero-zero UTC.
Over.

?

?

5.

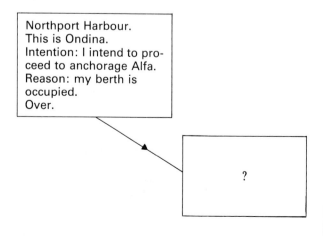

Northport Harbour.
This is Ondina.
Intention: I intend to proceed to anchorage Alfa.
Reason: my berth is occupied.
Over.

?

Ex. 4.G The Marking of Quantities, Codes, etc.

Put a suitable marker word in the blank spaces in front of the following pieces of information.

Example: time one-one-one-zero GMT

1. _____one-four-three-zero UTC.

2. _____buoy number two-two.

3. North Point _____ one-decimal five miles.

4. I am towing a cable _____ two-zero-zero metres.

5. Keep radio silence, _____ __ two hours.

6. _____ five sides beef.
   _____ six-zero-zero litres white paint.
   _____ two-zero litres detergent.

7. My salt water _____ is three-one metres

8. My _____(is) __ __ __ two-seven degrees true from South Point. _____ two miles.

9. My _____ is two-five-zero thousand tonnes. (Cargo lifting capacity).

10. Reduce speed _____ three knots.

ANSWERS

Ex. 4.A.1

Trans 1   Al Idrisi, Sierra Uniform Sierra Whiskey. Al Idrisi, Sierra Uniform Sierra Whiskey. This is Karat, Delta Alfa Kilo Sierra. Karat, Delta Alfa Kilo Sierra on VHF channel one-six. Over.

Trans 2   Karat, this is Al Idrisi. Over.

Trans 3   Al Idrisi. This is Karat. Switch to VHF channel one-two. Over.

Trans 4   Karat. This is Al Idrisi. Agree VHF channel one-two. Over.

Trans 5   Al Idrisi. This is Karat. INTENTION. I intend to alter course, after period: five minutes. New course: two-seven-zero degrees true. Over.

Trans 6   Karat. This is Al Idrisi. INTENTION RECEIVED: You intend to alter course after period: five minutes. Say again, new course. Over.

Trans 7   Al Idrisi. This is Karat. I say again new course two-seven-zero degrees true. Over.

Trans 8   Karat. This is Al Idrisi. Understood. New course: two-seven-zero degrees true. Stand by on VHF channel one-two. Over.

Trans 9   Al Idrisi. This is Karat. Standing by on VHF channel one-two. Out.

Ex. 4.A.2

Trans 1–6   same as above.

Trans 7   Al Idrisi, this is Karat. Break. Out.

Ex. 4.A.3

Trans 1–5   Same as in Exercise 4.A.1.

Trans 6   Karat. This is Al Idrisi. Message received. Over.

Trans 7   Al Idrisi. This is Karat. I say again. INTENTION: I intend to alter course after period: five minutes. New course: two-seven-zero degrees true. Please read back.

Trans 8   Karat. This is Al Idrisi. Read-back: INTENTION: you intend to alter course after period five minutes new course two-seven-zero degrees true. Over.

Trans 9   Al Idrisi. This is Karat. Read-back is correct. Over.

Trans 10   Karat. This is Al Idrisi. Stand by on VHF channel one-two. Over.

Trans 11   Same as Trans 9, Ex. 4.A.1.

Ex. 4.A.4

Trans 1–7   Same as in Ex. 4.A.1.

Trans 8   Karat. This is Al Idrisi. Understood. New course: one-seven-zero degrees true. Stand by on VHF channel one-two. Over.

Trans 9   Al Idrisi. This is Karat. Mistake. INTENTION: I intend to alter course after period five minutes new course: two-seven-zero degrees true. Over.

Trans 10   Karat. This is Al Idrisi. Correction. Understood: New course: two-seven-zero degrees true. Over.

Ex. 4.A.5

Insert stated phrases into appropriate spaces in conversation 4.A.1.

Ex. 4.B

1.   Instruction
2.   Advice
3.   Warning
4.   Information
5.   Information
6.   Request
7.   Information
8.   Warning
9.   Question
10. Question
11. Intention
12. Information
13. Request
14. Request
15. Information
16. Request
17. Advice
18. Question
19. Instruction
20. Intention

Ex. 4.C

(a)
1.   Question: Are buoy maintenance operations complete in Fairway Alpha.
2.   Question: What is your ETA at harbour entrance.
3.   Question: What is my berth number.
4.   Question: Which side for pilot ladder.
5.   Question: Is pilot service operating normally.
6.   Question: How many cranes operational at berth three-zero.
7.   Question: What is depth in main fairway.
8.   Question: Do you intend to leave by North fairway or South fairway.
9.   Question: What is position of bunkering terminal.
10. Question: Do you require radar assistance to navigation.

(b)
1.   Instruction: Stop your engines immediately.
     or Advice: Stop your engines immediately.
2.   Instruction: Alter course to: new course one-three-three true.
     or Advice: Alter course to: new course one-three-three true.
3.   Instruction: Make fast to the lock tail.
     or Advice: Make fast to the lock tail.
4.   Instruction: Keep clear for period: five minutes.
     or Advice: Keep clear for period: five minutes.
5.   Instruction: Push on port bow.
     or Advice: Push on port bow.

(c)
1.   Request: Permission to enter sector two.
2.   Request: Please supply fresh water quantity two thousand tonnes.
3.   Request: Please confirm your gross tonnage is one hundred and ten thousand tonnes.
4.   Request: Please supply following items. Rice quantity one tonne. Frozen lambs number: ten. Lube oil quantity two-zero-zero litres.
5.   Request: Please send a doctor.

(d)
1.   Warning: Icebreaker is aground.
2.   Information: ETA Pilot station one-one-zero-zero local time.
3.   Information: Wind direction: South West.
     Wind force: force four.
4.   Warning: We are not under command.
5.   Information: Pilotage service suspended.

(e)
1.   Intention: I intend to proceed to the anchorage.

2. Intention: I intend to close down radio. Time: now.

3. Intention: I intend to change course. New course: two-one-zero degrees true.

4. Intention: I do not intend to sail today.

5. Intention: I intend to be underway within period: one hour.

Ex. 4.D

(a)
1. Answer: Positive. Buoy maintenance operations are complete in Fairway Alpha.

2. Answer: ETA at harbour entrance is one-two-zero-zero GMT.

3. Answer: Your berth number is one-four Alpha.

4. Answer: Rig pilot ladder on starboard side.

5. Answer: Positive: Pilot service is operating normally.

6. Answer: Three cranes are operational at berth three-zero.

7. Answer: Depth in main fairway is three-five metres.

8. Answer: Intention: I intend to leave by South Fairway.

9. Answer: Bunkering terminal is at entrance to dock number two.

10. Answer: Negative: I do not require radar assistance to navigation.

(b)
1. Instruction received: Stop my engines immediately: Positive.

2. Instruction received: Alter course to: new course one-three-three true. Negative.

3. Advice received: Make fast to lock tail. Positive.

4. Advice received: Keep clear for period: five minutes. Positive.

5. Instruction received: Push on port bow. Positive.

(c)
1. Request received: You are permitted to enter sector two.

2. Request received: Supply fresh water quantity two thousand tonnes.

3. Request received: Gross tonnage one hundred and ten thousand tonnes. Negative. (*Note:* this message would normally be followed by a message Information: My gross tonnage is eleven thousand tonnes.

This message corrects the error made.)

4. Request received: Supply following items. Rice quantity one tonne. Frozen lambs number: ten. Lube oil quantity: two-zero-zero litres. Positive.

5. Request received: Send a doctor. Positive.

(d)
1. Warning received: Icebreaker is aground.

2. Information received: ETA Pilot Station is one-one-zero-zero local time.

3. Information received: Wind direction: South West. Wind force: force four.

4. Warning received: You are not under command.

5. Information received: Pilot service suspended.

(e)
1. Intention received: You intend to proceed to the anchorage.

2. Intention received: You intend to close down radio. Time: now.

3. Intention received: You intend to change course. New course two-one-zero degrees true.

4. Intention received: You do not intend to sail today.

5. Intention received: You intend to be underway within period: one hour.

Ex. 4.E

1. Instruction received: Leave berth number one-six immediately. Negative. Reason: Engine breakdown (*Note:* message probably followed by Request: Please send tugs.)

2. Request: Please send doctor. Reason: crewman has severe stomach pains. (*Note:* at sea this message would be prefixed by Pan-Pan.)

3. Information: Departure at zero-seven-three-zero local not possible. Reason: Bunkering delayed.

4. Eros, this is Spartan. Warning: I am unable to stop. Reason: Engine breakdown.

5. Warning: Dredger operating in Fairway. Proceed with extreme caution. (*Note:* If addressed to all ships, this message would be prefixed by Securite).

Ex. 4.F

1. Box 1. Navrom. This is Dragon. Advice. Over: Use the North Fairway. Over.

Box 3. Navrom. This is Dragon. Nothing more. Out.

2. Box 1. Nefterudovoz. This is Lizzonia. Question: What is your position. Over.

Box 3. Nefterudovoz. This is Lizzonia. Understood: Your position is bearing: one-zero-four degrees true from Star Point, distance one-six decimal five miles. Nothing more. Out.

3. Box 2. Oskar. This Osijek. Warning received: A vessel is aground near the main fairway. Advice received: Enter via the South Fairway. Positive. Over.

4. Box 3. Paisano. This is Shell Southport. Mistake. Information: Your bunkers will be ready at time: one-four-zero-zero local. Over.

Box 4. Shell Southport. This is Paisano. Correction. Information received: My bunkers will be ready at time: one-four-zero-zero local. Out.

5. Box 2. Ondina. This is Northport Harbour. Intention received: You intend to proceed to anchorage Alfa. Reason: Your berth is occupied. Over. (*Note:* This message would normally be followed by another giving approval of Ondina's action, or suggesting another suitable anchorage.)

Ex. 4.G

1. Time.
2. Position.
3. Distance.
4. Length.
5. Period.
6. Quantity.
7. Draft.
8. Position/bearing/distance.
9. Deadweight.
10. New speed.

SECTION 5

Major communication subjects

5.0   GENERAL INTRODUCTION

This section provides the user with examples of messages constructed according to the principles of SEASPEAK. The examples given are set out under the operational headings (Major Communication Subjects) listed below.

It must be emphasised that in most cases these examples are hypothetical. They are *not* set phrases for use in particular operations. They cannot be re-used 'parrot-fashion' because operational circumstances differ. For example, in 5.6 'Navigational Dangers (non-sécurité) Gulf Trader is *being warned* by Capitan Stanzoukas that the Jebel Ali fairway buoy is off position, but Gulf Trader, in different circumstances, could be *asking* Capitan Stanzoukas if the buoy is off position.

SECTION 5

Major communication subjects

Actual examples of Mayday, Pan-Pan and Sécurité messages are not given in this section because they are subject to strict internationally agreed conventions. These conventions are dealt with in Section 3 with examples.

5.0.1 List of Major Communication Subjects

This list includes the majority of subjects for which maritime VHF may be used. It provides guidance on the identification of individual subjects so as to facilitate the recommendations made in Section 4 about keeping different subjects separate during a VHF conversation.

1. Mayday
2. Pan-Pan
3. Sécurité
4. Search and rescue
5. Collision avoidance and manoeuvring
6. Navigational dangers (non Sécurité)
7. Navigational instructions (including routeing)
8. Navigational information (including tides, currents, etc.)
9. Meteorological reports, forecasts, and information
10. Movement reports
11. Breakdown reports
12. Special message formats
13. Medical information (non-urgent)
14. Ice
15. Special operations information
16. Anchor operations
17. Arrival details
18. Pilot arrangements
19. Tugs and towage
20. Berthing/unberthing
21. Departure details
22. Helicopter and aircraft operations
23. Port regulations
24. Telephone (telegram) link calls
25. Relaying (non-safety)
26. Cargo and cargo operations
27. Bunkering operations
28. Agency, business and commerce
29. Ship's stores
30. Unclassical messages
31. Radio checks
32. Closing down (shutting down)

5.1 MAYDAY

Communications relating to the request for and provision of immediate assistance to a ship, aircraft, or other vehicle which is threatened by grave and imminent danger.

Instructions and examples concerning this communication subject are given in Section 3.

5.2 PAN-PAN

Urgent messages concerning the safety of a ship, aircraft or other vehicle, or the safety of a person.

Instructions and examples concerning this communication subject are given in Section 3.

5.3 SÉCURITÉ

Messages containing an important navigational or important meteorological warning.

Instructions and examples concerning this communication subject are given in Section 3.

5.4 SEARCH and RESCUE

Instructions on how to conduct Search and Rescue operations are given in the IMO MERSAR Manual which is primarily designed for use by merchant ships. It contains descriptions of the communications that should be conducted during Search and Rescue operations.

If it is necessary to give more information about the condition of survivors (e.g. medical symptoms), medical aid, or the condition of the casualty (the ship in distress), this information should be the subject of a separate message following the conclusion of search report. In such cases the words *Stay on* would be included at the end of the conclusion of search report.

All the examples for the subject of search and rescue show how to use SEASPEAK in conjunction with the MERSAR Manual. The figures (5.16.1(a)), etc. refer to the appropriate section of the MERSAR Manual.

Examples:

a. **Arranging search patterns** (5.16.1.(a))

> Rose Maru. This is Gammon.
> INSTRUCTION: Search Mersar pattern number:
> two, start time: one-zero-two-zero GMT,
> initial course: two-four-zero degrees true,
> search speed: six knots.
> Over.

b. **Adjusting track spacing** (5.16.1.(e))

> Rose Maru. This is Gammon.
> INSTRUCTION: Adjust track spacing, new track spacing:
> two miles.
> Over.

c. **Requests for particular types of assistance in the SAR operation.** (6.1.12.)

> Brest Radio. This is Delphi.
> REQUEST: Please send a doctor to Rose Maru, reason:
> a survivor has broken legs.
> Over.

d.   **Conclusion of search reports (6.1.15.)**

Colombo Radio. This is State of Abidjan.

Conclusion of search report.

INFORMATION, one: Ship name: Rose Maru, destination: Bombay, is carrying quantity: five survivors.

INFORMATION, two: Ship name: State of Abidjan, destination: Singapore, is carrying quantity: six survivors.

Stay on.

Over.

ACKNOWLEDGEMENT TRANSMISSION

Colombo Radio. This is State of Abidjan.

Conclusion of search report continued.

INFORMATION, three: The condition of the survivors is fair* and medical aid is not required*.

INFORMATION, four: The casualty sank in deep water.*

Over.

---

*1.   *fair* is taken from the following alternatives: *good/fair/poor/bad*.

2.   *not required* is taken from the following alternatives: *required/not required*.

3.   *INFORMATION four*. This is a brief description of the state of casualty at the time of conclusion of search.

5.5

COLLISION AVOIDANCE and MANOEUVRING

This subject covers messages concerned with the avoidance of collision, manoeuvring, and the establishment of position and identity of stations in these circumstances.

Your attention is drawn to the recommendations and requirements of various administrations regarding the use of bridge to bridge radio telephone for this communication subject.

Always make certain that you are talking to the correct station. Do not make any assumptions in identifying another ship and use all means at your disposal to achieve positive identification e.g. VHF/DF, transponder systems, reference to a navigation mark, reference to a position, or reference to a charted feature.

Never, under any circumstances, make an attempt to identify another ship solely by reference to a relative bearing from your own ship.

Examples:

a.   **Identification of another VHF station** (geographical position)

All ships in West Cape area, all ships in West Cape area. Calling unknown ship. Position: bearing: two-seven-zero degrees true, from West Cape distance six miles. This is Gammon, position: bearing: three-zero-zero degrees true, from West Cape* distance six-decimal five miles.

On VHF channel one-six.

Over.

The reply to the above call should be given as follows:

> **Gammon. This is Fourah Bay. I say again, Fourah Bay, position: bearing: two-six-eight degrees true, from West Cape* distance six miles.**
> **Over.**

*No message marker is transmitted here because the positional information is part of the identification of Fourah Bay and Gammon.

b. **Description of intended action**

> **State of Abidjan. This is Star Vega.**
> **INTENTION: I intend to alter course, after period: five minutes, new course: two-seven-zero degrees true.**
> **Over**

c. **Asking a vessel to delay a sailing whilst another passes its berth**

> **Sydney Venture. This is Comet.**
> **ADVICE: Please do not leave your berth until I am clear of the lock entrance.**
> **Over.**

d. **Informing another vessel of your movements**

> **Gammon. This is Rose Maru.**
> **WARNING: I intend to operate astern propulsion.**
> **Over.**

e. **Identification of another VHF station** (visual)

> **All ships, all ships. Calling unknown ship. Position: now passing Jebel Ali fairway buoy, course: East. This is Gulf Trader, position: bearing: two-seven-zero degrees true, from Jebel Ali fairway buoy distance two miles.**
> **Over.**

5.6   NAVIGATIONAL DANGERS (Non-Sécurité)

This subject covers all messages about navigational dangers which are not urgent enough to justify being treated as Sécurité messages.

The master of a ship which meets with a dangerous derelict or any other danger to navigation must make a report to the appropriate land radio station and, if it is considered necessary, to do so to all ships.

Examples:

a. Inter-ship communication of non-urgent navigational dangers

> Gulf Trader. This is Capitan Stanzoukas.
> WARNING: Jebel Ali fairway buoy is not in the correct position.
> Over.

b. Secondary fairway buoy out of position

> Tasman Ferry. This is Port Phillip Radio.
> WARNING: Geelong fairway buoy number:
>   one is not in the correct position.
> Over.

c. Navigational aid not lit during daytime

> Offshore Star. This is Aberdeen Harbour.
> WARNING: The leading lights are not lit.
> Over.

5.7 NAVIGATIONAL INSTRUCTIONS (including routeing)

Communications within this subject will normally be started by a shore station or other coastal authority.

Examples:

a. Coast guard station advising ship to follow an IMO traffic separation scheme

> Elin Star. This is Coastguard Navigation Information Service.
> INSTRUCTION: Steer course: two-three-zero degrees true,
>   reason: to comply with the traffic separation
>   scheme.
> Over.

b. Port controlling entrance channel

> Texon Prince. This is Boulogne Harbour.
> INSTRUCTION: Alter course to starboard and keep clear of the
>   controlled fairway, reason: a tanker will leave
>   the harbour soon.
> Over.

*No message markers are used because the information given is part of the identification of the station.

c. Pilot station instructing ship on order of entry

> Olivia Queen. This is Sharjah Pilot.
> INSTRUCTION: Stop engines and wait for the ship ahead of you to
>   enter harbour.
> Over.

5.8 | NAVIGATIONAL INFORMATION (including tides, currents, etc.)

This subject covers a wide range of messages concerning navigational information including light characteristics, fairway depth, tide and currents.

Examples:

a. **Tidal height information**

> All ships in River Weser. This is Weser Riviere Radio.
> Navigational Information; heights of tide.
> INFORMATION, one: Position: Robbenplatz, height of tide: one-decimal-five metres, time: now.
> INFORMATION, two: Position: Fischereihafen, height of tide: one-decimal-four metres, time: now.
> Out.

b. **Depth of water in a fairway.**

> Genoa Harbour. This is Capitan Stanzoukas.
> QUESTION: What is the depth in the main fairway.
> Over.

The reply to the above call could be as follows:

> Capitan Stanzoukas. This is Genoa Harbour.
> ANSWER: The depth in the main fairway is depth: two-zero metres from seaward until position: buoy number: three, and depth: one-zero metres between position: buoy number: three and position: dry dock entrance.
> Over.

c. **Description of buoys, lights and other navigational aids.**

> Castor. This is State of Abidjan.
> INFORMATION: West Cape light shows: flash: two, interval: three-zero seconds, range: one-eight miles.*
> Over

*Description of the light is to be given in accordance with current IALA system, as shown on charts or in lists of lights.

d. **Positional Information**

> Star Vega. This is Eastport.
> INFORMATION: The fairway entrance is position: bearing: two-seven-zero degrees true, from Cap du Nord distance: three decimal five miles.
> Over.

5.9 METEOROLOGICAL INFORMATION

The master of a ship which encounters a tropical revolving storm (or winds of force 10 or more, about which no warning has been given) must make a report to a land radio station and if considered necessary to all ships. The report should contain:

— the position of the storm with date and time in UTC;
— the position, true course and speed of the ship at the time of the observation;
— the barometric pressure;
— the change in the barometric pressure over the last three hours;
— the true direction of the wind;
— the wind force;
— the sea state;
— the height and direction of the swell;
— the period and length of the swell.

Examples:

a. **Weather reports**

> **Meteorological Information, Weather Forecast area: Shannon, period: two-four hours.**
> **INFORMATION: The wind direction is: North West, force: five, ...**
> **Out.**

b. **Reports of sea state**

> **Livorno Harbour. This is Harriet.**
> **INFORMATION: The sea outside the harbour entrance is very rough and the swell is South West, steep and short.**
> **Over.**

c. **Description of weather**

> **Offshore Star. This is Platform Alpha.**
> **WARNING: The visibility, position: here, is distance: five-zero-zero metres, and the trend is: decreasing slowly.**
> **Over.**

5.10 MOVEMENT REPORTS

This subject covers messages concerning the movements of vessels. These may either be reports from ships to shore radio stations, or messages transmitted by shore radio stations giving information on the movements of vessels.

The occasions on which ships are required to make movement reports to shore radio stations are given in the regulations covering navigation in the relevant sea areas.

Examples:

a. **Position report to a vessel traffic centre**

> Vancouver Traffic. This is Oliver.
> INFORMATION: My position is: Sheringham Point, and my ETA:
> position: buoy Juliett Alpha is time: one-four-zero-zero local.
> Over.

b. **Report on arriving at a berth in a VTS system**

> New Orleans Traffic. This is Africa Express.
> INFORMATION: Berthing is completed at pier number: two, time:
> two-three-two-five local.
> Over.

c. **List of ship movements**

> Olivebank. This is Maas Centre.
> INFORMATION: The following ships are moving within your area:
> name: World Fusion from Europort
> E.T.D.: one-five-zero-zero local,
> name: Gammon from Europort
> E.T.D.: one-five-one-five local.
> name: Foxtrot Echo four-nine from Hook van Holland, E.T.D.: one-five-one-five local.
> Over.

d. **Request/Reports about how busy a harbour is**

> Northport Harbour. This is Aspen Carrier.
> REQUEST: Please advise me on traffic conditions, area:
> approaches to Northport.
> Over.

5.11 BREAKDOWN REPORTS

This subject covers all messages relating to breakdowns which will affect other ships, fixed structures or the coast.

Many countries require these reports to be made to shore stations in the event of breakdowns within specified distances of their coasts. Some of these distances can be quite large, particularly when oil or dangerous cargoes are involved. For example, the distance is fifty miles in the case of tankers off the French coast.

In most cases where reports are required by law, special message formats have been prescribed. These are given under Section 5.12 'Special Message Formats'.

Examples:

a.   **Report to shore station of main engine failure**

> West Cape Coastguard. This is Rose Maru.
> INFORMATION: I am drifting, reason: engine breakdown.
> INTENTION: I expect to be underway within period: one hour.
> Over.

b.   **Report to another ship of steering-gear failure**

> Comet. This is Star Vega.
> WARNING: I am unable to alter course, reason: steering-gear
>   breakdown.
> Over.

c.   **Report to port authority of inability to sail on time**

> Beline Harbour. This is Cool Trader.
> INTENTION: I do not intend to sail today, reason: windlass
>   breakdown.
> Over.

5.12   SPECIAL MESSAGE FORMATS

Special message formats are precisely laid down methods of transmitting specified information in certain circumstances. The message is preceded by a marker word (e.g. MAREP) to indicate its content, and each piece of information in the message is preceded by a code letter which is spoken using the phonetic alphabet.

Special message formats are referred to in SEASPEAK as fixed formats. The code letters, and hence the topics given in each fixed format, are designed to cover all the information required by the authorities. In some cases not all the topics will be relevant, or the appropriate information will not be available. In those cases the code letter and the associated topic should be omitted from the message.

When fixed formats are in use, as much of the requested information as possible must be supplied.

Fixed formats must be strictly adhered to when they are being used. Whenever the circumstances permit, a fixed format should be used in preference to free SEASPEAK. No attempt should be made to use fixed formats in circumstances other than those given in this manual, or in publications of individual ports or of national authorities dealing with communications.

The three types of fixed format given here (MAREP, SURNAV and IMO) are intended to show how to use the system. This is not a complete list of all fixed formats. It should be noted that MAREP and SURNAV largely conform to the IMO resolution on General Principles for Ship Reporting Systems. It is intended that any future system will also conform with this resolution.

The method of expression to be used with fixed formats differs slightly from that of SEASPEAK. The main difference is that, as each topic of the message is defined by a code letter, it is not normally necessary to state the items that are being measured, or the units being used, as is required by SEASPEAK for dealing with quantities (Section 1.6.1).

The table below explains how the topics are to be expressed when using fixed formats.

Topic	Method of Expression
Ship station identity	Name, nationality and callsign. As spoken in the rules for identification of stations (Section 1.3) with the nationality and registry of the ship spoken between its name and callsign.
Date and time (GMT/UTC)	A six-digit group giving the day of the month (first 2 digits), hours (second 2 digits), and minutes (last 2 digits), suffixed either by GMT or UTC.
Position (Latitude and longitude)	As in the rules for giving positions (Section 1.8) but omitting the prefixes *position, latitude,* and *longitude.*
Position (bearing and distance)	As in the rules for giving positions (Section 1.8) but omitting the prefixes *position, bearing,* and *distance* and the suffix *true.* All bearings given in fixed formats are to be bearings in 360 degree notation.
True course	True course in 360 degree notation. The prefix *course* and the suffix *degrees true* are to be omitted.
Speed	Speed through the water in knots and tenths of knots. The word *decimal* should be used to indicate the decimal point. The prefix *speed* and the suffix *knots* are to be omitted.
Destination	The name of the port or general area in which it is intended first to berth or anchor.
Radiocommunications	Radio watch being maintained, particularly VHF channels on which watch is being kept. The prefix *VHF channel* is to be omitted.
Maximum draught	Maximum draught in metres and tenths of metres. The word *decimal* is to be used to indicate the decimal point. The prefix *draught* and the suffix *metres* should be omitted.
Cargo type and quantity	Cargo type is to be given first, followed by the number of metric tonnes of that cargo, followed by the words *metric tonnes.*

Fixed format reports should be given in the following order:

1. The name of the system e.g. MAREP, SURNAV.
2. The name of the type of report e.g. POSREP, DEFREP, AVARIES.
3. The contents of the report given by using the code letters in alphabetical order (spoken as Alfa, Bravo, etc.) followed by the relevant information.

5.12.1 MAREP System — English Channel and Dover Strait

(Extract from U.K. Notice to Mariners 631/1986).

Ship Movement Reporting (MAREP)

Introduction

(1) The objective of the MAREP scheme is to assist the mariner, to improve safety of navigation in the English Channel and Dover Strait, and to reduce the risk of pollution of the coasts of the United Kingdom and France in this area. Participation in the scheme is voluntary and the International Maritime Organization (IMO), through its Maritime Safety Committee, has recommended that ships to which the scheme applies should participate. The transmission of reports is free of charge.

(2) The MAREP scheme provides for certain categories of ships to report-in to a number of designated shore stations when in the area of the Traffic Separation Schemes and associated Inshore Traffic Zones off Ushant, off Casquets and in the Dover Strait. Broadcasts will be made by shore stations on a regular basis and as required and will include information on any known situations which could affect the safe navigation of ships in these Traffic Separation Schemes or associated Inshore Traffic Zones.

(3) Ships with certain defects and ships in other categories are also invited to report when elsewhere in the English Channel.

Participation

(4) Ships of the following categories intending to enter the areas described in para. 5 below are invited to participate:-

(a) all loaded oil and chemical tankers and loaded gas carriers of 1600 gross registered tons and over;

(b) any ship "not under command" or at anchor in a traffic separation scheme or associated inshore zone;

(c) any ship "restricted in her ability to manoeuvre", ships engaged in towing, deep draught ships, or ships with a defect in their propulsion or steering;

(d) any ship with a defect in those navigational aids which could adversely affect her navigation under prevailing conditions.

When to Report

(5) Ships mentioned above are invited to report to the designated shore stations (para. 8 below) when intending to enter:-

(a) the Traffic Separation Schemes off Ushant and off Casquets, or their associated inshore traffic zones:

    (i) Reports should be made at a distance of ten (10) nautical miles before entering the areas described in (a) above;

(b) the Traffic Separation Scheme in the Dover Strait or the associated inshore traffic zones:

    (i) On proceeding eastward into this Scheme or its associated inshore traffic zones when arriving within two (2) nautical miles of a line joining the Royal Sovereign light tower and Bassurelle light-buoy and extended to the French coast;

    (ii) When proceeding south-westward, when arriving within two (2) nautical miles of a line from North Foreland extended through the Falls light vessel to the Belgian coast;

    (iii) When departing from a port within the associated inshore traffic zones.

(6) The phrase "entering a Traffic Separation Scheme" covers ships intending to use the traffic separation lanes, joining them from the side, or crossing the Schemes as described in Rule 10(b) and (c) of the International Regulations for Preventing Collisions at Sea, 1972.

(7) Any ship not under command or any ship of the categories described in para. 4(c) and (d) above wherever it is in the English Channel area (east of a line joining Ushant South-West Buoy and Bishop Rock Lighthouse and west of the line described in para. 5(b) (ii) above) is invited to report to a shore station. These ships may be asked to make subsequent pre-arranged reports to shore stations.

Reports and Shore Stations

(8) Ships with no defects should make a Position Report (POSREP). Ships with defects, i.e. when not under command, with a defect in propulsion or steering or as described in para. 4(d) above should make a Defect Report (DEFREP). Where appropriate a subsequent change Report (CHANGE-REP) should be made. Reports in the English language should be transmitted by VHF using the format at the Appendix and using for guidance the IMO Standard Marine Navigational Vocabulary and the International Code. The reports should be made to the following designated shore stations:-

Traffic Separation Zone	MAREP receiving Station	VHF Frequency
(a) Ushant	Quessant Traffic	16–11
(b) Casquets	Joburg Traffic	16–11
	Portland Coastguard	16–69

Channel 11 should be used for calling and working Ouessant and Jobourg Traffic, but these stations should be called outside the times set for broadcasts in paragraph 10.

Channel 69 should be used for calling and working Portland Coastguard.

(c) Dover Strait	Gris Nez Traffic	16–69
	Dover Coastguard	16–69

Channel 69 should be used for calling and working these stations.

(d)   Ships requiring further information or assistance may be transferred by the Centres at Ushant, Jobourg and Gris Nez Traffic to Channel 79 and by Dover Coastguard to Channel 80.

(9) Ships referred to in paragraph 7 should make their report to the nearest designated station. If unable to make contact with any of these stations the report should be made through a Coast Radio Station and addressed to one of the designated stations.

Information Broadcasts

(10) Routine broadcasts will be made by the Centres at Ushant, Jobourg, Gris Nez and Dover on VHF Channel 11 with additional routine broadcasts in restricted visibility at the following times:-

	Clear Weather	Restricted Visibility
Ushant Traffic	H+10	H+25
	H+40	H+55
Jobourg Traffic	H+20	H+05
Gris Nez Traffic	H+50	H+35
Dover Coastguard	H+10	H+25
	H+40	H+55

(11) Urgent broadcasts will be transmitted as necessary at any time.

(12) All broadcasts will be preceded by a forewarning on VHF Channel 16.

(13) Broadcasts will cover navigational and traffic information of immediate interest and information on movements of ships which appear to be navigating within a traffic separation scheme contrary to the requirements of Rule 10 of the International Collision Regulations.

Ship's Radio Watch

(14) In order to derive the fullest benefit from the MAREP scheme a continuous watch should be maintained between routine broadcasts on VHF Channel 16 (and on Channel 11 where two Channel reception is available).

Caution

(15) It is emphasised that the MAREP scheme does not absolve the Master from his sole reponsibility for the safe conduct of his ship.

5.12.2 SURNAV System

Area of use: French territorial waters (12 mile limit) and the approaches.

a.   Six hours before entering French territorial waters.

b.   Before sailing from a French port or anchorage.

Circumstances of use: See official publications e.g.

a.   Lists of Radio Signals

b.   UK Notice to Mariners

c.   Annual Summary to UK Notices to Mariners.

Must be used by:

a.   Tankers carrying hydrocarbons, and vessels carrying dangerous cargoes which are navigating in the approaches to France and intending to enter French territorial waters.

b.   Any of the above vessels, within 50 miles of the French coast, which are damaged or have defects which would result in damage to the vessel or her cargo.

c.   Any vessel going to the assistance of a vessel covered by (a) above.

d.   Any of the above vessels whose circumstances have changed since their last report.

VHF stations to use:

Any French Coast radio station or traffic information station.

The SURNAV report should be addressed for forwarding to 'Marine Brest' or 'Marine Cherbourg' when you are in Atlantic waters, and 'Marine Toulon' when you are in Mediterranean waters.

VHF channels to use:

The working channels of any French coastguard (callsign — CROSMA + name) or coast radio station. The coast radio stations are listed in the ITU 'List of Coast Radio Stations' and supplements.

The Initial Call is to be made on the working VHF channel.

Fixed formats:

a.   SURNAV FRANCE   — initial report

b.   SURNAV AVARIES (i)   — damage/defect report

c.   SURNAV AVARIES (ii)   — proceeding to assistance report.

Code letters: SURNAV FRANCE

ALFA	Ship.
BRAVO	Date and time (GMT/UTC) of report.
CHARLIE	Position in latitude and longitude.
DELTA	Position — bearing and distance
ECHO	Course.
FOXTROT	Speed.
INDIA	Destination.
JULIETT	Date, time (GMT/UTC) and position of entering French territorial waters or getting underway.
KILO	Date, time (GMT/UTC) and position of leaving French territorial waters or of arriving at destination in French waters.
NOVEMBER	R/T watch being maintained.
PAPA	Draught.
QUEBEC	Cargo type (as defined in MARPOL 73 Annex I, Appendix I List of Oils, Annex II, Appendix II, List of Noxious Liquid Substances carried in bulk) and quantity.
ROMEO	Whether manoeuvring ability is normal or impaired by defects in propulsion, steering or anchoring equipment.
SIERRA	Whether operational fitness is normal or impaired by defects in radar, radio, safety, or ballasting equipment.

Code letters: SURNAV AVARIES (i)

ALFA	Ship.
BRAVO	Date and time (GMT/UTC) of report.
CHARLIE	Position.
ECHO	Course.
FOXTROT	Speed.
INDIA	Destination.
JULIETT	Time (GMT/UTC) and nature of call for assistance or towage.
KILO	Name of assisting vessel, if it is already present, or ETA (GMT/UTC).
MIKE	Name and telegraphic address of owner, character and any French consignee.
NOVEMBER	Radio watch being maintained.
PAPA	Draught.
QUEBEC	Cargo, type (as defined in MARPOL 73) and quantity.
ROMEO	Nature of damage or development of the situation.
TANGO	Any other information.

SECTION 5

Major communication subjects

SURNAV AVARIES (ii)

ALFA	Ship.
BRAVO	Data and time (GMT/UTC) of report.
CHARLIE	Position.
ECHO	Course.
FOXTROT	Speed.
INDIA	Destination.
JULIETT	Date, time (GMT/UTC) and position of casualty.
KILO	Name, nationality and callsign of casualty.
LIMA	Course of casualty, or destination, if known.
MIKE	Speed of casualty, if known.
NOVEMBER	Radio watch being maintained.
QUEBEC	Cargo of casualty (as defined in MARPOL 73) and quantity, if known.
ROMEO	Damage/defect suffered by casualty.
TANGO	Any other information.

Examples:

a.   *Initial report*

SURNAV FRANCE	
ALFA:	Hirondelle, French, Foxtrot Foxtrot Foxtrot Foxtrot.
BRAVO:	Zero-two, one-five, four-five UTC.
CHARLIE:	Four-eight degrees zero-one minutes North, zero-zero-six degrees four-five minutes West.
ECHO:	Zero-three-zero
FOXTROT:	One-four-decimal-eight.
INDIA:	Havre-Antifer.
JULIETT:	Zero-two, one-eight, one-eight UTC.
KILO:	Zero-three, zero-seven, zero-zero UTC.
NOVEMBER:	One-one, one-six.
PAPA:	Two-three-decimal-two-five.
QUEBEC:	Crude oil, two-five-zero thousand metric tonnes.
ROMEO:	Normal.
SIERRA:	Normal.

b. *Surnav Avaries (i)*

SURNAV AVARIES	
ALFA:	Hirondelle, French, Foxtrot Foxtrot Foxtrot Foxtrot.
BRAVO:	Zero-two, one-nine, four-five UTC.
DELTA:	Three-five-zero degrees two-eight miles from Isle d'Ouessant.
ECHO:	Zero-three-zero.
FOXTROT:	Four-decimal-five.
INDIA:	Havre-Antifer.
JULIETT:	Zero-two, one-nine, three-zero UTC. Tug requested.
KILO:	Smitlloyd Three. Two-zero-three-zero UTC.
MIKE:	Consignee Elf Aquitaine. Telephone number: three-three-two-one-two-four, Paris.
NOVEMBER:	One-one, one-six.
PAPA:	Two-three-decimal-two-five.
QUEBEC:	Crude oil, two-five-zero thousand metric tonnes.
ROMEO:	Steering gear not working.

c. *Surnav Avaries (ii)*

SURNAV AVARIES	
ALFA:	Smitlloyd three, Dutch, Papa Hotel Alfa Alfa.
BRAVO:	Zero-two, one-nine, five-zero UTC.
DELTA:	Three-five-zero degrees one-eight miles from Isle d'Ouessant.
ECHO:	Three-five-zero.
FOXTROT:	One-eight-decimal-zero.
JULIETT:	Zero-two, one-nine, three-zero UTC. Three-five-zero degrees two-eight miles from Isle d'Ouessant.
KILO:	Hirondelle, French, Foxtrot, Foxtrot, Foxtrot, Foxtrot.
LIMA:	Havre-Antifer.
MIKE:	Four-decimal-five.
NOVEMBER:	One-one, one-six.
QUEBEC:	Crude oil, two-five-zero thousand metric tonnes.
ROMEO:	Steering gear not working.
TANGO:	Smitlloyd Three is a salvage tug.

5.12.3 | IMO ship reporting system

CODE	SPOKEN AS	INFORMATION REQUIRED
A	alpha	**Ship:** name and call sign or ship station identity.
B	bravo	**Date and time of event** A six digit group giving date of month (first two digits), hours and minutes (last four digits) if other than UTC state time zone used.
C	charlie	**Position:** A four digit group giving latitude in degrees and minutes suffixed with N(North) or S(South) and a five digit group giving longitude in degrees and minutes suffixed with E (East) or W (West);
or	or	
D	delta	**Position:** A true bearing *from* (first 3 digits) a clearly defined landmark and a distance in nautical miles.
E	echo	**True Course:** A three digit group
F	foxtrot	**Speed in knots and tenths of knot:** A three digit group.
G	golf	**Port of departure:** Name of last port of call.
H	hotel	**Date, time and point of entry into system:** Entry time as expressed in (B) and entry position expressed as in (C) or (D).
I	india	**Destination and expected time of arrival at defined ETA point:** Name of port and date time group expressed as in (B).
J	juliet	**Pilot:** State pilot requirements at VTS destination *or* state whether a deep sea or local pilot is already on board.
K	kilo	**Date, time and point of exit from system:** Exit time expressed as in (B) and exit position expressed as in (C) or (D).
L	lima	**Route information:** Intended track.
M	mike	**Radio communications:** State in full names of stations/frequencies guarded.
N	november	**Time of next report:** Date, time, group expressed as in (B).
O	oscar	**Maximum present static draught in metres:** Four digit group giving metres and decimals of metre.
P	papa	**Cargo/Ballast** (see *Ballast) Cargo and brief details of any dangerous cargoes including harmful substances and gases that could endanger persons or the environment: 1. approximate type, e.g. oil, gas, chemical. 2. quantity in tonnes. 3. type according to IMDG code.
V	victor	**Medical personnel:** Doctor, physician's assistant, nurse.
W	whiskey	**Total number of persons on board:** State number.
X	x-ray	**Miscellaneous:** Any brief information — give brief details.

Note: if blank occurs put 'nil'.

5.13 | MEDICAL INFORMATION (non-urgent)

This subject covers all medical information of a non-urgent nature. Urgent medical information, i.e. concerning the saving of life, is dealt with under urgency communications (Pan-Pan) Section 5.2, and in Section 3.3.4 Medical communications, in particular 3.3.4.4, — the use of the medical section of the International Code of Signals.

Examples:

a. **Port health messages**

> Göteborg Harbour. This is Star Vega.
> INFORMATION: My vessel is healthy.
> REQUEST: Please grant free pratique.
> Over.

b. **Advice on treatment of minor ailments**

> West Cape Coastguard. This is Rose Maru.
> INFORMATION: A man has minor burns.
> REQUEST: Please provide medical advice.
> Over.

5.14 | ICE

This subject covers messages relating to ice, or navigation in and near ice. This includes icing, the meteorological conditions associated with ice, ice-breaker co-ordination and ice convoy operations.

It is obligatory to make a report when:

a. **Encountering dangerous ice.**
    This report must be made in the form of a Sécurité message and must contain:
    — type of ice,
    — position(s) of ice.
    — date and time of observation (GMT or UTC).
    (This report may be the subject of a Pan-Pan message if necessary).

b. **Encountering air temperature below freezing associated with gale force winds and causing severe ice accumulation on ships.**
    This report should be made in the form of a Sécurité message and must contain:
    — date and time of observation (GMT or UTC),
    — position where the conditions were encountered,
    — the air and sea temperatures,
    — the force and direction of the wind.

Examples:

a.   **Icing conditions information**

> **Reykjavik Radio. This is Arctic Prince.**
> **QUESTION: Is icing expected tomorrow, position: area:**
> **   South of Iceland?**
> **Over.**

b.   **Requests for ice-breaker assistance**

> **Kotka Harbour. This is Comet.**
> **INFORMATION: My position is: at the ice edge.**
> **REQUEST: Please provide ice-breaker assistance.**
> **Over.**

c.   **Organisation of ice convoy**

> **Vista. This is Viikari.**
> **INFORMATION: Ice-breaker assistance is commencing now.**
> **INSTRUCTION: Keep watch on VHF channel one-three.**
> **Over.**

The reply to the above call might be as follows:

> **Viikari. This is Vista.**
> **INFORMATION-RECEIVED: Ice-breaker assistance is**
> **   commencing now.**
> **INSTRUCTION-RECEIVED: Keep watch on VHF channel**
> **   one-three, Positive.**
> **Over.**

The next call might be as follows:

> **Vista. This is Viikari.**
> **INFORMATION: Your place in the convoy is place number:**
> **   one behind me and Rose Maru will follow you.***
> **Over.**

*See Section 4.6.5. Two messages in one.

5.15   SPECIAL OPERATIONS INFORMATION

This subject covers messages about special operations. These operations are defined in the International Regulations for the Prevention of Collision at Sea. The subject also covers messages about operations which are not normally conducted by merchant ships.

Examples:

a.   **Warning of a survey line**

> **Derringer. This is Decca One.**
> **WARNING: I am towing a seismic survey gear, length:**
> **one-decimal five miles.**
> **INSTRUCTION: Keep clear.**
> **Over.**

b.   **Imposing radio silence before venting on an oil rig**

> **All ships. This is Swallow Alfa.**
> **Radio Silence.**
> **WARNING: There will be gas venting operations today.**
> **INSTRUCTION: Keep radio silence inside range:**
> **one-thousand metres from Swallow Alfa rig,**
> **start time: one-four-zero-zero GMT,**
> **period: three-zero minutes.**
> **Out.**

c.   **Arranging for clear passage for an unmanoeuvrable tow**

> **Star Vega. This is Tug Oscar.**
> **ADVICE: Please keep clear of me, reason: my tow restricts**
> **my ability to manoeuvre.**
> **Over.**

d.   **Arranging lightening operations**

> **Norseman. This is China Star.**
> **INFORMATION: I am ready for you to come alongside me,**
> **and I am stopping now.***
> **Over.**

*See Section 4.6.5. Two messages in one.

5.16   ANCHOR OPERATIONS

Messages relating to anchors, anchor handling and anchoring.

Examples:

a.   **Announcing anchor up**

> **Varberg pilot boat. This is Good Faith.**
> **INFORMATION: My anchor is up.**
> **Over.**

b.   Asking if anchor is dragging

> Comet. This is Port de Ouest.
> QUESTION: Is your anchor dragging?
> Over.

c.   Ordering anchor up

> Star Vega. This is Freetown Pilot.
> INSTRUCTION: Weigh your anchor.
> Over.

d.   Directing to anchorage

> Rose Maru. This is Cambex Terminal.
> INSTRUCTION: Anchor in area: Alfa until there is
>   enough water to enter.
> Over.

5.17   ARRIVAL DETAILS

The required content of arrival messages will be found in the regulations issued by individual ports and national administrations.

The following example relates to one particular port and is shown only to illustrate this communication subject. It does not apply to all ports.

Information should be sought in the appropriate official publications before transmitting arrival details.

Example:

> Grandport. This is Abel Matutes.
> INFORMATION: My ETA is: one-seven-zero-zero GMT,
>   destination: area port terminal, approach
>   direction: North, tonnage: one-five-thousand
>   gross metric tonnes, draught: eight metres.
> Over.

When entering a port without such regulations, the amount of information in each transmission should be approximately half that shown in the above example, and should be organised into messages according to SEASPEAK principles.

Example: (first message transmission)

> Petitport. This is Abel Matutes.
> INFORMATION, one: My approach direction is: North, and my
>   destination is: area port terminal.
> INFORMATION, two: My ETA is: one-seven-zero-zero GMT.
> Over.

5.18 | PILOT ARRANGEMENTS

Messages relating to the ordering of a pilot and the arranging of his boarding or disembarkation.

Examples:

a. **Asking for the position of the pilot vessel**

> **Northport Harbour. This is Axel.**
> **QUESTION: What is the position of the pilot vessel?**
> **Over.**

b. **Asking for pilot ladder position**

> **Northport Pilot. This is Axel.**
> **QUESTION: Which side do you want the pilot ladder?**
> **Over.**

The reply to the above call should be as follows:

> **Axel. This is Northport Pilot.**
> **ANSWER: I want the pilot ladder on the port side, height:**
> **one metre above the water.**
> **Over.**

c. **Asking for a lee to be made**

> **Axel. This is Northport Pilot.**
> **ADVICE: Alter course to port through: four-five degrees**
> **and slow down to your minimum safe speed.**
> **Over.**

d. **Pilot service broadcasts**

> **All ships. This is Northport Pilot.**
> **INFORMATION: Northport pilot service is suspended, reason:**
> **gales. I say again, Northport pilot service is**
> **suspended, reason: gales.**
> **Out.**

5.19 | TUGS AND TOWAGE

Examples:

a. **Arranging tug operations**

> **Northport Harbour. This is Star Vega.**
> **QUESTION: How many tugs do I need?**
> **Over.**

b. Rendezvous with tugs

> Northport Harbour. This is Star Vega.
> QUESTION: What position will tugs meet me?
> Over.

c. Instructions to tugs when berthing

> Huskey. This is Star Vega.
> INSTRUCTION: Push on my starboard bow.
> Over.

d. Instructions from tugs when underway

> Star Vega. This is Huskey.
> ADVICE: Slacken your anchor now.
> Over.

5.20 BERTHING/UNBERTHING

Examples:

a. Informing a vessel which berth to go to

> Oscar. This is Northport Harbour.
> INFORMATION: Your berth is number:
>   one-five at Bell Dock.
> Over.

b. Rope handling instructions

> Star Vega forecastle. This is Star Vega bridge.
> INSTRUCTION: Put out the forward back spring.
> Over.

c. Warning of unusual circumstances to be expected during berthing

> Star Vega. This is Northport Harbour.
> WARNING: Do not turn your cargo gear outboard before
>   berthing, reason: shore cranes are near the edge of the
>   dock.
> Over.

d. Arranging entry to a lock

> Gammon. This is Northport Harbour.
> INSTRUCTION: Make fast on the lock tail now, and enter the lock
>   at time: one-five-zero-zero local.
> Over.

5.21 DEPARTURE DETAILS

Messages containing the information required of ships before their departure from ports.

The required content of departure messages will be found in the regulations issued by individual ports and national administrations.

The following example relates to one particular port, and is shown only to illustrate this communication subject. It does not apply to all ports. Information should be sought in the appropriate official publications before transmitting departure details.

Example:

> **Westport traffic. This is Gammon.**
> **INFORMATION: I am at berth number: two-five.**
> **INTENTION: I intend to leave via: the Narrows and Slow Pass.**
> ***INFORMATION: My ETA at position: The Narrows is time:**
>   **one-five-zero-zero local.**
> ***REQUEST: Please permit me to proceed.**
> **Over.**

*Transmissions should not normally contain more than two marked messages. However, in cases when SEASPEAK message marking principles are being applied to *regulation* transmissions (as in this example), the number of marked messages will be greater than two.

5.22 HELICOPTER and AIRCRAFT OPERATIONS

This subject covers messages relating to the operation of helicopters and aircraft in association with ships. It does not cover messages concerned with Search and Rescue operations. These are covered in Search and Rescue — Section 5.4.

Detailed guidance on the operation of helicopters with ships both in normal and emergency operations is given in the publication 'Guide to Helicopter/ Ship Operations' published by the International Chamber of Shipping. It lists the information that will be required by a helicopter going to a ship, and the types of messages that will be exchanged during the operations.

Examples:

a. **Discussion between ship and helicopter about conditions on deck**

> **Voyager. This is Helicopter Alfa Bravo.**
> **QUESTION: What is the relative wind direction and wind speed**
>   **across your deck?**
> **Stay on.**
> **Over.**

The conversation might proceed as follows:

Helicopter Alfa Bravo. This is Voyager.

ANSWER: The relative wind direction is: three-zero degrees on the port bow, and the relative wind speed is: two-five knots.

Over.

Voyager. This is Helicopter Alfa Bravo.

Understood. Relative wind direction: three-zero degrees on the port bow, relative wind speed: two-five knots.

QUESTION: What is the pitch and roll?

Over.

Helicopter Alfa Bravo. This is Voyager.

ANSWER: The pitch and roll is moderate.

Over.

---

b. **Information from ship about landing time**

Helicopter Alfa Bravo. This is Voyager.

ADVICE: Wait.

INFORMATION: I expect to be ready for you to approach after period: one-five minutes.

Over.

---

c. **Report of oil pollution**

Spray Tug. This is Aircraft Bravo Charlie.

INFORMATION: There is an oil slick from position: latitude: five-zero degrees three-zero minutes North, longitude: zero-six-two degrees zero-seven minutes West, length ten miles, direction: North-east.

Over.

---

d. **Cautionary message from aircraft patrol to fishing vessel**

Boston Rover. This is Aircraft Watchdog Three.

INFORMATION: You are fishing in a prohibited area.

INTENTION: I intend to report you to your national authorities.

Over.

5.23 PORT REGULATIONS

This subject covers messages relating to regulations applying when the ship is alongside in individual ports.

Examples:

a.   Cautionary message from port authority about engine trials.

> **Kalong Treasure. This is Southport Harbour.**
> **INFORMATION: You are not permitted to run your main**
>   **engine when you are at the berth.**
> **Over.**

b.   Informing incoming vessel of mooring regulations

> **Kalong Treasure. This is Southport Harbour.**
> **INFORMATION: Rat guards are mandatory at Southport.**
> **INSTRUCTION: Make ready rat guards for all your**
>   **lines before berthing.**
> **Over.**

c.   Request from ship to exchange stores.

> **Southport Harbour. This is Kalong Treasure.**
> **REQUEST: Please permit me to change stores with the ship**
>   **at the next berth.**
> **Over.**

5.24   TELEPHONE (TELEGRAM) LINK CALLS

This subject covers all messages between ship and coast radio stations relating to the making of telephone link calls or the transmission of telegrams.

The content of the telephone call or telegram itself is not included in this communication subject.

Examples:

a.   Message from coast radio station about standby channel and turn number

> **Isabella. This is Land's End Radio.**
> **ADVICE: Standby on VHF channel eight-three.**
> **INFORMATION: Your turn number is: four.**
> **Over.**

b.   Asking for a ship's accounting code

> **Isabella. This is Land's End Radio.**
> **QUESTION: What is your accounting code?**
> **Over.**

c.   Asking for the price of a call just made

> **Land's End Radio. This is Isabella.**
> **QUESTION: What was the charge for my call?**
> **Over.**

5.25 | RELAYING (non-safety)

This subject covers the relaying of all types of messages except those concerned with distress, urgency and safety which are dealt with in Section 3.

Relaying should not be conducted without the agreement of the originating station.

The station which is relaying a message must indicate clearly that the message originates from another station.

When the message has been successfully relayed the originating station should be informed.

Example:

> **Swatow Harbour. This is Cobalt Three.**
>
> **Relay message from Hansa to Swatow Harbour.**
>
> **INFORMATION: The ETA of Hansa at Swatow Harbour is time: two-three-zero-zero GMT.**
>
> **Over.**
>
> ---
>
> **Cobalt Three. This is Swatow Harbour.**
>
> **Relay message from Swatow Harbour to Hansa.**
>
> **INFORMATION-RECEIVED: The ETA of Hansa at Swatow Harbour is time: two-three-zero-zero GMT.**
>
> **Over.**
>
> ---
>
> **Hansa. This is Cobalt Three.**
>
> **Relay message from Swatow Harbour to Hansa.**
>
> **INFORMATION: Swatow Harbour received your message.**
>
> **Over.**

5.26 | CARGO and CARGO OPERATIONS

This subject covers all operations related to cargo, e.g. description of the cargo, unloading, stowage, segregation, loading, and securing. It does not include commercial and business matters (See Section 5.28).

Examples:

a. **Reporting type of cargo to a coastguard station**

> **Southport Coastguard. This is Paisano.**
>
> **INFORMATION: My cargo is: type: Arabian crude oil, quantity: two-four-zero thousand metric tonnes.**
>
> **Over.**

b. **Instruction from a port station for a ship to have its deck cargo ready for discharging.**

> **Paisano. This is Southport.**
>
> **ADVICE: Make ready your deck containers for discharging.**
>
> **Over.**

c.   Reporting location of cargo to a shore facility

> Bulkport Harbour. This is Astra.
> INFORMATION: The cargo for discharging is in hold number:
>   three, and hold number: four.
> Over.

d.   Giving cargo information to a ship

> Pacer. This is Bulkport Operations.
> INFORMATION: We have a cargo for you: type: phosphate,
>   quantity: one-four thousand metric tonnes.
> Over.

5.27   BUNKERING OPERATIONS

This subject covers all messages relating to fuelling operations.

Examples:

a.   **Request for bunkers**

> Shell Southport. This is Paisano.
> REQUEST: Please supply bunkers: quantity: two thousand metric
>   tonnes.
> Over.

b.   **Question about type of bunkers required**

> Paisano. This is Shell Southport.
> QUESTION, one: What is the oil type and redwood number?
> QUESTION, two: What is the maximum rate of delivery?
> Over.

c.   **Information about bunkering facilities**

> Bunkerage One. This is Paisano.
> INFORMATION: My main bunkering connection is aft, distance:
>   five metres forward of the superstructure.
> Over.

d.   **Information about time and method of delivery of bunkers**

> Paisano. This is Shell Southport.
> INFORMATION: Your bunkers will arrive by road tanker at time:
>   one-four-zero-zero local.
> QUESTION: Will you be ready?
> Over.

5.28 | AGENCY, BUSINESS and COMMERCE

This subject covers all messages relating to agency, business and commerce. These include messages about Charter Party arrangements, disciplinary matters and crewing.

Examples:

a. **Asking for De-rat Exemption Certificate to be renewed**

> **Maritime. This is Star Vega.**
> **REQUEST: Please arrange the renewal of my De-rat Exemption Certificate.**
> **Over.**

b. **Informing the charterer that the ship is ready to load**

> **Eastport Agency. This is Gammon.**
> **INFORMATION: The ship is prepared according to the Charter Party terms and I am ready to load.**
> **Over.**

c. **Asking for transportation for crew**

> **Maritime. This is Star Vega.**
> **INFORMATION: The new chief engineer will arrive at Mombasa on flight number: XA three-zero-one, time: zero-five-zero-zero local.**
> **REQUEST: Please send a car to meet him.**
> **Over.**

d. **Instruction from charterers' agent that ship is to proceed to a different destination.**

> **Gammon. This is Eastport Agency.**
> **ADVICE: Proceed to Southport, reason: there is a cargo for you.**
> **Over.**

5.29 | SHIP'S STORES

This subject covers messages relating to ship's stores which can include engineering stores and fresh water.

Examples:

a.   **Informing agent of stores required**

> **Maritime. This is Star Vega.**
> **Ship's stores list.**
> **REQUEST: Please deliver:**
> > **quantity: two metric tonnes potatoes,**
> > **quantity: four sides beef,**
> > **quantity: two-zero-zero litres deck paint, green**
> > **quantity: two-zero-zero litres lube oil,**
> > **quantity: four-five metric tonnes fresh water.**
> **Over.**

b.   **Describing spares needed**

> **Maritime. This is Gammon.**
> **REQUEST: Please deliver an injector, manufacturer: Bosch, part**
> > **number: Bravo-stroke-seven-nine-stroke-zero-one-**
> > **two-one-four-hyphen-two, type: one-five-Bravo.**
> **Over.**

c.   **Requesting equipment for ship.**

> **Maritime. This is Gammon.**
> **REQUEST: Please supply welding equipment and quantity: four**
> > **sets of gas bottles, reason: urgent repair.**
> **INFORMATION: We have qualified welders on board.**
> **Over.**

5.30   UNCLASSIFIED MESSAGES

This subject covers messages relating to any subject which is not listed as a major communication subject.

Example:

> **Paisano. This is Gammon.**
> **QUESTION: Is John Dawson chief engineer, still?**
> **Over.**

5.31   RADIO CHECKS

This subject covers messages about the checking of radio equipment. This does not include reports on overall readability which are dealt with in Section 2.2.4.

Guidance on how to conduct radio checks is given in Regulations 5058–5060 and Appendix 15 of the ITU Radio Rules (1982 ed.).

The SINPFEMO code set out in Section 2.2.4 provides a system for reporting on R/T signals.

Examples:

a. Request for a report on radio interference

> Bergen Radio. This is Pacer.
> QUESTION: What is the effect of interference on my transmission: Over.

b. Report on modulation of received signals

> Axel. This is Leningrad Radio.
> INFORMATION: The modulation of your transmission is poor. Over.

c. Request for a report on signal strength for maintenance purposes

> Yokohama Radio. This is Brisbane Queen.
> REQUEST: Please provide a full SINPFEMO report on my signals, reason: maintenance.
> Over.

5.32   CLOSING DOWN (Shutting down)

This subject covers all messages about the closing down of a radio station. In certain ports it is obligatory to make these transmissions.

Examples:

a. **Report to harbour authority on closing down after berthing.**

> Westport Harbour. This is Cleopatra.
> INFORMATION: Berthing at berth number: two-five is completed.
> INTENTION: I intend to close down now.
> Over.

b. **Report to coastguard station on closing down for emergency radio repairs whilst in a traffic separation scheme.**

> East Cape Harbour. This is Gammon.
> INFORMATION: I intend to close down my VHF station now, period: one-five minutes, reason: aerial repairs.
> Over.

c. **Broadcast by an oil rig on closing down for operational purposes**

> All ships. This is Swan Alfa.
> INFORMATION: We intend to close down all radio frequencies now, reason: gas venting.
> Over.

SECTION

6

Full conversations

6.0 GENERAL INTRODUCTION

This section contains three complete VHF conversations organised according to the principles of SEASPEAK. These examples show how the various features of SEASPEAK: VHF procedure, prefixing of quantities, message checking, message marking, standard phrases, message length, message patterns, transmissions length, and so on, control the conversation.

In all three examples the standard phrases e.g. This is ...., are underlined; the standard marker words are followed by a colon e.g. distance:, time:, period:, and message markers are in capital letters and are also followed by a colon e.g. WARNING:, QUESTION:, INSTRUCTION:

N.B. Conversations will not normally contain as many transmissions as are given here; these particular examples have been specially constructed to demonstrate how certain problems, such as loss of contact, interruption, and mistakes are dealt with in SEASPEAK.

6.1 EXAMPLE 1. Inter-ship

Nippon Maru is at sea in the South Atlantic and is on passage from Buenos Aires to Yokohama. She sees Gulf Trader going in the opposite direction. Knowing that there is congestion at Buenos Aires, Nippon Maru calls up Gulf Trader to inform her of the current situation and its cause. As this is an inter-ship exchange, the Initial Call is made on VHF channel 16.

Nippon Maru	**Gulf-Trader, Gulf Trader.** *This is* **Nippon Maru[1], Juliett-Sierra-Alfa-Alfa; Nippon Maru, Juliett-Sierra-Alfa-Alfa.** *On VHF channel* **one-six[2].** *Over.*
Gulf Trader	**Nippon Maru, Juliett-Sierra-Alfa-Alfa.** *This is* **Gulf Trader, Alfa-Six-Zulu-Zulu.** *Over.*
Nippon Maru	**Gulf Trader,** *This is* **Nippon Maru.** *Switch to VHF channel* **zero-six.** *Over.*
Gulf Trader	**Nippon Maru.** *This is* **Gulf Trader.** *Agree VHF channel* **two-six.** *Over.*
Nippon Maru	**Gulf Trader.** *This is* **Nippon Maru.** *Mistake. Switch to VHF channel* **zero-six.** *I say again.* *Switch to VHF channel* **zero-six.** *Over.*
Gulf Trader	**Nippon Maru.** *This is* **Gulf Trader.** *Correction. Agree VHF channel* **zero-six.** *Over.*

Switch-over rules	**Both stations listen for a short period on VHF channel 16.**
	Both stations switch to VHF channel 06.
	Both stations listen for a short period on VHF channel 06.
	
	    However, another conversation is heard in progress on VHF channel 06.
	    The Controlling Station (Nippon Maru) switches back to the calling VHF channel (16).
	    Gulf Trader hearing nothing from Nippon Maru switches back to the calling VHF channel (16).
	    The Controlling Station then re-establishes contact on the calling VHF channel (16).

Nippon Maru	**Gulf Trader.** *This is* **Nippon Maru.** *On VHF channel* **one-six.** *Over.*
Gulf Trader	**Nippon Maru.** *This is* **Gulf Trader.** *Over.*
Nippon Maru	**Gulf Trader.** *This is* **Nippon Maru.** *Switch to VHF channel* **zero-eight[3].** *Over.*
Gulf Trader	**Nippon Maru.** *This is* **Gulf Trader.** *Agree VHF channel* **zero-eight.** *Over.*
Switch-over rules	**Both stations listen for a short period on VHF channel 16.** **Both stations switch to VHF channel 08.** **Both stations listen for a short period on VHF channel 08.**

	VHF channel 08 is not in prior use, therefore they proceed with the exchange.
Nippon Maru	**Gulf Trader.** *This is* **Nippon Maru.** **QUESTION: What is your destination?** *Stay on.* *Over.*
Gulf Trader	**Nippon Maru.** *This is* **Gulf Trader.** **ANSWER: My destination is Buenos Aires.** *Over.*
Nippon Maru	**Gulf Trader.** *This is* **Nippon Maru.** **Understood, Buenos Aires.** **INFORMATION: A vessel is aground, position: near Practicos Interseccion Light Vessel.** *Stay on.* *Over.*
Gulf Trader	**Nippon Maru.** *This is* **Gulf Trader.** *Say again,* **all after position.** *Over.*
Nippon Maru	**Gulf Trader.** *This is* **Nippon Maru.** *I say again.* **Position: near Practicos Interseccion Light Vessel.** *Over.*
Gulf Trader	**Nippon Maru.** *This is* **Gulf Trader.** **INFORMATION-RECEIVED: A vessel is aground position: near Practicos Interseccion Light Vessel.** *Over.*
Nippon Maru	**Gulf Trader.** *This is* **Nippon Maru.** **INFORMATION: A delay is expected in the approaches, period: four-eight hours.** *Over.*
Gulf Trader	**Nippon Maru.** *This is* **Gulf Trader.** **INFORMATION-RECEIVED: A delay is expected in the approaches, period: four-eight hours.** *Thank you.* *Over.*
Nippon Maru	**Gulf Trader.** *This is* **Nippon Maru.** *Nothing more.* *Out*[4].
	Both stations listen on VHF channel 08 for a short period in order to allow either to renew the exchange if necessary. **Both stations switch back to VHF channel 16.**

Note 1.   Nippon Maru is the Controlling Station as he is making the Initial Call.

Note 2.   Nippon Maru states which VHF channel the call is made on in case Gulf Trader is keeping dual watch.

Note 3.   VHF channel 08 was picked as it is number two in priority of choice for use in inter-ship communication (see Section 1.2.2 which gives a table showing ITU approved usage of VHF channels).

Note 4.   The Controlling Station terminates the call.

6.2 EXAMPLE 2. Shore Radio Station

Western Sky, approaching Singapore via the East Johore Strait, calls up Singapore Port Operations to confirm her time of arrival (ETA) at the pilot station. Western Sky has looked up Singapore Port Operations' working VHF channel and therefore makes the Initial Call on that VHF channel (channel 12).

Star Vega is another ship approaching Singapore. She fails to listen on the working channel before making her Initial Call and therefore causes an interruption which is dealt with by Singapore Port Operations. It is important to note that Singapore Port Operations becomes the Controlling Station (CS), although it did not make the Initial Call, because it is a Shore Radio Station.

	Western Sky listens on VHF channel 12 before making the Initial Call on this channel to make sure that he is not interrupting.
Western Sky	**Singapore Port Operations, Singapore Port Operations.** *This is* **Western Sky, Nine-Victor-Alfa-Tango; Western Sky, Nine-Victor-Alfa-Tango.** *On VHF channel* **one-two.** *Over.*
Singapore Port Ops.	**Western Sky, Western Sky.** *This is* **Singapore Port Operations.** *Over*[1].
switch-over rules	These do not need to be applied.
Western Sky	**Singapore Port Operations.** *This is* **Western Sky.** **INFORMATION: My ETA position: East Johore Pilot station is time: one-three-four-five UTC.** *Over.*
Singapore Port Ops.	**Western Sky.** *This is* **Singapore Port Operations.** *Mistake.* **Time is: one-four-three-zero UTC now.** *Stay on.* *Over.*
Western Sky	**Singapore Port Operations.** *This is* **Western Sky.** *Correction.* **My ETA is: one-five-four-five UTC.** *Over.*

SECTION

6

Full conversations

Singapore Port Ops.	**Western Sky.** *This is* **Singapore Port Operations.** **INFORMATION-RECEIVED: Your ETA position: East Johore pilot station is time: one-five-four-five UTC.** **INSTRUCTION: Anchor in the General Purpose Anchorage, reason: your berth is occupied.**
Star Vega	**Singapore Port Operations[2], Singapore Port Operations.** *This is* **Star Vega, Golf-Alfa-Alfa-Alfa; Star Vega Golf-Alfa-Alfa-Alfa.** *On VHF channel* **one-two.** *Over.*
Singapore Port Ops.	*Interruption[3].* **Star Vega.** *This is* **Singapore Port Operations.** *Stop transmitting.* *Out.*
Singapore Port Ops.	**Western Sky.** *This is* **Singapore Port Operations.** *Please acknowledge,* **anchorage instruction.** *Over.*
Western Sky	**Singapore Port Operations.** *This is* **Western Sky.** **INSTRUCTION-RECEIVED: Anchor in the General Purpose Anchorage.** *Nothing more.* *Over.*
Singapore Port Ops.	**Western Sky. This is Singapore Port Operations.** *Out.*
termination rules	Both stations listen on VHF channel 12 for a short period. Both stations resume watch on the appropriate watch-keeping channel.

Note 1.   Singapore Port Operations is a shore radio station and therefore becomes the Controlling Station.

Note 2.   Interruption by a non-involved station.

Note 3.   Controlling Station deals with interruption.

6.3   EXAMPLE 3. Broadcast

Kotka Radio in Finland is making a regular broadcast about the ice conditions in the Gulf of Riga. The broadcast message content is repeated to allow recipients time to write it down.

Kotka Radio	**All ships in Gulf of Riga; all ships in Gulf of Riga.** *This is* **Kotka Radio, Kotka Radio.** Ice information. *Switch to VHF channel* **two-five.** *Over.*
switch-over rules	Kotka Radio listens on VHF channel 16 for a short period in case any station required a repeat of the working VHF channel number. Kotka Radio switches to VHF channel 25.

Kotka Radio	**All ships in Gulf of Riga, all ships in Gulf of Riga.** *This is* **Kotka Radio, Kotka Radio.**
	Ice information, area: Gulf of Riga.
	INFORMATION: The ice type is: winter fast ice,
	                     ice change: no change,
	                     ice navigation: ice-breaker assistance is necessary.
	I say again.
	INFORMATION: The ice type is: winter fast ice,
	                     ice change: no change,
	                     ice navigation: ice-breaker assistance is necessary.
	Out.

termination rules	Kotka Radio listens on VHF channel 25 for a short period to allow stations to respond to the broadcast should they wish to do so. Kotka radio resumes normal VHF watchkeeping.

SECTION 6.
EXERCISES

The following exercises should be attempted *after* practice with the full conversations in the section has been completed. Guidance on the use of those conversations for practice purposes is given in the training introduction to the section (page 149)

These exercises are designed to give learners an opportunity to simulate full SEASPEAK conversations and by so doing to practise a wide range of the recommendations made in the manual.

Up to this point the exercises provided at the end of sections have concentrated on particular aspects of Seaspeak. Here is a reminder:

— In Section 1 the emphasis was on the transmission of *numbers, letters, callsigns, positions.*

— In Section 2 the emphasis was on the *pattern* of the total conversation, and on the *content, sequence* and *form* of the transmissions required to make and maintain contact.

— In Section 3 the emphasis was on the special format of *distress communications.*

— In Section 4 the emphasis was on the use of *standard phrases* (the simple language tools used to make and maintain contact and manage the conversation), and on the *construction of messages.*

— In Section 5 the emphasis was on practising the language recommendations in the context of a variety of communication purposes.

Performance of the exercises which follow will require the simultaneous operation of many of those aspects, with very few directions to guide you. Working from the information provided, it is necessary for the learner to assume the rôle of a communicator at one of the VHF stations given and to conduct a satisfactory conversation with the other station. This can be done between pairs of students of equal proficiency, between student and teacher, or between already competent students and those less advanced.

A brief resumé of the information known to each station is given, and it is the job of the communicators to make contact and to exchange that information in the most efficient manner. If communication links can be set up so that the participants can operate in positions remote from each other, so much the better. Indeed, once a degree of procedural and language competence is achieved, the more that can be done to simulate actual VHF radio conditions, the more valuable the training becomes.

In the early stages of practice with these exercises, it may be necessary for learners to refer to other parts of the Manual. Initially, therefore, it will be of help if the conversations are planned and written out by the participants, in advance of their engaging in voice communication. However, the ultimate test of competence is of course the ability to work directly from the brief notes provided.

As in the case elsewhere in this manual, the exercises provided can be manipulated, extended and enhanced infinitely, by making changes to the data given and by the introduction of complicating yet germane influences, such as noise, interference, and interruption.

Ex. 6.1

A VHF conversation takes place between two ships at sea. Ship "SAINT ROSE" heading for an area where new oil rigs have been established. The other ship "DESTREHAN" knows the exact position of these rigs and passes on the information, in response to a question from SAINT ROSE. Initial contact is made on VHF channel 16 and a suitable working channel is selected.

SAINT ROSE knows that new oil rigs are established in the following positions:

Rig Alfa	25°	02.2′N
	90°	06.2′W
Rig Bravo	25°	07.0′N
	90°	36.0′W
Rig Charlie	25°	11.2′N
	89°	58′W

SAINT ROSE also knows that safety fairways are established in direction 278° from

25° 03.0′N		
90° 06.0′W	to	25 08′N
		90 37′W

DESTREHAN asks for the width of the safety fairway.

SAINT ROSE replies stating that the fairway is one mile wide and that oil rig Alfa is close to the south side of the fairway.

Ex. 6.2

A VHF conversation takes place between a tanker (BLUE SKY) and an oil terminal (MOBIL SABINE) some time before the ship arrives in the vicinity of the terminal. The initial call is made on a known working VHF channel.

The information known to the ship is as follows:

The cargo is 50,000 tonnes of crude oil of the type known as 'Arabian Light'.
The maximum discharge rate is 7,500 tonnes per hour.
The ship has discharge pipelines on the port side only.
The draught of the ship is 12 metres 20 cms.
E.T.A Sabine Pilot 04.00 March 18th.

The information known to the oil terminal is as follows:

The maximum permitted draft is 12 metres. There are lighters to discharge surplus. The capacity of the lighters is 1,000 tonnes. The terminal is able to provide only two lighters per day. The maximum permitted discharge rate into lighters is 500 tonnes per hour. The maximum permitted pumping rate ashore is 5000 tonnes per hour. Lighters will be available after 6 hours. Ship must be fully inerted at all times.

A suggested sequence for this conversation is as follows:

1. The ship calls the terminal and gives details of draught and cargo.

2. The terminal acknowledges the information, informs the ship of the draught limitations and indicates that it has more to say.

3. The ship acknowledges the fresh information.

4. The terminal gives the information about lighters and shore facilities.

5. The ship acknowledges the fresh information and asks what time will the lighter operation begin.

6. The terminal indicates a delay of six hours.

    N.B. The terminal does not talk about the port side restriction, because they are able to manage the restriction without further discussion.

Ex. 6.3

The ship "Fruit Express" is approaching Wandelaar Pilot Station (working VHF channel 06) en route to Antwerpen. She has information to transmit to both the Pilot Station (Wandelaar Pilot) and her Agent (Belge Fruit). The Agent may be contacted through Ostend Radio, using a link call on VHF channel 66. Ship is number 5 on list. Commercial information must be sent via the Coast Station. Sort the information, make Seaspeak conversations accordingly. Agent's number is 32–3–448–73–52.

The information known to the ship is as follows:

    The cargo is bananas (2,000 tonnes)

    The ship requires berthing priority

    The normal berth used is called Geest

    The ship's draft is 6.3 metres

    The ship's present speed is 23 knots

    The ETA at Wandelaar Pilot is 06.40 local on September 24th

    The ship has no defects

The information known to the agent is as follows:

    A berth will be available.

    The name of the berth is Fyffe

    Discharge will begin immediately after berthing is completed

    The discharge will be 6 hours

The information known to the pilot is as follows:

    There is a pilot delay of one hour

    The maximum speed in the river is 18 knots

Ex. 6.4

A VHF conversation takes place between a ship "Atlantic Rover" and a coastguard station Falmouth Coastguard following the discovery, by the ship, of some wreckage. Initial contact is made on VHF channel 16 and a suitable working VHF channel is then selected.

The ship has observed the wreckage of a yellow and black yacht, of the type known as a catamaran. The name is not visible and no survivors are sighted. It looks like an old wreck. Its position is 49° 20.25′ N 07° 32.6′ W.

The coastguard acknowledges the information and asks the ship to confirm the position. The coastguard also asks the ship to check that the wreck is a catamaran because a trimaran is reported missing.

The ship is unable to provide more information but it does repeat that the wreck is probably old because of seaweed on the hull.

Ex. 6.5

A VHF conversation takes place prior to a berthing operation. The shore station (Goteborg Port Traffic) calls the ship (Silja Queen) on a working channel (VHF channel 12).

The shore station tells the ship that the berth is called *Skeepsbron Number 2* and that the ship will be expected to berth *port side alongside.*

The shore station suggests the following arrangement of tugs:

    Take: — one tug on the port bow

            — one tug on the starboard bow

            — one tug on the starboard quarter

The shore station advises the ship to have heavy wires ready fore and aft, and to keep the passenger gangway stowed.

The shore station informs the ship that a gangway will be provided by the shore.

The ship asks what lines are required, and the shore station answers that the forward lines required are: three headlines, two breastropes and two springs. The aft lines required are three sternlines, two breastropes and two springs. The shore station also informs the ship that rat guards are required.

Ex. 6.6

An urgent VHF conversation takes place between a ship (EVERGLADES) and a shore (CIENFUEGOS) because the ship has suffered a major breakdown and requires immediate assistance. The rules governing the special communications necessary here are covered in Section 3 of this manual.

The information known to the ship is as follows:

    There is a major engine breakdown.

    The position of the ship is

                21° 30′N
                81° 30′W.

    Port repair facilities are required.

    The ship is directly in the path of a hurricane (code name EDNA).

    The hurricane is 500 miles away from the ship on a bearing of 105°.

    The immediate assistance of a salvage tug is required.

    The shore station transmits the following information after having confirmed the information from the ship:

        The salvage tug *Liberdad de los Pueblos* will leave after two hours.

        The tug will be at the ship's position after 6 hours.

ANSWERS

Ex. 6.1

1. Destrehan, Destrehan. This is Saint Rose, Saint Rose, on VHF channel one-six. Over.

2. Saint Rose. This is Destrehan. Over.

3. Destrehan. This is Saint Rose. Switch to VHF channel zero-six. Over.

4. Saint Rose. This is Destrehan. Agree VHF channel zero-six. Over.

5. Destrehan. This is Saint Rose. Question: Are there new oil rigs in sea area position Latitude two-five degrees North; Longitude zero-nine-zero degrees West. Over.

6. Saint Rose. This is Destrehan. Answer: Positive: There are new oil rigs in sea area position: Latitude two-five degrees North; Longitude zero-nine-zero degrees West. Information one: Rig Alpha Position: Latitude two-five degrees zero-two decimal two minutes North; Longitude zero-nine-zero degrees zero-six decimal two minutes West Stay on. Over.

7. Destrehan. This is Saint Rose. Information one received: Rig Alpha Position Latitude two-five degrees zero-two decimal two minutes North; Longitude zero-nine-zero degrees zero-six decimal two minutes West. Over.

8. Saint Rose. This is Destrehan. Information two: Rig Bravo Position Latitude two-five degrees zero-seven minutes North; Longitude zero-nine-zero degrees three-six minutes West. Stay on. Over.

9. Destrehan. This is Saint Rose. Information two received: Rig Bravo Position Latitude two-five degrees zero-seven North; Longitude zero-nine-zero degrees three-six minutes West. Over.

10. Saint Rose. This is Destrehan. Information three: Rig Charlie Position Latitude two-five degrees one-one decimal two North; Longitude zero-eight-nine degrees five-eight minutes West. Stay on. Over.

11. Destrehan. This is Saint Rose. Information three received: Rig Charlie Position Latitude two-five degrees one-one decimal two North; Longitude zero-eight-nine degrees five-eight minutes West. Over.

12. Saint Rose. This is Destrehan. Information four: Safety fairway is established in direction two-seven-eight degrees from position: Latitude two-five degrees zero-three North; Longitude zero-nine-zero degrees zero-six minutes West to position Latitude two-five degrees zero-eight minutes North; Longitude zero-nine-zero degrees three-seven minutes West. Over.

13. Destrehan. This is Saint Rose. Information four received: Safety fairway is established in direction two-seven-eight degrees from Latitude two-five degrees zero-three North; Longitude zero-nine-zero degrees zero-six minutes West to position Latitude two-five degrees zero eight minutes North; Longitude zero-nine-zero degrees three seven minutes West. Question: What is the width of the safety fairway. Over.

14. Saint Rose. This is Destrehan. Answer: Safety fairway is one mile wide. Information: Rig Alpha is close to South side of safety fairway. Nothing more. Over.

15. Destrehan. This is Saint Rose. Understood: Safety fairway is one mile wide. Information received: Rig Alpha is close to South side of safety fairway. Nothing more. Thank you. Out.

Ex. 6.2

1. Mobil Sabine, Mobil Sabine. This is Blue Sky, Blue Sky on VHF channel 68 Alpha. Over.

2. Blue Sky. This is Mobil Sabine.

3. Mobil Sabine. This is Blue Sky. Information one: ETA Sabine Pilot zero-three-one-eight zero-four-zero-zero local. Stay on. Over.

4. Blue Sky. This is Mobil Sabine. Information one received: ETA Sabine Pilot March one-eight zero-four-zero-zero local. Over.

5. Mobil Sabine. This is Blue Sky. Information two: Draft is one-two decimal two-zero metres. Stay on. Over.

6. Blue Sky. This is Mobil Sabine. Information two received: Draft is one-two decimal two-zero metres. Over.

7. Mobil Sabine. This is Blue Sky. Information three: Cargo is five-zero thousand tonnes Arabian light crude. Maximum discharge rate seven decimal five thousand tonnes per hour. Stay on. Over.

8. Blue Sky. This is Mobil Sabine. Information three received: Your cargo is five zero thousand tonnes Arabian light crude. Maximum discharge rate seven decimal five thousand tonnes per hour. Over.

9. Mobil Sabine. This is Blue Sky. Information four: This ship has discharge pipelines on port side only. Over.

10. Blue Sky. This is Mobil Savine. Information four received: Your ship has discharge pipelines on port side only. Information one: Maximum permitted draft one-two metres. Information two: Surplus cargo to be discharged into lighters. Stay on. Over.

11. Mobil Sabine. This is Blue Sky. Information one received: Maximum permitted draft one-two metres. Information two received: Surplus cargo to be discharged into lighters. Over.

12. Blue Sky. This is Mobil Sabine. Information three: Two lighters per day. Capacity each lighter one thousand tonnes. Maximum permitted discharge rate into lighters five-zero-zero tonnes per hour. Stay on. Over.

13. Mobil Sabine. This is Blue Sky. Information three received: Two lighters per day. Capacity each lighter one thousand tonnes. Maximum permitted discharge rate into lighters five-zero-zero per hour. Over.

14. Blue Sky. This is Mobil Sabine. Information four: Maximum permitted discharge rate ashore five thousand tonnes per hour. Instruction: Ship must be inerted at all times.

15. Mobil Sabine. This is Blue Sky. Information four received: Maximum permitted discharge rate ashore five thousand tonnes per hour. Instruction received: Ship must be inerted at all times. Positive. Question: What is ETA of first lighter. Over.

16. Blue Sky. This is Mobil Sabine. Answer: ETA of first lighter is six hours after your arrival. Nothing more. Over.

17. Mobil Sabine. This is Blue Sky. Nothing more. Out.

Ex 6.3

Conversation with Wandelaar Pilot

1. Wandelaar Pilot, Wandelaar Pilot. This is Fruit Express, Fruit Express on VHF channel one-six. Over.

2. Fruit Express. This is Wandelaar Pilot. Switch to VHF channel zero-six. Over.

3. Wandelaar Pilot. This is Fruit Express. Agree VHF channel zero-six. Over.

4. Fruit Express. This is Wandelaar Pilot on VHF channel zero-six. Over.

5. Wandelaar Pilot. This is Fruit Express.
   Information: ETA Wandelaar zero-six-four-zero local
   Draft: six decimal three metres
   Speed: two-three knots
   No defects
   Stay on. Over.

6. Fruit Express. This is Wandelaar Pilot.
   Information received: ETA Wandelaar zero-six-four-zero local
   Draft: six decimal three metres
   Speed: two-three knots
   No defects
   Question: What is your cargo. Over.

7. Wandelaar Pilot. This is Fruit Express. Answer: Cargo is two thousand tonnes bananas. Request: Request berthing priority. Over.

8. Fruit Express. This is Wandelaar Pilot. Request received: You request berthing priority. Information: Pilot delay is one hour. Maximum permissible river speed one-eight knots. Question: Do you have berth allocated. Over.

9. Wandelaar Pilot. This is Fruit Express. Information received: Pilot delay is one hour. Maximum river speed one-eight knots. Answer: No berthing information available. Wait one-zero minutes. Nothing more. Over.

10. Fruit Express. This is Wandelaar Pilot. Request: Call on VHF channel zero-six when berthing information available. Over.

11. Wandelaar Pilot. This is Fruit Express. Request received: Call on VHF channel zero-six when berthing information received. Positive. Over.

12. Fruit Express. This is Wandelaar Pilot. Nothing more. Out.

Conversation with Agent, Belge Fruit
(Note: This conversation is by "link call", duplex telephone, therefore no necessity for word "over".)

1. Ostend Radio, Ostend Radio. This is Fruit Express, Fruit Express. Over.

2. Fruit Express. This is Ostend Radio. Switch to VHF channel six-six. Over.

3. Ostend Radio. This is Fruit Express. Agree VHF channel six-six. Over.

4. Fruit Express. This is Ostend Radio on VHF channel six-six. Over.

5. Ostend Radio. This is Fruit Express. Request: Link call to number three-two-three-four-four-eight-seven-three-five-two. Over

6. Fruit Express. This is Ostend Radio. Request: Link call to number three-two-three-four-four-eight-seven-three-five-two. Positive. Advice: Turn number five. Stand by on VHF channel six-six. Over.

7. Ostend Radio. This is Fruit Express. Advice received: Standing by on VHF channel six-six. Over.

8. Fruit Express. This is Ostend Radio. Nothing more. Out.

LATER

9. Fruit Express. This is Ostend Radio. Over

10. Ostend Radio. This is Fruit Express. Over

11. Fruit Express. This is Ostend Radio. Link call for you on VHF channel six-six. Over.

PAUSE

page 158

12. Fruit Express. This is Belge Fruit.

13. Belge Fruit. This is Fruit Express.

14. (Belge Fruit speaking) Information: Berth Fyffe available time: now. Discharge will commence on arrival. Discharge complete in period: six hours. Question: What is your ETA Wandelaar.

15. (Fruit Express speaking) Information received: Berth Fyffe available time: now. Discharge will commence on arrival. Discharge complete in period: six hours. Answer: ETA Wandelaar zero-six-four-zero local. Information: Maximum river speed one-eight knots.

16. (Belge Fruit speaking) Information received: ETA Wandelaar zero-six-four-zero, maximum river speed one-eight knots. Nothing more.

LATER

Conversation with Wandelaar

1. Wandelaar Pilot. This is Fruit Express on VHF channel zero-six. Over.

2. Fruit Express. This is Wandelaar Pilot. Question: Do you have berth available. Over.

3. Wandelaar Pilot. This is Fruit Express. Answer: Positive. Berth available time: now. Name: Fyffe. Over.

4. Fruit Express: This is Wandelaar Pilot. Advice: Approach Pilot station. Nothing more. Out.

5. Wandelaar Pilot. This is Fruit Express. Advice received: Approach Pilot station. Positive. Nothing more. Out.

Note: Initial conversation with Wandelaar can be made using a fixed format message.

Ex. 6.4

1. Falmouth Coastguard, Falmouth Coastguard. This is Atlantic Rover, Atlantic Rover. Over.

2. Atlantic Rover. This is Falmouth Coastguard. Switch to VHF channel one-one. Over.

3. Falmouth Coastguard. This is Atlantic Rover. Agree VHF channel one-one. Over.

4. Atlantic Rover. This is Falmouth Coastguard. On VHF channel one-one. Over.

5. Falmouth Coastguard. This is Atlantic Rover. Information one: Wreckage sighted in position: Latitude four-nine degrees two-zero decimal two-five minutes North; Longitude zero-zero-seven degrees three-two decimal six minutes West. Information two: Wreckage of yacht type: catamaran. Colour: black and yellow. Stay on. Over.

6. Atlantic Rover. This is Falmouth Coastguard. Information one received: Wreckage sighted in position: Latitude four-nine degrees two-zero decimal two-five minutes North; Longitude zero-zero-seven degrees three-two decimal six minutes West. Information two received: Wreckage of yacht type: catamaran. Colour: black and yellow. Question: Are there any survivors. Over.

7. Falmouth Coastguard. This is Atlantic Rover. Answer: Negative. There are no survivors. Information three: Wreckage is old. Hull is covered in seaweed. Over.

8. Atlantic Rover. This is Falmouth Coastguard. Information three received: Wreckage is old. Hull covered in seaweed. Request: Please confirm position and type of yacht. Information: Yacht type trimaran missing in area. Over.

9. Falmouth Coastguard. This is Atlantic Rover. Request received: Positive. Position and type of yacht. Correct. Wreckage is old. Hull covered in seaweed. Information: No trimaran sighted. Nothing more. Over.

10. Atlantic Rover. This is Falmouth Coastguard. Information received. Nothing more. Out.

Note: Falmouth Coastguard would probably broadcast a Securite message concerning the wreckage immediately after the conversation above.

Ex 6.5

1. Silja Queen. Silja Queen. This is Goteborg Port Traffic. Goteborg Port Traffic. On VHF channel one-two. Over.

2. Goteborg Port Traffic. This is Silja Queen. Over.

3. Silja Queen. This is Goteborg Port Traffic. Information one: Your berth Skeepsbron number two. Port side alongside. Stay on. Over.

4. Goteborg Port Traffic. This is Silja Queen. Information one received: My berth Skeepsbron number two. Port side alongside. Over.

5. Silja Queen. This is Goteborg Port Traffic. Information two: Tugs provided quantity: one for port bow; quantity: one for starboard bow; quantity: one for starboard quarter. Stay on. Over.

6. Goteborg Port Traffic. This is Silja Queen. Information two received: Tugs provided quantity: one for port bow; quantity: one for starboard bow; quantity: one for starboard quarter. Over.

7. Silja Queen. This is Goteborg Port Traffic. Advice: Have heavy wires ready fore and aft. Keep passenger gangway stowed. Stay on. Over.

8. Goteborg Port Traffic. This is Silja Queen. Advice received: Have heavy wires ready fore and aft. Keep passenger gangway stowed. Positive. Question: What lines are required. Over.

9. Silja Queen. This is Goteborg Port Traffic. Answer: Forward: three headlines, two breastropes and two springs. Aft: three sternlines, two breastropes and two springs. Please read back. Over.

10. Goteborg Port Traffic. This is Silja Queen. Read back: Forward: three headlines, two breastropes and two springs. Aft: three sternlines, two breastropes and two springs. Over.

11. Silja Queen. This is Goteborg Port Traffic. Read back is correct. Information three: Gangway will be provided by shore. Information four: Ratguards are required. Over.

12. Goteborg Port Traffic. This is Silja Queen. Information three received: Gangway will be provided by shore. Information four received: Ratguards are required. Over.

13. Silja Queen. This is Goteborg Port Traffic. Nothing more. Out.

Note: Information on tugs and lines frequently is provided by the Pilot, and is not transmitted on VHF.

Ex. 6.6

1. Pan-Pan, Pan-Pan, Pan-Pan. This is Everglades, Everglades, Everglades. Pan-Pan. This is Everglades, Kilo Gulf Mike Xray. Position: Latitude two-one degrees three-zero minutes North; Longitude zero-eight-one degrees three-zero minutes West. Engine breakdown. Salvage tug assistance urgently required. Over.

2. Pan-Pan. Everglades. This is Cienfuegos. Pan-Pan received. Over.

3. Pan-Pan Cienfuegos. This is Everglades. Information one: Position: Latitude two-one degrees three-zero minutes North; Longitude zero-eight-one degrees three-zero minutes West. Information two: Major engine breakdown. Port repair facilities required. Information three: We are in path of hurricane EDNA. Request: Immediate assistance from salvage tug. Over.

4. Pan-Pan. Everglades. This is Cienfuegos. Information one received: Your position Latitude two-one degrees three-zero minutes North; Longitude zero-eight-one degrees three-zero minutes West. Information two received: Major engine breakdown. Port repair facilities required. Information three received: You are in path of hurricane EDNA. Request received: You require assistance from salvage tug. Stand by VHF channel one-six. Period: five minutes. Over.

5. Pan-Pan. Cienfuegos. This is Everglades. Standing by on VHF channel one-six. Over.

LATER

6. Pan-Pan. Everglades. This is Cienfuegos. Information one: Tug Liberdad de los Pueblos ETD after period: two hours. Information two: ETA of tug your position period: six hours after departure this port. Stand by on VHF channel one-six. Nothing more. Over.

7. Pan-Pan. Cienfuegos. This is Everglades. Information one received: Tug Liberdad de los Pueblos ETD after period: two hours. Information two received: ETA of tug my position period: six hours after departure Cienfuegos. Standing by on VHF channel one-six. Nothing more. Over.

8. Pan-Pan. Everglades. This is Cienfuegos. Final Call. Out.

NOTES

1. SEASPEAK messages are formed entirely from words within the English language.

2. The total vocabulary used in SEASPEAK comprises 3 kinds of words and expressions:

   (i) **The vocabulary of 'general' English.** Knowledge of the non-specialised vocabulary of English is assumed, and so it is not listed in the SEASPEAK Vocabulary.

   (ii) **Words in general maritime use.** These words occur frequently in maritime communications, and are listed in Section I, as Categorised General Maritime Vocabulary.

   (iii) **Words in specialised maritime use.** These words and expressions may occur only rarely in general maritime use, but frequently in particular circumstances or for specific communication subjects. They are listed in Section II under the Major Communications Subjects.

   N.B. This vocabulary may be used in conjunction with Seaspeak bilingual vocabulary supplements.

SECTION I
**Categorised
general maritime
vocabulary**

Ship, boat and aircraft types

air cushion vessel
aircraft
barge ...
    drilling barge
    self dumping barge
cable ship
carrier ...
    aircraft carrier
    barge carrier
    bulk carrier
    combination carrier
    (COMBI)
    ULCC ultra large crude
    carrier (see tanker)
    VLCC very large crude
    carrier (see tanker)
collier

container ship
corvette
cruiser
derelict
destroyer
dredger
drifter
drill ship
drilling rig
factory trawler
ferry ...
    chain ferry
fishery protection ship
fishing boat ...
    gill net fishing boat
    purse seine fishing boat
    ring net fishing boat
    trawler
fleet ...
    fleet auxiliary
foreign-going ship
freighter ...
    package freighter
frigate
heavy lift vessel
helicopter
hovercraft
hydrofoil
ice-breaker
jetfoil
LASH (lighters aboard
    ship)
landing craft
lighter
liner ...
    passenger liner
minelayer
minesweeper
motor ship (motor vessel)
navy
non-displacement craft
nuclear ship

OBO ship (ore/bulk oil
    ship)
pipe-laying vessel
power driven vessel
refrigerated ship
ro-ro ship
sailing vessel ...
    sail training ship
    sailing boat
    sailing dinghy
    sailing ship
    sampan
salvage vessel
school ship
scow
seaplane
self-unloading ship
semi-submersible
small craft
steamship
submarine ...
    submarine escort
submersible
tanker ...
    chemical tanker
    liquefied gas tanker
    oil tanker
    ULCC
    VLCC
tow boat
towing vessel
trawler
troopship
tug
twin-screw ship
vessel
warship
whale catcher (whale
    chaser)
wreck
yacht

Appendix

Seaspeak maritime vocabulary

On-board terminology (general)

abaft ...
   abaft the beam
abeam
abreast
aboard
aft
after
ahead
alongside
amidships
athwart
beam
bodily sinkage
by the head
by the stern
damaged
draught
emergency
even keel
fire
heave away (to heave
     away)
heel
height
hoist (to hoist)
in ballast
lee
length
navigation satellite
port
signal ...
   signal letters
starboard
steering
trim (by head)
trim (by stern)
warping

On-board terminology (parts and equipment)

accident boat
accommodation ladder
  (gangway)
anchor
  anchor cable
  stern anchor
auto pilot
auxiliary steering gear
bitt
boarding ladder
boat
bollard
bow
bridge
compass
crane
Decca
derrick
emergency apparatus

emergency radio and
    batteries
emergency steering
engine
fathometer
fender
fire appliance
fire extinguisher ...
  foam extinguisher
    fixed carbon dioxide
      extinguisher
    foam monitor
      extinguisher
    halon extinguisher
    portable carbon dioxide
      extinguisher
fuel
fumes
gangway
gear
heaving line
hawser
hoist
inflatable ...
  inflatable boat
  inflatable dinghy
  inflatable life raft
ladder
lee side
life raft
light ...
  all round navigation light
  masthead light
  port light
  starboard light
  stern light
line-throwing appliance
loran
machinery ...
  propulsion machinery
navigational aid
oars
port side
pump
propeller ...
  controllable pitch
    propeller
radar
radio ...
  portable radio
raft
rocket ...
  rocket apparatus
rudder
side
signal lights
starboard side
steering gear ...
  auxiliary steering gear
stern
transponder
thruster ...
  bow thruster
  lateral thruster

transverse thruster
towing wire
twin-screw
warp

Engineering

aerial
after peak
air ...
  air compressors
  air filter
alarm
alternator
ammeter
amplifier
anode antifouling
armature
automatic control system
auxiliary steering gear
ballast ...
  ballast pump
  ballast tank
battery
bearing
bilge
blade (propeller)
boiler ...
  boiler room
  boiler tubes
bolts
bow
bow door
bulb
bulkhead ...
  bulkhead door
    (watertight)
cable
capstan
casting
circuit
circulate (to circulate)
circulation ...
  circulation pump
  circulation water
commutator
compartment
compressor
condenser
console
control gear
controllable pitch propeller
controls
cooling cargo chamber
crankshaft
current
diesel ...
  diesel-electric
  diesel engine
dynamo
electric ...
  electric cables
  electric circuit
  electric current *page 161*

Appendix

Seaspeak
maritime
vocabulary

SECTION I
**CATEGORISED
GENERAL
MARITIME
VOCABULARY**

SAFETY
NAVIGATION
AND PILOTAGE

electric fittings
electric heater
electric installations
electric motor
emergency ...
    emergency apparatus
    emergency power supply
    emergency steering
engine ...
    engine room
    engine part
equipment
evaporator
forecastle deck
fuel ...
    fuel filter
    fuel oil
    fuel supply
fumes
gas turbine
gasket
gauge
generator ...
    emergency generator
gland
grease
hand steering gear
hand pump
hatch
hinge
hub
hull
impeller
indicator
inert gas system
insulation
kerosene
lagging
lifting device
lines ...
    lines (engine cooling
        system)
linkage
machinery
machinery space
main engine
main inlet
main turbine
manual steering
motor
mountings
nuts
oil ...
    oil barrel
    oil filter
    oil heater
    oil pressure gauge
overload
packing
pintle
piston ...
    piston ring
plate
plug

power ...
    power supply
pressure lines
propeller
propeller nut
propshaft
pulley
pump
pump motors
refrigerating machinery
regulator
rudder
rudder actuator
rudder pintle
rudder plate
safety valve
screws
sea water pump
separator (oily water)
shaft bearing
spare ...
    spare anchor
    spare part
    spare piston
    spare propshaft
steam turbine
steering gear ...
    steering gear motor
stern door
tail shaft
telemotor system
thrust block
thruster
transmission
turbine ...
    turbine blades
watertight doors
welding
welding equipment
winch
wiring

Safety, navigation and pilotage

abnormal
about (to go about)
accident
action
adrift
advance
advance (in advance)
advance (to advance)
advice
advise (to advise)
afloat
against the stream
aground
ahead (in front)
ahead (to go ahead)
alongside
alter course (to alter course)
alteration of course

AMVER
anchor ...
    at anchor
    anchor is clear
    anchor is dragging
    anchor (to anchor)
    anchor is foul
    clear to drop anchor
    drop anchor
answer the helm
apparent wind
approach (to approach)
approaching
ARPA
arrival
ashore
attendance (in attendance)
authorisation
authorise (to authorise)
available
avoidance
awash
aweigh
bad weather
beneaped
berth (to berth)
blocked
boarding
bound (to be bound for)
breakers
buoyage ...
    IALA'A' system buoyage
    IALA'B' system buoyage
category
clear
close quarters situation
close to the surface
closest point of approach
    (CPA)
collision ...
    collision course
    collision regulations
        (COLREG 72)
    risk of collision
contact
continuous bad weather
control ...
    out-of-control
convoy
corrective action
course
crash stop
crossing ...
    crossing ahead
    crossing course
    crossing situation
    crossing traffic
    crossing vessel
current
dangerous quadrant
dangerous semi-circle
dead slow
deep
deep water route

Appendix

Seaspeak maritime vocabulary

departure
departure course
depth
depth of water
destination
detention
direction ...
   recommended direction of
    traffic flow
disabled
disembark
distance
distinguishing number
distress
ditch
downstream
draught
dredging
drift ...
   direction of drift
    drifting
drop astern (to drop astern)
east
easterly
eastern
eastward
ebb
ebb tide
echo
embark
embarkation
emergency ...
   emergency signal
   emergency stop
engine breakdown
enter harbour (to enter
   harbour)
enter port (to enter port)
entry
estimated time of arrival
   (ETA)
estimated time of departure
   (ETD)
explosion
eye of storm
fishing ...
   fishing gear
   fishing lights
flashing
flood stream
flood tide
flotation
fog ...
   fog bank
   fog patches
   fog signal
fresh water allowance
   (FWA)
full astern
full rudder
full speed ahead
gather way (to gather way)
give way (to give way)
go ahead (to go ahead)

go astern (to go astern)
great circle
half speed
hard-a-port
hard-a-starboard
hazard
head
head-on
head-on situation
head for (to head for)
head to wind
headway
high water
homing
hove-to
hurricane
ice patrol
identification signal
immediate action
immersed
impede
increasing wind
initial ...
   initial course
   initial position
inland waters
inshore
inshore waters
keep clear
landfall light
latitude
launching
lee
lee shore
lee side
leeward
life raft
lighten draught
load draught
longitude
lookout
lose way
low water
maintain
make (to make)
make fast (to make fast)
   made fast
make no way (to make no
   way)
   making no way
make port (to make port)
make way (to make way)
   making way
man overboard ...
   man overboard light
manoeuvrability
manoeuvre (to manoeuvre)
   manoeuvring
medical advice
mines
minimum speed
moderate
moor alongside (to moor
   alongside)

navigation ...
   navigation light (ship's)
   navigation warning
non-displacement mode
north
northerly
northern
northwards
not under command
notice to mariners
nuclear accident
obstruct
obstruct (to obstruct)
off course
offshore
oil ...
   oil platform
   oil pollution
   oil rig
   oil slick
operation ...
   operational
order
outward bound
over the ground
overboard
overdue
overtake (to overtake)
   overtaken
   overtaking
own vessel
parachute flare
pass (to pass)
past
pilot ...
   pilot boat
   pilot station
   pilot vessel
pilotage ...
   compulsory pilotage
   pilotage district
   pilotage waters
pipeline
port speed
prohibited area
racon
radar ...
   anti-collision radar
   radar bearing
   radar clutter
   radar plot
   radar search
   radar surveillance
   radar target
radio ...
   radio communications
rain
reduce (to reduce)
reducing speed
reduction
refloat
refloating
RAS (replenishment-at-sea)
rescue (to rescue).. *page 163*

Appendix

Seaspeak
maritime
vocabulary

SECTION I
CATEGORISED
GENERAL
MARITIME
VOCABULARY

BUSINESS AND
MISCELLANEOUS

rescue aircraft
rescue helicopter
rescue ship
restrict (to restrict)
restricted manoeuvrability
restricted visibility
rhumb line
right of way
round turn
rudder ...
   rudder hard over
   jammed rudder
   lost rudder
run aground
safe speed
sailing plan
salvage
sandbank
search and rescue
searchlight
seaward
seine fishing
set
set and drift
shallow
sheer
ship's heading
ship's position
shipping lane
shipwreck
shore
sight (in sight)
signal (to signal)
   signalling
signals ...
   recognition signals
single up (to single up)
   singled up
sink (to sink) ...
   sinkage
sinking
slow ahead
smoke
south
southerly
southern
southward
special area
speed ...
   safe speed
spill
stand-on-vessel
station (to keep station)
station keeping
stationary
steer for (to steer for)
steerage way ...
   bare steerage way
stern on
stern to
stern first
sternway
stop (to stop) ...
   stopped

stopping distance
storm
submarine cable
survival
suspended
swell
swing (to swing) ...
   swinging basin
   swinging circle
   swinging room
take way off (to take way
   off)
target
target area
terminal
through the water
tide ...
   falling tide
   rising tide
time zone
tow (a tow)
tow (to tow)
   towing
track ...
   recommended track
traffic control signals
traffic lane
traffic separation scheme
trawl (to trawl)
   trawling
turn (to turn) ...
   turning
   turning basin
under way
underkeel clearance
unmanageable
vessel constrained by her
   draught
vessel engaged in fishing
vessel restricted in her
   ability to manoeuvre
vessel traffic service (VTS)
visibility
visible
voyage
walkie-talkie
warning
watch
watch ...
   fresh water
   open water
   salt water
waterway
weather
west
westerly
western
westward
windward
worsen (to get worse)
wreck ...
   dangerous wreck
wreckage
_____

Business and miscellaneous

agent
agree (to agree) ...
   agreed
   agreement
assign (to assign)
   assigned
authorities
bunker (to bunker) ...
   bunkering
   bunkers
burn (to burn)
   burning
casualty ...
   casualty (ship)
classification
classification society
competent authority
confuse (to confuse) ...
   confused
de-rat certificate
de-rat (to de-rat)
de-ratting
deck repairs
deck stores
dock regulations
doctor
drinking water
duty
embargo
engine stores
harbour authorities
injure (to injure) ...
   injured
International Code of
   Signals (INTERCO)
International Sanitary
   Certificate
international sanitary
   requirements
labour
lighterman
medical
nationality
naval
number of crew
number of passengers
officer in charge
outport
passenger
piracy
pirates
pollution control
pollution (marine)
port ...
   port authorities
   port charges
   port refuge
   port police
   port regulations
   port sanitary authority
pratique

public health authorities
quarantine ...
   quarantine anchorage
   quarantine buoy
   quarantine flags
rabies ...
   rabies control
radiocommunications
regulations
shipping agent
stores

Buoys, lights and beacons

beacon ...
   light beacon
   radar beacon
   radio beacon
   transponder beacon
   unlighted beacon
buoy(s) ...
   bell buoy
   bifuraction buoy
   cable buoy
   can buoy
   cardinal buoy
   conical buoy
   cylindrical buoy
   dan buoy
   isolated danger buoy
   lanby buoy
   lateral buoy
   light buoy
   military buoy
   new danger buoy
   nun buoy
   outfall buoy
   pillar buoy
   port buoy
   preferred channel buoy
   recreational zone buoy
   safe water buoy
   secondary channel buoy
   spar buoy
   special buoy
   spherical buoy
   spoil buoy
   starboard buoy
   topmark buoy
   traffic separation buoy
   transition buoy
   unlighted buoy
   watch buoy
   whistle buoy
buoyage ...
   IALA'A' system
   IALA'B' system
character (lighted aid to
   navigation)
leading line
light ...
   floodlight
   intermittent light

leading light
light beacon
light vessel
lighthouse
navigation light (ship's
   navigation light)
searchlight
vessel light
light characteristics ...
   alternating
   fixed
   flashing
   fixed and flashing
   group flashing
   long flashing
   single flashing
   isophase
   morse code
occulting ...
   composite group occulting
   group occulting
   single occulting
quick ...
   continuous quick
   group quick
   interrupted quick
   very quick
radar ...
   anti collision radar
   radar surveillance
   radar target
roundabout
routeing system
traffic control signals
ultra quick ...
   continuous ultra quick
   interrupted ultra quick
very quick ...
   continuous very quick
   group very quick
   interrupted very quick

Port and coast features and installations

anchorage ...
   emergency anchorage
   prohibited anchorage
   quarantine anchorage
anchored vessel
approach wall
approaches
archipelago
ARPA
bank
bar
bay
beach
beacons (see Buoys, Lights
   and Beacons)
bend
berth
boat

boom
bottom
boundary
breakers
breakwater
bridge ...
   bridge pier
   floating bridge
   swing bridge
buoys (see Buoys, Lights
   and Beacons)
cable area
canal
chart
cliff
coast radio station
coastguard
coastline
container crane
coral reef
dock ...
   dry dock
   dock gate
   floating dock
dockyard
dredged fairway
entrance
fairway ...
   dredged fairway
   mid-fairway
   narrow fairway
ferry terminal
fjord
foul ...
   foul anchorage
   foul berth
   foul bottom
harbour ...
   harbour master
   harbour pilot
   harbour radar
   icebound harbour
inland waters
inshore ...
   inshore waters
jetty
junction
land
landing stage
lane
lateral buoy
leading lights
leading line
left bank
lifting device
light vessel
lighthouse
lights (see Buoys, Lights
   and Beacons)
lock ...
   lock entrance
   lock gate
   lock still
   lock tail

Appendix

Seaspeak maritime vocabulary

SECTION I
**CATEGORISED
GENERAL
MARITIME
VOCABULARY**

BUOYS, LIGHTS
AND BEACONS
PORT AND COAST
FEATURES AND
INSTALLATIONS

Appendix

Seaspeak maritime vocabulary

low water height
mid-fairway
middle ground
mooring buoy
mooring(s) ...
   single point mooring
    (SPM)
narrow fairway
narrow waters
narrows
navigation aid
navigation light
nets
obstruction
pier
pilot ...
   pilot boat
   pilot station
   pilot vessel
pilotage ...
   pilotage district
   pilotage waters
pipeline
pipelines
port
port speed
port (side) bank
prohibited area
prohibited anchorage
quay
racon
radio
radio station
rig
right of way
right bank
ro-ro system
rock (dangerous rock)
roundabout
routeing system
sandbank
sea buoy
searchlight
separation zone
ship canal
shipping lane
shipwreck
shoaling
shore
special area
stand-on vessel
starboard bank
strait
submarine cable
suction bank
swing bridge
swinging basin
swinging circle
swinging room
target ...
   target area
terminal
tide ...
   falling tide

rising tide
track ...
   recommended track
traffic ...
   traffic lane
   traffic separation scheme
   traffic sector
   traffic zone
turning basin
two-way route
vessel-restricted-in-her-
    ability-to-manoeuvre
vessel traffic service (VTS)
walkie-talkie
warehouse
waters ...
   inland waters
   inshore waters
waterway
way point
wharf
wreck ...
wreck buoy
   dangerous wreck
wreckage

SECTION II
Major communication subjects

Mayday, Pan-Pan and Sécurité 1., 2. & 3.

abandon (to abandon)
abandon ship
accident boat
accommodation
after peak
air compressors
alarm
bayou
beacon (see Buoys, Lights
   and Beacons)
beam sea
bergy bits
beset
bilged
boarding nets
boiler repairs
boiler room
breaking seas
breaking up
breathing apparatus
breeches buoy
broach to
watertight bulkhead door
bulkhead door
bulwark
buoyancy ...
   buoyancy aid
   buoyancy apparatus
   buoyancy jacket
   buoyancy reserve
   buoyancy tank
buoyant lifeline
buoys (see Buoys, Lights
   and Beacons)
capsize
carbon monoxide
cargo securing equipment
cargo is shifting
carry away (to carry away)
casualty
cement box
chain ferry
character (lighted aid to
   navigation)
cofferdam
collision bulkhead
collision mat
compartment
container
control ...
   out of control

Decca navigator system
Deccometer
deck line
detector (fog)
disabled
distress ...
   distress calls
   distress procedure
   distress receiver
   distress signal
   distress transmitter
docking signals
doctor
dyke
earthquake
eddy currents
effective range
emergency ...
   emergency compressor
   emergency escape
   emergency exit
   emergency signal
   emergency steering
   Emergency Position
     Indicating Radio
     Beacon (EPIRB)
   emergency power supply
EPIRB
escape ...
   escape slide
inflatable escape slide
estimated position
extinguisher (see also
   on-board terms)
fast
fathom
fathom chart
fire ...
   fire damage
   fire extinguished
   fire extinguisher
   fire in accommodation
   fire in the cargo
   fire in the machinery
     space
   fire monitor
   fire line
   fire pump
fishing gear
flare
red flare
flash
flash point
flood
flotsam
fog bell
fog horn
force 8 (gale)
force 9 (strong gale)
force 10 (storm)
force 11 (violent storm)
force 12 (hurricane)
foul
free surface

frogman
gale ...
   gale warning
   gate
   severe gale
gauge
generator ...
   emergency generator
growler
head
heel
heel over
hurricane
ice ...
   black ice
   covered with ice
   ice breaker
   ice chart
   iceberg
   ice floe
   ice pack
inert gas system
injure (to injure)
   injured
   injury
intensity
intercoastal
jettison
Loran C
lantern
launch
launch the lifeboat
lifebelt
lifeboat ...
   lifeboat engine
   lifeboat equipment
   lifeboat lines (and
     painter)
   lifeboat man
   lifeboat station
   lifeboat transmitter
   lifeboat winch
lifebuoy
lifebuoy light
lifejacket
lighthouse
lights (see Buoys, Lights
   and Beacons)
line throwing apparatus
low water height
Mayday
Mersar
magnetic disturbance
making water
mines
minimum safe speed
muster
muster of passengers
mutiny
neaped
night errors
Omega system
object
open boat

overboard
overtake (to overtake)
overtaking
parachute
path
petroleum
pick up (to pick up) ...
     pick up a sick person
pilot ...
   mechanical pilot hoist
   pilot hoist
   pilot ladder
   pilot vessel
pollution
pooped
port hand mark
power supply ...
   emergency power supply
propeller foul
radio silence
radio station
radiotelephone (R/T)
raft
recurvature
repairs
rescue boat ...
   inflatable rescue boat
ro-ro ramp
rudder damage ...
   jammed rudder
   lost rudder
run aground
run aground (to run
   aground)
S.O.S. signal
salvage vessel
satellite navigation
sécurité
searcher
searchlight
secondary
secure
send a boat
shift of cargo
ship canal
shipwreck
shoaling
signal letters
silence period
sinking
slick
smoke helmet
smoke signal
speed control
spring a leak
squat
stand by (to stand by)
stand off (to stand off)
steering assistance
steering gear
storm ...
   storm bound
   storm oil
   storm surge

Appendix

Seaspeak
maritime
vocabulary

SECTION II
**MAJOR
COMMUNICATION
SUBJECTS**

4.
SEARCH AND
RESCUE

storm warning
stove in
sunk
survival suit
survivor
swept away
thermal protective aid
thieves
tidal wave (tsunami)
train of waves
unseaworthy
urgency signal
VHF channel
Williamson turn
warning
watch buoy
water ...
   waterlogged
   water spout
   watertight
   watertight doors
   wave
   weather (see
      Meteorological
      Reports,
      Forecasts and
      Information)
weather forecast
wind direction
wind force
wind speed
windward
worsen

Search and rescue 4.
abandon (to abandon) ...
   abandon ship
accident ...
   ocean accident
acknowledgement
alarm
alight
assistance
bends
blanket ...
   thermal blanket
board liferaft
boarding nets
boat ...
   boat rope
   open boat
breaking seas
breeches buoy
bunkers
capsize
casualty
coast ...
   coastal incident
   coastline
contact
co-ordinator surface search
   (CSS)

day ...
   daylight signalling lamp
dead
debris
Decca navigator system
difference ...
   difference of latitude
   difference of longitude
direction finder (D/F)
distress ...
   distress area
   distress calls
   distress incident
   distress procedure
   distress receiver/
      transmitter
   distress signal
dive
downdraught
downwind
drogue
dye marker
elapsed time
embarkation into liferafts
emergency ...
   emergency message
   emergency position
      indicating radio
      beacon (EPIRB)
   emergency signal
endurance
expanding square search
   pattern
flooding
funnel
gale
gust (of wind)
hand flares
harness
hatch
head to wind
heliograph
hoisting cable
hover (to hover)
hulk
hull
identification signal
illumination
lane count
latticed charts
launching the liferaft
leak
lee side
less
lifeboat ...
   lifeboat canopy
   lifeboat equipment
   open lifeboat
   partially enclosed
      lifeboat
   totally enclosed lifeboat
lifebuoy ...
   lifebuoy light
lifejacket ...

lifejacket light
lifesaving equipment
lifesaving rocket
light vessel
line throwing appliance
lower the lifeboat
main deck
Mayday
Mersar
meteorological report
miles, nautical miles
morse code
morse lamp
motor boat
motor lifeboat
name of ship
on scene commander
      (OSC)
on scene communications
on scene co-ordination
parachute flare
personal flotation device
pick up sick person (to ...)
plane
position of distress
position reporting system
pyrotechnic
raft
refuge
relative wind
rescue ...
   rescue aircraft
   rescue basket
   rescue helicopter
   rescue ladder
   rescue net
   rescue sling
   rescue suit
restricted visibility
rocket ...
   rocket apparatus
rope ...
   buoyant rope
sail (to sail)
   sailing
scramble net
sea fog
search ...
   search initiation
   search pattern
   search speed
   search target
search pattern ...
      parallel track search
      pattern
searcher
searchlight
seasick
seasickness
seaward
sector ...
   sector search pattern
send a boat
severe

SECTION II
**MAJOR
COMMUNICATION
SUBJECTS**

**5.
COLLISION
AVOIDANCE
AND
MANOEUVRING**

shift of cargo
ship's doctor
shipwreck
smoke ...
   smoke signal
S.O.S. signal
station keeping
stormbound
stove in
stretcher
survival craft
termination
timber ...
   timber deck cargo
total loss
unmanageable
upperworks
vessel ...
   vessel search
weather report
Williamson turn
winch cable
winch reel
wreckage

Collision avoidance and manoeuvring 5.

accordance (in accordance
   with ...)
anchor cable
angle
area to be avoided
aspect
athwartships
bank ...
   left bank
   port bank
   right bank
   starboard bank
   suction bank
bearing ...
   clearing bearing
   constant bearing
   relative bearing
   true bearing
blast ...
   prolonged blast
   short blast
blind sector
bound ...
   eastbound
   inbound
   northbound
   outbound
   southbound
   upbound
   westbound
break out (to break out)
   breaking out
bridge pier
brought up
buoys (see Buoys, Lights
   and Beacons)

canal effect
clear astern
close ...
   close quarters
   close to the surface
   closest point of approach
     (CPA)
come to anchor (to come to
   anchor)
counter current
crossing ...
   fairway crossing
   traffic lane crossing
danger signal
dead stop
deep water route depth
deterioration
distance off
downbound
end on
enter fairway (to enter
   fairway)
fairway ...
   out of fairway
flotsam
force-land
heave to (to heave to)
helm order
hold (to hold) ...
   hold back (to hold back)
   hold on (to hold on)
holding ground
hold on (to hold on)
impede
inbound
inshore traffic zone
interaction
join (to join)
   joining
lay (to lay)
   laying
local special rule
manoeuvring signal
mine clearance
mid-fairway
navigation ...
   navigation hazard
   navigation mark
passage ...
   safe passage
past and clear
pilotage ...
   compulsory pilotage
port side
power failure
precautionary area
rain squall
rudder ...
   rudder jammed
searoom
separation line
separation zone
signal ...
   signal of intent

sound signal
siren
slip the tow (to ...)
   slipping the tow
speed ...
   increasing speed
   reducing speed
   speed over the ground
   speed reduction
   safe speed
   speed through the water
stand by (to stand by)
standing by
stand off (to stand off)
steady
steering gear failure
   (... failure)
stern current
stopping distance
swinging circle
thruster ...
   bow thruster
   transverse thruster
time to CPA
   (closest point of
     approach)
tow ...
   towage
   tow line
   tow rope
   towing cable
   towing light
track ...
   recommended track
traffic ...
   traffic density
   traffic lane
traffic flow ...
   established traffic flow
   direction of traffic flow
transfer
true ...
   true bearing
true course ...
   true course made good
   true course through the
     water
   true motion display
turning
   turning basin
   turning circle
   turning short round
under power
weigh anchor (to weigh
     anchor)
   weighing anchor
whistle
Williamson turn

Appendix

Seaspeak maritime vocabulary

SECTION II
MAJOR COMMUNICATION SUBJECTS

6.
NAVIGATIONAL DANGERS (NON-SÉCURITÉ)

7.
NAVIGATIONAL INSTRUCTIONS (INCLUDING ROUTEING)

Navigational dangers (non-sécurité) 6.

beacons (see Buoys, Lights and Beacons)
buoys (see Buoys, Lights and Beacons)
coral reef
danger ...
   isolated danger
depth charge
dive (to dive) ...
   diver
   diving
drying height
dust
earthquake
fishing ...
   fishing equipment
floating mark
ground swell
gun ...
   gunfire
heavy weather
hulk
jettison
lights (see Buoys, Lights and Beacons)
light ...
   electric light
   light characteristics (see Buoys, Lights and Beacons)
   lights exhibited by vessels
navigation mark
night error(s) (Decca)
paravane
periscope ...
   periscope depth
plane
radio
revolving storm
rock
settling tank
shoal ...
   shoal waters
shoot (to shoot)
small craft
snorkel
snort
stationary
stern first
stove in
submersibles
take the ground (to take the ground)
topmark
underpowered
waterspout
wave
whirlwind

Navigational instructions 7. (including routeing)

(see also Port and Shore Features and Installations)
abandon (to abandon)
acknowledge (to acknowledge) ...
   acknowledgement
acquisition
airborne
arrest
beacons (see Buoys, Lights and Beacons)
bridge
buoys (see Buoys, Lights and Beacons)
captain
chart signs and abbreviations
clearing ...
   clearing bearing
   clearing mark
cliff
coastline (see also Port and Coast Features ...)
come to anchor (to come to anchor)
command
courtesy flag
deep water route
depth ...
   critical depth
   trawling depth
deviation
directional radio beacon
distress calls
dive (to dive) ...
   diving
drift (to drift also drift (noun)) ...
   direction to drift
dye marker
economical speed
established direction of traffic flow
fathom ...
   fathom chart
fix position (to fix position)
flare ...
   hand flare(s)
   red flare
flood
flotsam
forward of the beam
heave to (to heave to)
helm orders
hulk
inshore traffic zone
International Code of Signals (INTERCO)
International Convention for Safety of Life at Sea (SOLAS)
isophase light
jetsam
knuckle
lane ...
   lane count
   lane slip
latticed charts
launch
leave to port
leave to starboard
leeway
left bank
left rudder
lights (See Buoys, Lights and Beacons)
lighten ship
lighthouse characteristics
navigable semicircle
navigation mark
optional pilotage
outfall (buoy)
periscope depth
pick up a mooring
pick up a sick person
pillar
pilotage ...
   compulsory pilotage
port hand mark
port side
port speed
position of distress
precautionary area
proceed to sea
raft
recommended direction of traffic flow
recommended track
   roundabout
reef
relative track
right bank
routeing system
round turn
sailing directions
sailing orders
separation zone or line
set ...
   set and drift
shoal waters
silence periods
sinkage, bodily
slack water
slow ahead
small craft
smoke
snorkel/snort
special charts
standby
stand ...
   stand off
   stand off and on
   stand-on vessel
starboard ...

SECTION II
MAJOR COMMUNICATION SUBJECTS

8.
NAVIGATIONAL INFORMATION, INCLUDING TIDES, CURRENTS, ETC.

9.
METEOROLOGICAL REPORTS, FORECASTS AND INFORMATION INCLUDING TIDES AND CURRENTS

starboard hand
station keeping
stationary
steerage
stern …
   stern first
   stern to
   stern way
stop (to stop) …
   stopping
storm surge
strait
Suez davit
Suez lights
tide …
   height of tide
   low tide
   set of tide
   spring tide
   tide atlas
traffic lane
traffic separation scheme
track …
   track angle
true …
   true course
   true course made good
   true course through
     water
   true track
   true track of target
turn
two-way route
under way
weather side

Navigational information, including tides, currents, etc. 8.

allowance
bench mark
bore
bottom
canal effect
channel
chart datum
current chart
current …
   coastal current
   counter current
   eddy current
   tidal current
decreasing
drift …
   drift angle
duration of fall
duration of rise
dyke
easterly
eddy
high water …
   high water height

high water neap
high water spring
knot
low water …
   low water height
   low water springs
   low water neaps
mean …
   mean high water
   mean high water springs
   mean low water
   mean low water springs
   mean sea level
neap
northerly
overfalls
rate
refloat (to refloat)
rip
rise
rode
secondary fairway
set and drift
ship canal
sill
slack water
southerly
stand
surface
surge …
   storm surge
   tidal surge
tidal …
   tidal atlas
   tidal basin
   tidal current charts
   tidal datums
   tidal predictions
   tidal range
   tidal set
   tidal stream
   tidal stream atlas
   tidal waters
   tidal wave (tsunami)
tide …
   height of tide
   high tide
   neap tide
   range of tide
   rise of tide
   rising tide
   spring tide
   tide rode
   tide table
water level
wave
westerly
(see also Buoys, Lights and
   Beacons)

Meteorological reports, forecasts and information including tides and currents 9.

air
altitude
altostratus
anabatic wind
aneroid barometer
anticyclone
arctic sea smoke
arctic zone
area
atmosphere …
   atmospheric pressure
   atmospherics
Azores anticyclone
backing
baro …
   barograph
   barometer
   barometric pressure
   barometric tendency
Beaufort notation
black ice
breaking seas
breeze
brickfielder
Celsius
calm
cloud
col
cold …
   cold air front
   cold front
   cold sector
cumulonimbus
cumulus
cirrocumulus
cirrus
cumulostratus
cyclone
cyclonic rain
cyclonic wind
decrease (to decrease)
   decreasing
depression
dew point
drift (to drift)
   drifting
drizzle
dry …
   dry bulb
earthquake
extra-tropical storm
fog, advection
forecast
force (of wind) …
   Force 0 = calm
   Force 1 = light air
   Force 2 = light breeze
   Force 3 = moderate
     breeze   *page 171*

Appendix

Seaspeak maritime vocabulary

SECTION II
**MAJOR
COMMUNICATION
SUBJECTS**

10.
MOVEMENT
REPORTS

Force 4 = gentle breeze
Force 5 = fresh breeze
Force 6 = strong breeze
Force 7 = near gale
Force 8 = gale
Force 9 = strong gale
Force 10 = storm
Force 11 = violent storm
Force 12 = hurricane
freshen
frigid zone
frost
front …
    arctic front
gale …
    gale warning
gust
hail
haze
heavy swell
high pressure (anti-cyclone)
humidity
hurricane
icing
imminent
increase (to increase)
    increasing wind
isobar
katabatic wind
land breeze
line squall
low pressure area
marine barometer
maritime …
    maritime air mass
    maritime polar mass
meteorological
millibar
mirage
mist
mistral
moderate
monsoon
navigable semicircle
nimbostratus
nimbus
occluded front
okta
overcast
polar front
precipitation
pressure
prevailing wind
radiation fog
rain …
    rain showers
    rain squall
recurvature
relative wind
rising
Roaring Forties
rough sea
route
scirocco

sea breeze
sea fog
severe
shift of wind
short seà
shower
sleet
snow
southward
speed
squall
state
steep sea
storm warning
stratus
stratocumulus
surf
surface
swell
synopsis
synoptic chart
thunderstorm
tornado
track
train of waves
tropical …
    tropical revolving storm
    tropical storm
        approaching
trough
true wind
typhoon
variable wind
veer (to veer) …
    veering
velocity
    velocity of waves
warm front
warm sector
warning
waterspout
weather …
    weather chart
    weather facsimile
    weather forecast
    weather report
    weather routeing
    weather ship
wet bulb thermometer
whirlwind
wind …
    wind direction
    wind force
    wind speed
windward
winter
(see also Vocabulary for
    Ice)

Movement reports 10.

(see also Port and Coast
Features and Installations)
anchor …
    anchor cable
    anchor foul
approaches
approach wall
area to be avoided
beacons (see Buoys, Lights
    and Beacons)
bend
beset
booming ground
bridge …
    swing bridge
buoys (see Buoys, Lights
    and Beacons)
cable …
    cable area
    cable crossing
    cable laying
calibration
canal effect
calling in point (CIP)
clearing line
close up
compass adjustment
conning position
controlling depth
convoys
critical depth
cut
dead ship
dccp water route
designated frequency
deviation report
direction finder, VHF
downbound
dock …
    dock gate
    floating dock
drag (to drag)
    dragging
dredge (to dredge)
    dredging
eastbound
escort
established direction of
        traffic flow
hamper (to hamper)
    hampered
heave up (anchor)
hold back (to hold back)
holding ground
hydrographic survey
inbound
in transit
inshore traffic zone
interaction
lights (see Buoys, Lights
    and Beacons)
limitation

Appendix

Seaspeak
maritime
vocabulary

SECTION II
**MAJOR
COMMUNICATION
SUBJECTS**

11.
BREAKDOWN
REPORTS

12.
MEDICAL
INFORMATION
NON-URGENT

marine traffic ...
   marine traffic instruction
   marine traffic regulating
    centre
   marine traffic regulator
Mediterranean moor
mid-fairway
navigate with caution
northbound
operating procedure
out of position
outbound
person in charge of the
   deck watch
pollutant
precautionary area
prohibited ...
   prohibited anchorage
   prohibited area
   overtaking prohibited
radiotelephone beacon
range lights
report, final
reporting point
route information
seismic survey
shorten tow
spoil ground
traffic ...
   traffic clearance
   traffic congestion
   traffic directive
   traffic flow
   traffic instruction
   traffic sector
   traffic zone
turning basin
two-way route
upbound
way point
wind rode

Breakdown reports 11.
(see also Engineering
Terms)
answer the helm
   (to answer the helm)
anti-collision radar
ARPA
automatic control systems
automatic helmsman
   (autopilot)
automation
auxiliary ...
   auxiliary machinery
   auxiliary steering gear
ballast water
blade ...
   propeller blade
bilge
boiler ...
   boiler repairs

boiler room
boiler tubes
by the ...
   by the head
   by the stern
cargo (see also Cargo and
   Cargo Operations) ...
   cargo handling equipment
   cargo heating coil
   cargo equipment
   cargo plan
   securing cargo
cement box
circulation pump
circulation water
closing arrangements
compressor
condenser
cooling cargo chamber
cooling system
crankshaft
Decca navigation system
diesel-electric
door, bow
door, stern
dynamo
echo sounder
electric ...
   electric circuit
   electric current
   electric installation
   electric motor
   electric propulsion
   electric repairs
electrician
engine ...
   diesel engine
   engine-room
   main engine
engineer
evaporation
fuel filter
fuel oil
full ...
   full rudder
   full speed ahead
   full speed astern
gas turbine
generator
gun
gunfire
hand steering gear
hard
hard-a-starboard
inert gas system
instruction books
insulation
left rudder
loran
Loran C
machinery space
main and alarm receiver
main inlet
main turbine

means of propulsion
oil filter
Omega system
overload (to overload)
pintle
piston ...
   piston ring
power ...
   emergency power supply
   power supply
propeller ...
   fouled propeller
   lost propeller
   propeller blade
   propeller nut
propeller repairs
propulsion machinery
pump motors
radar ...
   radar spares
   radar transmitter and
    receiver
radio ...
   radio aids
   radio installation
   radio receiver
   radiotelephone
reduce (to reduce) ...
   reducing speed
refrigerating machinery
repairs
rudder ...
   rudder actuator
   rudder pintle
   rudder plate
   rudder repairs
safety valve
sea water pump
separator, oily water
shaft bearing
slow steaming
spare ...
   spare anchor
   spare part
   spare piston
   spare propeller shaft
steering ...
   emergency steering
   manual steering
   steering gear motor
tail shaft
telemotor system
thrust block
turbine ...
   gas turbine
   steam turbine
   turbine blades
welding

Medical information non-urgent 12.

absentee

Appendix

Seaspeak maritime vocabulary

SECTION II
**MAJOR
COMMUNICATION
SUBJECTS**

13.
ICE

air condition
ankle
antiscorbutics
anus
arctic
armpit
arm, upper
artery
assistants
back
backbone
back of ...
   back of hand
   back of head
   back of knee
   back of lower arm
   back of neck
   back of shoulder
   back of thigh
   back of upper arm
bill of health
bite
bladder
blanket
blister
blue
body
boil
bottle
brain
breast
bring up
brow
bunk
bury (to bury)
buttock
cabin
calf
cancer
case
cat
Celsius
central lower abdomen
central upper abdomen
chest ...
   mid chest
choke
cholera
circulation
cramp
clothes
colour blindness
complement
confused
cover
crew
crew's quarters
cure
dead
dog
elbow
electric shock
eye
eyelid

face
fatigue
female
fever
fingers
first aid
equipment
foot
forearm
frostbite
front of leg
frontal region of head
genitals
groin
gullet (oesophagus)
gums
healthy
heart
injection
injured
instruments
International Code of
   Signals
     (INTERCODE)
International Medical
   Guide for Ships (IMGS)
intestine
isolate
jaw
joint
kidney
knee
knuckle
labour
lateral abdomen
lime juice
lime wash
lip lower
lip upper
liver
lower ...
   lower abdomen
   lower chest region
   lower thigh
lumbar (kidney region)
lungs
male
medical advice
medical box
Medical First Aid Guide
   (MFAG)
medical guide
medical supplies
middle thigh
mouth
neck front
needle
nose
palm of hand
pancreas
patella
penis
public health authorities
rabies

rib
sacral region
scorbutic
scrotum
scurvy
seizure
ship's doctor
Ship's Captain's Medical
     Guide
shiver (to shiver)
shoulder
sick bay
sick berth
side ...
   side of head
skin
spinal column ...
   lower spinal column
   middle spinal column
   upper spinal column
spleen
stomach
stretcher
stroke
suffocation
temperature ...
   temperature reports
testicles
thumb
toes
tongue
tonsils
tooth (teeth)
top of head
upper abdomen
upper thigh
urethra
uterus
vein
voice box (larynx)
whole ...
   whole abdomen
   whole arm
   whole back
   whole chest
   whole leg

Ice 13.

ablation
accumulation
aged ridge
anchor ice
arctic ...
   arctic circle
antarctic ...
   antarctic circle
bare ice
belt
bergy bit
bergy water
beset
big floe

Appendix

Seaspeak
maritime
vocabulary

SECTION II
**MAJOR
COMMUNICATION
SUBJECTS**

14.
SPECIAL
OPERATION
INFORMATION

bight
brash ice
bummock
calving
close pack ice
compacted ice edge
compact (to compact) ...
    compacting
compact pack ice
concentration ...
    concentration boundary
consolidated pack ice
consolidated ridge
crack
dark nilas
deformed ice
difficult area
diffused ice edge
diverging
dried ice
easy areas
fast ice ...
    fast ice boundary
    fast ice edge
finger rafted ice
finger rafting
firm
first year ice
flaw ...
    flaw lead
    flaw polynya
floating ice
floe
floeberg
flooded ice
fracture ...
    fracture zone
fracture (to fracture)
    fracturing
frazil ice
friendly ice
frost smoke
giant floe
glaciated
glacier ...
    glacier berg
glacier ice
glacierised
glacier tongue
grease ice
grey ice
grey-white ice
grounded hummock
grounded ice
growler
hoarfrost
hostile ice
hummock
hummocked ice
hummocking
iceberg
ice ...
    ice tongue
ice blink

ice bound
ice boundary
ice breaker
heavy ice breaker
ice breccia
ice buoy
ice cake
ice conditions
ice canopy
ice chart
ice clause
ice cover
ice covered
ice edge
ice fender
ice field
ice foot
ice free
ice fringe
ice front
ice island
ice jam
ice keel
ice limit
ice of land origin
ice massif
ice patch
ice piedmont
ice port
ice report
ice rind
ice shelf
ice stream
ice strengthening
ice under pressure
ice wall
lake ice
large fracture
large ice field
lead
level ice
light nilas
mean ice edge
medium first year ice
medium floe
medium fracture
medium ice field
moraine
multi-year ice
new ice
new ridge
nilas
nip
nunatak
old ice
open water
pack ice ...
    open pack ice
    very close pack ice
pancake ice
pingo
polar circle
polynya
puddle

rafted ice ...
    rafting
ram
recurring polynya
ridge
ridged ice ...
    ridged ice zone
ridging
rime
river ice
rotten ice
sastrugi
screwing
sea ice
second year ice
shearing
shore lead
shore polynya
shuga
skylight
slush
small ...
    small floe
    small fracture
    small ice cake
    small ice field
snow barcham
snow covered ice
snowdrift
snow line
standing floe
stranded ice
strip
submarine pingo
tabular berg
thaw holes
thick first year ice
thin first year ice
tide crack
tongue
vast floe
water sky
weathered ridge
weathering
white ice
young coastal ice
young ice

Special operation
information 14.
(see also ship types)
arbitration
burner
burning
degaussing
depth charge
dive (to dive)
    diving
diver
dredge net
drill (to drill)
drilling

page 175

Appendix

Seaspeak maritime vocabulary

SECTION II
**MAJOR
COMMUNICATION
SUBJECTS**

15.
ANCHOR
OPERATIONS

16.
ARRIVAL DETAILS

existing ship
fish
fisherman
fisher
fishing lights
fishing line
gun
gunfire
harmful substance
harbour authorities
hulk
incident
instantaneous rate of
    discharge (of oil tank)
international oil pollution
    prevention certificate
major conversion
minelayer
minesweeper
navigation lights
navigation mark
nearest land
nets
new ship
noxious ...
    noxious liquid substance
oily mixture
oil ...
    fuel oil
    oil pollution
    oil rig
    oil tanker
    persistent oil
organisation
permeability
periscope ...
    periscope depth
protocol
rabies control
segregated ballast
searchlight
seine net
sewage
snorkel/snort
sonar
spill (a spill)
spill (to spill)
stand-on vessel
tank ...
    centre tank
    holding tank
trawl ...
    beam trawl
    floating trawl
    warp trawl
violation
wing tank
zone

_____

Anchor operations 15.

anchor ...
    anchor aweigh
    anchor bearings

anchor bell
anchor broken out
anchor buoy
anchor cable
anchor cable on short
    stay
anchor cable leading up
    and down
anchor light
anchor lowered out of
    pipe
anchor (is) ready to let go
anchor shackle
anchor sighted
anchor stock
anchor watch
anchor windlass
    bow anchor
    stockless anchor
bring up
chain locker
chain stopper
clear anchor
cross (in cable)
ebb stream
elbow (in cable)
fix, position
fluke
foul bottom
gipsy
ground tackle
hawsepipe
heave up anchor (to heave
    up ...)
holding ...
    holding ground
    holding on
    holding power
kedge ...
    kedge anchor
kedge (to kedge)
    kedging
port chain
ride out storm
riding light
securing anchor chain
shank
short stay
shorten in
shoulder pipe
starboard chain
surge the cable
swing ...
    swing at anchor
vast
veer (to veer) ...
    veer the cable
    veering
walkie-talkie
watch buoy
weigh ...
    weigh anchor
wind rode
windlass

Arrival details 16.

anchor is ready to go
ballast ...
    ballast water
beam
bearing in degrees
break bulk
cargo (see also Cargo and
    Cargo Operations)
    bag cargo
    bale cargo
    bulk cargo
    cargo carrier
    cargo handling
    dry cargo
    light cargo
    port cargo
    refrigerated cargo
    steel cargo
cereals
clearance inward
cranage
crew list
cruise
customs declaration
customs entry
dead weight tonnage
declaration
density
discharge (to discharge)
    discharging
displacement ...
    displacement tonnage
double summertime
fuel
gross tonnage
harbour dues
ice breakers
ice stengthening
identification signal
immigration regulations
light dues
liner
motor boat
net tonnage
notice of readiness
noting protest
optional pilotage
parcel
passenger list
put into harbour
relative density
repairs
repatriation of seaman
report list
ro-ro system
safe port
salinity
salt water
separation
signal (to signal)
    signalling
signal mast
stern first

Appendix

Seaspeak maritime vocabulary

SECTION II
**MAJOR
COMMUNICATION
SUBJECTS**

17.
PILOT
ARRANGEMENTS

18.
TUGS AND
TOWAGE

stowaway
Suez Canal tonnage
Suez davit
Suez lights
terminal
tidal current
tidal datum
tonnage
waterline ...
    waterline length
without cargo

Pilot arrangements 17.

advance distance
anchor is ready to let go
attendance
auto-pilot
automatic helmsman
ballast
beam ...
    beam sea
boat rope
bore
breaking seas
bridge
bring up (to bring up)
clearance ...
    area clearance
    movement clearance
    time clearance
clearing line
come to anchor
command
commanding officer
conning ...
    conning position
continuous bad weather
control
cross (in cable)
cruise
dead weight tonnage
deck light
diameter
dimension
directives ...
    emergency directive
    information directive
    procedural directive
disembark
distance
dockyard
dolphin
drag (to drag)
    dragging
ebb stream
explosives anchorage
extra power
eye (of rope)
finished with engines
floodlight
fog anchorage
fresh water allowance
    (FWA)

full ...
    full rudder
    full sea speed
    full speed astern
    full speed ahead
half tide
hard over
heave short
heaving line
heavy swell
height of tide
hoist
hoisting gear
increase (to increase)
    increasing speed
inboard
joint responsibilities
junction
lashing (a lashing)
lashing (to lash)
lee shore
leeway
licensed pilot
line
linesman
low water height
marine
manoeuvring revolutions
maximum manoeuvring
    power
maximum revolutions
messenger rope
miles
minimum speed
moor ...
    Mediterranean moor
    running moor
    standing moor
oil tank
outboard
Panama lead
pilot ...
    mechanical pilot
    pilot assistance
    pilot cutter
    pilot ladder
    pilot lift
    pilot light
    pilot line
    pilot signals
    pilot vessel
propeller ...
    controllable pitch
      propeller
    lefthand propeller
    righthand propeller
radio
range line
relative density
shackles
ship control
ship directive
single crew
slow ahead

stand off
stand off and on
steady
stopped
strait
tension winches
terminal
thrust
thrusters ...
    transverse thrusters
traffic management
transfer distance
transverse thrust
turning circle
twin screw
unable to weigh anchor
vessel traffic service
    (VTS) ...
    VTS — elements of
    VTS — passive
VTA — vessel traffic
    adviser
VTC — vessel traffic co-
    ordinator
voyage
walk back
weather side
weigh anchor
wharf
windlass
windward
without cargo

Tugs and towage 18.

bollard ...
    bollard pull
broad on the bow
catenary
constant-tension winch
deck ...
    aft deck
    main deck
    poop deck
    forecastle deck
    foredeck
fast
girding
gob line
hawsepipe
hawser
headline
headway
heave tight
heaving line
horsepower
lateral thruster
leeway
let go (to let go)
make fast (to make fast)
pilotage
push (to push)
    pushing
pusher

Appendix

Seaspeak maritime vocabulary

SECTION II
MAJOR COMMUNICATION SUBJECTS

19.
BERTHING AND UNBERTHING

20.
DEPARTURE DETAILS

21.
HELICOPTER AND AIRCRAFT OPERATIONS

rudder damage
rudder lost
salvage agreement
Schmitt stopper
scope
short stay
shorten in (to shorten-in)
shorten tow (to shorten tow)
shoulder pipe
slack (to slack) ...
    slack away
    slack off
slip (to slip)
slipping the tow
slow ahead
standard salvage agreement
take in the slack
tow line
two rope
towage ...
    towage clause
towing ...
    automatic towing winch
    towing bollard
    towing bridle
    towing cable
    towing light
    towing lines
    towing winch
tugmaster
waist pipe
walkie-talkie
warp

Berthing and unberthing 19.

after breastline
apron
avast
bitt
bollard
bow ...
    bow clear
    bow fast
    bow line
    bow thruster
breast rope
bridle
capstan
cast off
clear astern
constant-tension winch
container crane
coil
distance off
double up
dropping moor
fairlead
fall astern
finished with engine
flake down

forecastle deck
foredeck
forward ...
    forward breast rope
foul lead
FWA — fresh water allowance
gantry
harness
hatch ...
    feeder hatch
    hatch covers
    survey hatch
headline
head spring
heave astern
heaving alongside
heaving line
inert gas system
knuckle
landing stage
make fast (to make fast) ...
    (to) make fast forward
    (to) make fast aft
mean draught
messenger line
moor
mooring boat
mooring lines
outport
pay out
pier
pipelines
port side
relative density
ro-ro system
roller fairlead for mooring lines
rubber
rubbing piece
running moor
salinity
salt water
Schmitt stopper
scupper ...
    scupper shoot
shore connection
shoulder pipe
side
single up (to single up) ...
    singling up
slack (to slack) ...
    slack away
    slack off
slip ...
    slip rope
    slip wire
snatch block
snubbing
springs (mooring)
standing moor
starboard side
stern ...
    stern door

stern fast
stern line
stevedore
stopper ...
    stopper off
take a turn
take in the slack
telephone
telegraph (engine room or docking telegraph)
thrusters (bow and transverse)
tidal basin
tier
tow line
tow rope
turning basin
turning gear
unmoor (to unmoor)
    unmooring
waist pipe
warehouse
warp
wire ...
    flexible wire rope
    insurance wire
    wire splice
    wire stopper

Departure details 20.

batten down
bow thruster
break out
clear of berth
ETD — estimated time of departure
even keel
FWA — fresh water allowance
pilot ...
    mechanical pilot hoist
    pilot away
    pilot ladder
put to sea (to put to sea)
ready for sea
single up
spring off
transverse thrust
trim
undock (to undock)
unmoor (to unmoor) ...
    unmooring

Helicopter and aircraft operations 21.

abandon (to abandon)
ADF — automatic direction finder
aiming circle
alight
casevac

SECTION II
**MAJOR
COMMUNICATION
SUBJECTS**

**22.
PORT
REGULATIONS**

chute
clear zone
container stack
down-draught
ejection seat
foam nozzles
full landing area
hoisting procedures
hook handlers
hovering
main rotors
manoeuvre (to
    manoeuvre) ...
    manoeuvring zone
marshalling batons
medevac
obstacles (helicopter)
overhead
relative wind
rendezvous
restricted landing area
rotor
scuppers
spray
static
strop
tail rotor
to serve you
underslung load
winch hook
winching zone
winchman
wire cutters

Port regulations 22.

absentee
accommodation ladder
    (gangway)
anchor ball
anchor buoy
area
arrest
ballast ...
    ballast water
barge
beach
bilge water
bitt
bollard
bonded stores
bonding wire
buoys (see Buoys, Lights
    and Beacons)
captain
cargo ...
    cargo handling
    cargo handling
        equipment
    cargo light
    cargo manifold
    cargo plan
cat

certificate ...
    burning certificate
    certificate of clearance
    certificate of pratique
    certificate of registry
    grain certificate
clear customs
clearance ...
    clearance inwards
    clearance outwards
commanding officer
commercial code
complement
consignee
contents bill
contraband
courtesy flag
cranage
crane wire
crew list
customs declaration
customs of port
deserter
disbursement
discharge
discrimination
dock dues
dock worker
docking signals
dog
dunnage
emigrant
extinguisher ...
    foam extinguisher
    portable extinguisher
    powder extinguisher
fenders
fire ...
    fire access
    fire alarm
    fire engine
    engine-room fire
    fire extinguisher
    fire prevention
    fire protection
    fire signal
    fire watchman
    fire wire
fireman
fireproof
first aid equipment
foreign going ship
free surface
fuel oil
fumigation
galley
gas free
gasoline
gate
goods
grain cargo certificate
gross tonnage
hazardous cargo
harbour dues

healthy
hook
hose
immigration regulations
import
in ballast
incorrect description of
    goods
international convention
    safety of life at sea
    (SOLAS)
international sanitary
    requirements
international shore
    convention
inward clearance
landing stage
lay up (to lay-up)
light dues
livestock
load ...
    load line convention
    load line rules
marine insurance
marine surveyor
marking of goods
master's declaration
material hazardous in bulk
maximum speed
minimum speed
nationality ...
    nationality flag
navigate
outward clearance
permission to load/
    discharge explosives
petroleum
police
port charges
port clearance
put into harbour
    (to put into harbour)
put out the gangway
put to sea
rat guard
refugee
refused material
repatriation of seamen
reporting
right of search
ro-ro system
safety hook
safety net
segregated ballast
ship's papers
shipment
shipowner
sign off
spoil ground
spoil ground mark (or
    buoy)
stevedore
storm warning
stowaway

Appendix

Seaspeak maritime vocabulary

surf
swell
tank cleaning
tank tests
terminal
tidal basin
tidal river
under way
undock
unmoor (to unmoor)
  unmooring
victualler
walkie-talkie
warehouse
warning signal
weatherbound
weigh anchor

Telephone (telegram) link calls 23.

accounting code
address
charges
Coast Radio Station
commercial
connected
duration of call
go ahead
link-call
non-commercial
serial number
service instructions
service message
signature
telegram
telephone number
text
traffic ...
  traffic list
turn number

Cargo and cargo operations 24.

abrasion
abrasives
acid
animals
bad lashing
bad ventilation
badly stowed
bag ...
  bag cargo
bale ...
  bale cargo
  bale space
ballast ...
  ballast pump
  ballast tank
  clean ballast
  dirty ballast
  ballast water

barrel, oil
batten ...
  batten decks
  batten down
bilge ...
  bilge water
boom
box
brake
break ...
  break bulk
broken stowage
bulk ...
  bulk cargo
  bulk cargo code
  bulk oil
bulkhead
buoys (see Buoys, Lights
  and Beacons)
calculation
calibration
can
carbon monoxide
care
cargo ...
  cargo battens
  cargo block
  cargo capacity
  cargo carrier
  cargo classification
  cargo damage
  cargo documents
  cargo handling
  cargo handling
    equipment
  cargo has shifted
  cargo hatch
  oil cargo heating
  cargo holds
  cargo labelling
  cargo light
  cargo manifold
  mechanically vented
    cargo
  naturally vented cargo
  cargo net
  cargo officer
  cargo plan
  cargo runner
  cargo segregation
  cargo winch
  dangerous cargo
  deck cargo
  perishable cargo
  port cargo
  precious cargo
  securing cargo
  stowing cargo
cargocaire vent system
carrier
case
cask
ceiling
cellular system

cement
cereals
certificate of fitness
chemical
chute
clean
cluster
coal
coaling station
coaming ...
  coaming stanchion
cold store
compartment
connection ...
  shore connection
consignee
consignment
container ...
  container crane
  container pool
  container straddle carrier
  freight container
cradle
crane wire
cross trees
damp
dangerous goods rules
deadweight cargo
deadweight tonnage
deck ...
  deck crane
  deck fitting
  deck house
  deck light
  deck plan
  main deck
derrick ...
  derrick guy
  derrick head
  heavy derrick
  derrick post
  jumbo derrick
deterioration
dew point
discharge
discharging
dry
dry cargo
explosive(s) ...
  discharging or loading
    explosives
flammable (same meaning
  UK: inflammable)
flash point
forehold
fore deck
gas ...
  gas freeing
  liquid natural gas (LNG)
  liquid petroleum gas
    (LPG)
  poison gas
general cargo
goods

Appendix

Seaspeak maritime vocabulary

timber deck cargo
time sheet
tom
toxin
trans-ship
transfer (to transfer)
truck
tween deck
ullage ...
   ullage plug
union ...
   union purchase
unload discharge
van
vehicle
ventilation
ventilator ...
   mushroom ventilator
warehouse
watchman
water ballast
water damaged goods
wharf

Bunkering operations 25.

air pipe
back pressure
barrel (oil)
blanking plate
bunker fuel oil
calibration
capacity
charter ...
   charter party
chief engineer
cubic capacity
diesel engine
diesel oil
flash point
forward tank
fuel ...
   diesel fuel
   fuel consumption
   fuel filter
   fuel oil
   fuel oil separator
   fuel oil supply
   high viscosity (HVP) fuel
   low sulphur fuel
   non distillate fuel
   residual fuel
furnace
gauge
gravity feed
handbooks
heater
heating coil
heavy diesel fuel
hydrocarbon
ignition ...
   ignition point

ignition temperature
import
instruction books
kerosene (paraffin)
kinematic viscosity
lay
list (to list)
   listing
litre
load ...
   load draught
load (to load)
   loading
log book
lube oil system
lubricate
main engine
main turbine
measure
motor
oil ...
   black oil
   heavy diesel oil
   lubricating oil
   mineral oil
   oil consumption
   oil filter
   oil gauge
   oil heater
   oil pollution
   oil samples
   oil separator
   oil tank
propulsion machinery
pump ...
   pump room
pump (to pump)
   pumping
quantity
redwood seconds
road tanker
scupper(s)
second engineer
settling tank
sludge ...
   sludge tank
spill
spray
take in
take off
tank ...
   tank cleaning
   tank tests
   tank top
test
trimming tank
turbine ...
   gas turbine
   steam turbine
ullage
vent ...
   vent pipe
viscosity

Agency, business and commerce 26.

able seaman
abroad
absentee
acknowledgement
application
arbitration
assistance
assistants
average
bareboat charter
bill ...
   bill of lading
   original bill of lading
boat note
bonded stores
break bulk
broken stowage
cable certificate
cancel
cancellation ...
   cancellation clause
cancelling date
capacity ...
   capacity plan
captain
capture
car
cargo ...
   cargo damage
   cargo documents
   cargo officer
   perishable cargo
   precious cargo
   stowing cargo
cargo (see also Cargo and
   Cargo Operations)
carrier
certificate ...
   certificate of
     classification
   certification of clearance
   certificate of competency
   certificate of origin
   certificate of proficiency
     in survival craft
   certificate of registry
   certificate of safety
   certificate of
     seaworthiness
   crew accommodation
     certificate
   discharge certificate
   dry docking certificate
   freeboard certificate
   grain cargo certificate
   lifeboatman certificate
   machinery certificate
chandlery
charter ...
   charter party
   charterer

Appendix

Seaspeak maritime vocabulary

chartering
chief engineer
chief officer
claim
class
classification ...
   classification societies
clean bill of health
clear customs
clearance ...
   clearance inwards
commander
commanding officer
commercial code
commission
commodore
compass adjustment
   certificate
consignee
consignments
construction rules
constructive total loss
consular ...
   consular fees
contamination
contents bill
contraband
contract
cost, insurance and freight
   (CIF)
courtesy flag
crew ...
   crew list
   crew's quarters
custom house
custom of port
customary dispatch
customs ...
   customs port
dangerous goods rules
   (IMDG Code)
dead ship
deadweight cargo
deadweight certificate
deck boy
deck hand
declaration
demise charter
demurrage
derelict
deserter
despatch
deviation
discipline
discrimination
displacement tonnage
disqualification
distressed seaman
dock dues
dock worker
dry cargo
duty free
efficient deck hand
emigrant

engineer ...
   engineer officers
entering in
entering out
entry ...
   entry form
equipment survey
exemption certificate
FAS (free alongside)
fees
fire ...
   fire insurance
   fire watchman
firearm
first mate
fisherman
flotsam
foreign going ship
free in and out
free on board (FOB)
freeboard certificate
general average
general cargo
goods
grain ...
   grain cargo certificate
greaser
guarantee
Hague rules
harbour
hatch survey
hull survey
husband
ice clause
IMO
incorrect description of
   goods
inspection
insurance ...
   insurance premium
invoice
jetsam
laid up
lagan
lay ...
lay days
licensed pilot
list
Lloyds ...
   Lloyds open form
loading port survey
log book
lorry
machinery ...
   machinery register
   machinery survey
mail
make port
manifest
manning certificate
marine insurance
marine surveyor
mariner
maritime ...

maritime law
maritime lien
Master ...
   Master's Bond
   Master's declaration
mate ...
   mate's log
   mate's receipt
memorandum
mercantile marine office
merchant seaman
mortgage
motorman
name of ship
nation
national flag of ship
nationality
naval architect
naval officer
navigation officer
new building
notice ...
   notice of readiness
noting protest
number of crew
offer
office
officer
official log book
offshore
oil pollution
oiler
on board
on shore
ordinary seaman
out clearance
outport
owner
Panama canal tonnage
passage
passenger ship certificate
penalty ...
   penalty clause
people
periodic survey
pilotage, voluntary
police
policy
port clearance
proceed
prohibit
property
protest
provisions
qualification
radio ...
   radio regulations
   radio safety certificate
   radio survey
rating
receiver of wreck
refuge
refugee
registered ...

Appendix

Seaspeak maritime vocabulary

SECTION II
**MAJOR
COMMUNICATION
SUBJECTS**

27.
SHIP'S STORES

registered breadth
registered length
registered tonnage
registration
regulations
repatriation of seaman
report (to report)
  reporting
  reporting day
  report list
return port
right of search
rummage
safety ...
  radiotelephony safety
    certificate
  safety equipment
    certificate
  safety precautions
sailing orders
sailor
salvage agreement
salvage money
seafarer
seafaring
seaman
seaworthiness
seaworthy
second engineer
second officer
seize
ship, substandard
ship's officers
ship's papers
ship owner
shipper
shipping ...
  shipping dues
  shipping office
sign on
sign off
signed under protest
sister ship
skipper
slick
sling
smoking
smuggler
smuggling
special survey
specific gravity
state
stevedore
steward
stoker
storage
store ...
  storekeeper
  stores list
storm bound
stow
strike ...
  strike clause
sue and labour clauses

Suez Canal tonnage
supercargo
survey
surveying
surveyor
sweating and water damage
tally
technician
thieves
third engineer
third officer
through bill of lading
time ...
  dead time
  time charter
  time chartering
  time policy
  time schedule
  time sheet
total loss
towage ...
  towage clause
translator
tug
under protest
unseaworthy
venture
victualler
warehouse
water damaged goods
way bill
work
working days
written warranty
York Antwerp rules

Ship's stores 27.
(see also Engineering)
abrasion
abrasives
acceleration
accelerator
aerial
air ...
  air compressors
  air condition
  air filter
alarm
alternator
ammeter
ampere
amp-hour
amplifier
anode
antifouling
armature
Automatic Radar Plotting
  Aid (ARPA)
attachment
attendance
auto-pilot
automatic
auxiliary ...

auxiliary machinery
auxiliary steering gear
available
bag
balance
ballast pump
ballast tank
barrel (oil)
battery
blanket
block
boiler ...
  boiler repairs
  boiler room
  boiler survey
  boiler tubes
bolts, nuts and screws
bonded stores
bottle
bucket
bulb
buoyancy aid
burner
Butterworth system
cam
can
carrier
case
cask
casting
cell
cereals
chandlery
chart ...
  Decca lattice chart
  Loran chart
  metric chart
clean
clock
clothes
cold store
commutator
condenser
contact system
cordage
corrective maintenance
corrosion
covering note
cranage
crude oil washing (COW)
damp
data
deck maintenance
delivery
dish
disposable
drinking water
dunnage
dynamo
electric ...
  electric fittings
  electric heater
  electric installation
  electric motor

Appendix

Seaspeak maritime vocabulary

electric repairs
engine ...
   engine part
equipment ...
   lifeboat equipment
evaporator
epoxy
extinguisher ...
   foam extinguisher
   portable extinguisher
   powder extinguisher
ferro-cement
fill
fine
first aid equipment
fish
fit
fitting
fix
flares ...
   red flares
floodlight
food ration
free
fuel ...
   fuel filter
fuse
galley
gas welding
gasket
gasoline
generator
gland
glass
grease
hammer
hand flares
hand pump
handbooks
hard
hawser
helmet, safety
hinge
hoist (to hoist) ...
   hoisting gear
hose
hub
impeller
instruments
insulation
kerosene (paraffin)
key
kit
knife
lagging
lamp
lantern
large
lens
lifebelt
lifeboat motor
lifeboat equipment
lighting
lime ...

lime juice
lime wash
line
liner
litre
lock
lorry
machinery
mail
maintenance ...
   corrective maintenance
   preventive maintenance
manifest
manrope
marine
mat
matches
mildew
mineral oils
missing
mooring lines
mooring wire
motor ...
   motor boat
nail
name (of ship)
nautical ...
   nautical almanac
   nautical tables
navigation equipment
navigation instruments
nets
numbers
offer
office
offshore
oil ...
   lubricating oil
   multigrade oil
   oil filter
   oil gauge
   oil heater
   oil samples
   vegetable oil
on board
outfit
overhaul
packing
pad
paint
painter
pallet
part
pattern
pilferage
pipe
piping
piston rings
plank
plug
propeller repairs
provisions
provision store
pulley

pyrotechnic
radar spares
radio spares
ration
receive
receiver
record
refit
reflector ...
   radar reflector
repairs man
replacement
rope ...
   rope guard
   rope ladder
rust
safety equipment
scrap
screw
send
serve
service
ship chandler
ship's stores
shop
short delivery
sling
smoke signal, buoyant
software
spare part
spare piston
storage
store ...
   store-ship
strike
substitute
table
tarpaulin
telephone
test
thieves
tidetable
time, schedule
tonne
tool
tools, non-spark
top up
transistor
tray
type
unit
unload (to unload)
use (to use)
van
vehicle
victualler
voyage
warehouse
water
weight
welding
wet
wiring
wood

work (to work)
  working
worn (to wear)

Appendix

Seaspeak maritime vocabulary

SECTION II
**MAJOR
COMMUNICATION
SUBJECTS**

28.
RADIO CHECKS

Radio checks 28.

bad
commercial
degrading effect
excellent
FM — frequency
  modulation
fading
fair
frequency of fading
good
interference
maintaining check
marginally commercial
modulation …
  depth of modulation
  quality of modulation
noise
not commercial
overall rating
poor
propagation …
  anomalous propagation
  disturbance propagation
rating scale
readability …
  readability code
signal quality
signal strength
SINPFEMO code
VHF Channel

System Identifier	MAREP	
Type of Report	POSREEP DEFREP CHANGEREP	(Position report) or (Defect Report) or (Change Report)

Appendix

Ship Reporting System

Heading	Text	Explanation or example
Identification of message	MAREP	
Type of message		POSREP
Identity of ship	ALFA+name of ship plus call sign	
Group date/hour	BRAVO+6 figure (Zulu)	date of month: 2 figures Hours and minutes: 4 figures.
Position	CHARLIE+latitude-longitude or CHARLIE+name of port of departure or DELTA+bearing-distance in relation to a sea mark	latitude: 3 figs followed by N or S, longitude: 5 figs followed by E or W. If the vessel is sailing from a port in the coastal zone. Bearing: 3 figs in degrees Distance: 2 figs in miles from land/sea mark indicated.
True Course	ECHO+true course	3 figs in degrees from north.
Speed	FOXTROT+speed in knots and tenths of knots	3 figures.
Destination	INDIA+name of port of destination and probable time of arrival	
Radio-communications	MIKE+VHF channel number	Give number of VHF channel monitored and if applicable number of second channel monitored.
Draught	OSCAR+maximum present draught	4 figures in metres and centimetres.
Cargo	PAPA+industrial name of product or IMDG Code No. +quantity	Nature of cargo. Quantity expressed in tonnes.
Navigational restrictions	QUEBEC+brief description in clear	Stopped, moored, hampered by draught, generally any restriction on manoeuvrability.
Additional comments	X-RAY+brief particulars	Any other information which may be useful.

Note: The headings QUEBEC and X-RAY can be omitted when there is nothing to report.

Glossary

The Glossary contains and defines those words and expressions, related to communications, that are unique to SEASPEAK, or defined in a special way, or which have one meaning selected for use in SEASPEAK to the exclusion of other meanings.

The approved **International Telecommunications Union (ITU)** definitions of some words and phrases are also included.

ADDRESS	The name, callsign, or other identification of the station which is being called.
BROADCAST	A transmission(s) to which a reply is not normally expected. The conduct of a broadcast is dealt with under **Broadcast Procedure** (Section 2.6).
CAPTURE EFFECT	During an exchange, the transmissions of a non-involved station may be heard. Because of the short range of VHF, it is possible that these extraneous transmissions may be heard by only one of the stations conducting the exchange. The other station(s) may be unaware of an interruption. This is called **Capture Effect.**
CHANNEL	An assigned frequency in the **Maritime Mobile Service,** e.g. VHF channel 16. The word channel is not to be used to refer to the navigable part of a waterway — see FAIRWAY.
CLARIFICATION	A request for explanation of a message which has been received.
COAST RADIO STATION	A radio station, situated ashore, whose main function is the handling of public correspondence. A Coast Radio Station is defined by the **ITU** as: a land station in the Maritime Mobile Service.
COMMUNICATION	Any form of contact between radio stations, either direct, as in an exchange, or indirect, as in a broadcast.
CONFIRMATION	A request for a check to be made on the accuracy or authenticity of a message which has been received.
CONTACT (to contact)	To establish communication with another station.
CONTROLLING STATION (CS)	The radio station which controls the conduct of communications in any specific situation.
CONVENTION	Agreed and established usage, procedures or standard practices, e.g. in the pronunciation of letters of the alphabet, numbers, etc. Where conventions exist they must be put into practice at all times when using VHF radio.
CO-ORDINATED UNIVERSAL TIME (UTC)	A time scale maintained by the **International Time Bureau.** For most practical purposes **UTC** is equivalent to mean solar time at the Prime Meridian (0 degrees longitude) i.e. GMT.
ELEMENT	Sub-section of a transmission, e.g. a single transmission may have the elements: address, identify, state VHF channel.
EMERGENCY POSITION INDICATING RADIO	An EPIRB is a transmitter which is designed to be used in an emergency to transmit signals which will enable the position of the ship in distress to be determined by radiolocation techniques (mainly DF). **EPIRB,** is defined by the ITU as a station in the Mobile Service, the emissions of which are intended to facilitate search and rescue operations.
EXCHANGE	Communications conducted between two or more radio stations. The conduct of an exchange is dealt with under **Exchange Procedure** (Sections 2.3 and 2.4).
FAIRWAY	Navigable part of a waterway. Note that in non-specialised usage fairway and channel are presently interchangeable.

Glossary

Except as part of a place name, e.g. English Channel, only fairway should be used. Messages that include such place names should be carefully framed so as to avoid confusion with radio channel.

FIXED FORMAT
A message whose elements are arranged in an agreed order. Each element is preceded by a letter of the alphabet which acts as a marker for the conduct of that element. The message as a whole is preceded by a word which acts as a marker identifying the subject of the message, e.g. MAREP, SURNAV FRANCE.

IDENTIFICATION
The name, callsign, or other identification of a radio station which is making a transmisson.

LOST CONTACT
When two or more stations which are in the process of communicating become unable to do so for any reason.

MAJOR COMMUNICATION SUBJECTS
The subjects which together form the bulk of maritime VHF conversation are listed in Section 6. When using VHF communication, deal with one subject at a time.

MARITIME MOBILE SERVICE
The official title of the maritime communication service. The ITU definition is: a mobile service between coast radio stations and ship stations or between ship stations, or between associated on-board communication stations; survival craft stations and emergency positions indicating radio beacon stations may also participate in this service.

MESSAGE
The main information-bearing part of a communication, i.e. other than VHF conventions, procedures, or standard phrases, e.g. *How do you read?* is normally a standard phrase, whereas *QUESTION: What is your ETA?* is a message.

MESSAGE CHECK
A system for ensuring that both stations agree on what has been said. They include techniques for confirmation of received information and for correction of mistakes.

MESSAGE CHECKING STEP
The separate tranmissions necessary to ensure that the content of a message is agreed by both stations.

MESSAGE MARKER
A word or phrase used to indicate the type of message which immediately follows. It is to be used as the first word or words of every message in a message-bearing transmission. The seven message markers and their related reply markers are listed and explained in Section 4.2.

MESSAGE PATTERN
Recommended rules for the construction of messages. See Section 4.3.

MESSAGE TYPE
This term is used to describe the function of the message, e.g. question, instruction, request, etc. There are seven message types. See Section 4.2 **Message Markers.**

PLACE
This word is used to refer to named locations or named geographical places. When expressing places in SEASPEAK the rules for giving positions are to be observed.

PORT OPERATIONS SERVICES
The official title of that part of the maritime communication service concerned with the movement of ships in or near a port. The ITU defines it as: a maritime mobile service in or near a port, between coast stations and ship stations, or between ship stations, in which messages are restricted to those relating to the operational handling, the movement and

Glossary

the safety of ships and, in emergency, to the safety of persons. Messages which are of a public correspondence nature shall be excluded from this service. See VESSEL TRAFFIC SERVICES.

PORT STATION — A coast station in the Port Operation Service.

POSITION — This word is used to describe locations that are normally expressed in navigational or maritime terms. The rules for giving positions in SEASPEAK are given in Section 1.8.

PROCEDURE — The rules and methods of operating that are required to be observed in order to make and maintain contact on VHF radio. They are explained in Sections 1, 2 and 3 or the Manual.

PUBLIC CORRESPONDENCE — Any communication between ships and persons or organisations ashore which must be routed via the official inland communication system. The ITU defines this as: any telecommunication which a station must, by reason of its being at the disposal of the public, accept for transmission.

RADIO STATION — One or more transmitters or receivers or a combination of transmitters and receivers, including the accessory equipment, necessary at one location for carrying on a radiocommunication service, or the radio astronomy service. Each station shall be classified by the service in which it operates permanently or temporarily.

READBACK — The re-transmission of information received in the previous transmission. Instructions on reading back are given in Section 4.4 **Message Checks.**

REPLY — The response to a message. A reply is the whole of a message which is transmitted using a reply marker, e.g. INSTRUCTION—RECEIVED, WARNING—RECEIVED, etc. See Section 4.2.5 **Message Markers.**

REPLY MARKER — The response to a message marker; the words or phrases which immediately precede the response to a message. Each message marker has a related reply marker which is to be used in the same manner as the message markers. The reply markers are given in Section 4.2.5.

SHIP DESCRIPTION — One of the information groupings recommended by SEASPEAK. The information group consists of those items of a ship's description which do not usually change, i.e. type of ship, colour of hull, superstructure arrangements, any other items.

SHIP MOVEMENT SERVICE — The official title of that part of the maritime communication service concerned with the movement of ships outside ports. It is defined by the ITU as: a safety service in the Maritime Mobile Service other than a port operation service, between coast stations and ship stations or between ship stations, in which messages are restricted to those relating to the movement of ships. Messages which are of a public correspondence nature shall be excluded from this service.

SHORE RADIO STATION — A radio station which is situated ashore and performs any function other than those performed by a coast radio station.

STANDARD PHRASES — Words or phrases whose meaning has been precisely defined for use in SEASPEAK procedures. e.g. *This is, Over, Please read back.* The standard phrases are listed, defined and explained in Section 4.1.

Glossary

STANDARD UNITS OF MEASUREMENT

In SEASPEAK it is recommended that only certain standard units of measurement are used. These units are drawn from the Système International d'Unités and from standard maritime practice. For purposes of uniformity it is advisable to adhere to this system. The standard units used in SEASPEAK are listed in Section 1.6.

SURVIVAL CRAFT STATION

A radio station in a survival craft. The ITU defines this as: a mobile station in the Maritime Mobile or Aeronautical Mobile Service intended solely for survival purposes and located in a lifeboat, life-raft, or other survival equipment.

SWITCH-OVER

The act of changing from one VHF channel to another and the associated procedural rules. These are covered in SEASPEAK by the **Switch-Over Rules** (Section 2.4.5).

TERMINATION

The act of finishing an exchange. The associated procedural rules are covered in SEASPEAK by the **Termination Procedure** (Sections 2.4.8 and 2.4.9 entitled **End Transmission** and **End Procedure**).

TRANSMISSION

Everything that is done or said between pressing the transmit switch before talking and releasing it afterwards. An exchange or broadcast will consist of a number of transmissions.

TYPE OF PROCEDURE

In VHF usage there are three different types of procedure: *exchange, broadcast,* and *distress/safety.* These are each dealt with separately in the Manual.

UNDERSTOOD

Understood means '*This is what I heard*'.

VESSEL TRAFFIC SERVICES

This term generally has the same meaning as PORT OPERATIONS SERVICES (p. 189) and is normally abbreviated to VTS. In everyday usage the official ITU term Port Operations Services is disappearing in favour of VTS.

VOCABULARY

The SEASPEAK vocabulary contains words and expressions specific to maritime usage. It does not contain words which are common to all English usage, e.g. and, the, etc. See Appendix, SEASPEAK Vocabulary.

Index

Index

Index

Index

Index

Index